Your HR Ally: Kickstart your human resources career

Melissa Hume

First Published in Australia by Aurora House
www.aurorahouse.com.au

This edition published 2021
Copyright © Melissa Hume 2021

Typesetting and e-book design: Prepress Plus
Cover design: Donika Mishineva

The right of Melissa Hume to be identified as Author of the Work has been asserted in accordance with the Copyright, Designs and Patents Act 1988.

ISBN number: 978-1-922403-89-6 (Paperback)

 A catalogue record for this book is available from the National Library of Australia

Distributed by:
Ingram Content: www.ingramcontent.com
Australia: phone +613 9765 4800 | email lsiaustralia@ingramcontent.com
Milton Keynes UK: phone +44 (0)845 121 4567 |
email enquiries@ingramcontent.com
La Vergne, TN USA: phone +1 800 509 4156 | email inquiry@lightningsource.com

Gardners UK:
www.gardners.com
phone +44 (0)132 352 1555 | email sales@gardners.com
Bertrams UK:
www.bertrams.com/BertWeb/index.jsp
phone +44 (0)160 364 8400 | email sales@bertrams.com

DEDICATION

THIS BOOK IS DEDICATED to my lovely Nanna Doris. She has always been supportive and someone I admire.

ABOUT AUTHOR

MELISSA HUME IS ALSO the author of *Career Guidance for Now and for the Future*. Melissa's first book is suitable for anyone trying to get their foot in the door in any type of profession. *Career Guidance for Now and for the Future* delves into how to write attention grabbing resumes and cover letters, and how to succeed in an interview – and much more!

Disclaimer

All examples used in this book are fictitious and do not refer to any existing business, organisation, political or government bodies, persons or organisational representatives. Case studies have been created for learning purposes only. As I am not a qualified lawyer, the general advice and guidance provided in this book has been created for learning purposes only.

CONTENTS

PREFACE

When I first embarked on my career, I wish I had a compass. Something or someone pointing me in the right direction, telling me what to say and how to act in the business world. Being very new to business and the human resources profession was overwhelming at times and I made a lot of mistakes! In the first few years of my career, I had researched and looked for answers on how to navigate company nuances and accelerate my own learning. Unfortunately, articles, books and other sources of information were vague and fell short of what I needed. There was no single guide that could help me comprehend the jungle of corporate politics. This was my motivation for writing this book. *Your HR Ally* is a book written for those eager to prove their worth in the first few years of their HR career or for anyone looking to understand human resources practices. This book provides a comprehensive insight into the important pillars of human resources from the beginning of the employee life cycle, starting with recruitment to the cessation of employment and beyond. This book also addresses topics that authors have traditionally avoided such as corporate politics and internal tensions that can arise from being a HR practitioner. *Your HR Ally* will teach you how to become a proficient player in an organisation's political arena and kickstart your human resources career.

Melissa Hume

1

BUILD YOUR PERSONAL BRAND

CONGRATULATIONS ON TAKING OWNERSHIP of your human resources career and setting yourself up for success. This book will give you the necessary exposure to areas of human resources, which you may not have had the opportunity to gain in the first few years of your career. Unlike other books, I will not neglect the negative aspects of the Human Resources (HR) profession so that you gain a holistic understanding as a reader. You need to know what it means to work in HR; what challenges you will face and just how rewarding it can be. Before I launch into the beginning of the employee life cycle, it is important for you to understand how you need to position yourself from the onset of your career. It is critical for you to create and build a personal brand and identity. As a HR professional, people within your network need to know who you are, what you stand for, and testify on your behalf to the quality of your work. Having a positive reputation is key and this falls into what I call a personal brand.

Before you can start to build your personal brand, you need to conduct your own self-evaluation. You need to assess your career goals and what your aspirations are. If you are starting out in your career, then this is the perfect opportunity for you to understand what you would like to achieve in your first few years: What is your preferred industry? How would like to build your network?

By using the questions below to prompt your ideas, you can formulate these goals. I recommend writing these in a journal and dating each page as you progress. I personally use this method so that I can track how my thoughts, feelings and perspective on events and changes to my career evolve over time. Self-reflection is key to you building a good personal brand.

The first few questions are geared towards your degree of self-awareness:

- What current skills and experience do you have related to HR? Or what skills do you have that are transferable to HR?
- What areas need improving?
- What can you do to address these areas?
- What would you like to do day-to-day in a job?
- How much do you want to get paid?
- How much do you believe you can potentially be paid for this job considering your current skill set and level of experience?
- What are your main motivations for pursuing a career in human resources?

Try and answer these questions as honestly as possible, as it will allow you to understand what job opportunities you are best positioned for.

The next set of questions focus on what you want to achieve once you have gotten your foot in the door and are planning your career growth.

As an entry level HR professional, you will start from a zero baseline in terms of your personal brand. Most likely, your network of other HR professionals and general colleagues would be non-existent or quite small and it is up to you to start growing this network. As you are gaining the first few years of experience, you should be actively thinking about how you can ensure you have ample opportunities in the future and how you will shine among all the other candidates out there in the market. This is where setting goals and having a personal brand comes into play.

Starting with career goals, you should again use your journal to note down what you would like to achieve in the next one to three years, and then in the long term:

- What are your family commitments at present?
- What will they be in the next few years?
- What are your financial goals? Are you looking to become financially independent in the immediate or near future?
- Will you instead concentrate on climbing the corporate ladder and establishing your career in the business world?
- What salary are you looking to earn in the next five and ten years of your career? What salary would you like to earn at the age that you retire?

These questions are to prompt you to think about what you would like to achieve and to start setting deadlines.

Once you have all these in your journal, you have essentially built the foundation of an action plan for your career. From conducting an initial self-assessment and answering these questions, you may even realise that working for organisations or other people is not for you.

You may discover that you would be willing to continue working for other people in the interim to build your network, skills and knowledge, and then the end goal is to venture out on your own.

Having an entrepreneurial spirit and mindset is fantastic and is a hard road to travel. This endeavour is not for everyone, as everyone has their own personal circumstances and reasons for wanting to work independently.

If you are unsure of how to venture out or you do not know how to even get started, you don't have to give up your primary source of income to kick-start your business venture. You can work for your current employer simultaneously while building your own income stream and side hustle. By continuing to work for an employer while gradually working on your own ideas and building your own business, the money you earn from your job can be then invested into building your future. This may be only one of the ways you see yourself gaining financial independence or achieving your career goals. If this is something you would like to personally strive for then having a strong personal brand is even more critical for you. You become what customers associate with your service and/or product, and when they or anyone thinks of you, they must associate this with only positive experiences.

Whether you're working for an organisation or have started to venture out yourself in the business world, you need to establish your public identity. With your goals and career aspirations now journalised, you need to understand how you would like those inside or outside your network to see you.

How will you start building your brand? Will you build a personal brand on a strong digital footprint such as a LinkedIn profile, your own personal website, personalised business cards, or something else that would separate you from the average HR practitioner?

When I was thinking about building my own personal brand, it was with the goal of creating career opportunities for myself. Strengthening your professional digital footprint is an excellent starting point; this is what people can find out about you by running online searches.

You may wish to start with creating a basic LinkedIn profile, with a professional display picture and an outline of your HR career, certificates and any qualifications you have. LinkedIn is an excellent networking tool and platform used by professionals and recruitment agencies when they are looking for candidates to fill client vacancies. Having your information available means you can be found and acts as a pseudo-CV to recruitment consultants looking for someone like you. If you do decide to create a LinkedIn or another type of professional profile online, they are only useful and relevant as long as you continue to update them with your career changes and any work you would like your network to know about.

Social media tools like LinkedIn allow you to add connections with people you have worked with in the past, acquaintances, or people you would like to engage in work with. With the newsfeed functionality, you can keep up to date with your network's movements, subscribe to industry groups and organisations you would like to follow and interact with.

As a platform member, you may also use your profile to write articles and blogs to build your online presence and generate discussions on topics you are passionate about. This is one way to build your personal brand. However, when you do start to publish material you need to be aware that you are at some point going to receive feedback or comments you may not like. This is the very nature of social media today; people will make comments or give feedback that may be negative and you may not appreciate them. This should not dissuade you to publish at all, as it is incredibly beneficial to your personal brand. You can also use the platform to publish any other works you have produced, release videos marketing your own services and/or products and anything else you would like your network to see. The more relevant and popular content you publish, the more of a following you will generate online, which will boost your personal brand.

Another method of publishing your work, services and any product you're offering is to build a website. This website can be a component of your own business or a personalised website dedicated to showcasing your career. Any website needs to be designed and laid out in a professional manner, with consistent themes, style and that also presents well to viewers. If your aim is to impress recruitment consultants and prospective employers, a personalised website may include a running blog and a section where they can directly download a copy of your CV. An interactive website looks more appealing than having a static website; static websites have a plain layout with simple click and flick through to the next page. Having an interactive website integrates colours, movements and a combination of text, video, and sound to give a positive user experience. Creating this type of website is in line with the professional personal brand you are trying to build. If you only have a small budget to work with, there are a lot of free website builder platforms available. The one minimum expense you will need to purchase is the domain name. You will then need to link this to the free website builder of your choice. There is also an option to purchase an email address with the domain name, so that you have a matching contact email with the website address. This is recommended if you are going to market this website to gain prospective employment opportunities and/ or clients, and this email address will also be referenced on business cards.

Having a personalised website and an online profile are important steps towards building your personal brand. However, a lot of people have taken these steps. These will not differentiate you as a stand-out candidate or as someone with flare. You need to show how you are different and have your personal brand reflect this fact. How can you differentiate yourself from other HR professionals you are competing with?

What is something only you can offer or have contributed during your career that is desirable and demonstrates your level of skills, knowledge, and experience? These are the questions I asked myself early on in my career. I wanted to be different and progress my career at an accelerated pace. Within the first few years of my HR career, I took on multiple unpaid internships in various organisations and widely read different books and articles online. I became a sponge learning what made some people more successful than others. From conducting my own research and trying to find my own method of what would set me apart from the other HR officers and consultants in Sydney, I decided to write a book: *Career Guidance for Now and for the Future.*

My first book was a means to organise my thoughts in a cohesive manner and construct a text that would be marketable and promote my personal brand. For me, this is how I was able to differentiate myself during job interviews and demonstrate that I was not the average HR professional. I was able to complete a project from beginning to end; writing and editing the manuscript was difficult, let alone organising the publishing, printing and promotion of the end product. Personally, it was a huge achievement! I wanted to leverage this as much as possible and would make sure I always had a book with me when I attended interviews and met with hiring managers. They were fascinated and some even ended up reading the book cover to cover.

Now, I am not saying that to be different you need to get out there and start writing! I am also not referring to my own experiences as an opportunity for myself to brag. I am trying to articulate the importance of you starting to brainstorm what you can do with your own capabilities to make yourself stand out and launch your personal brand. Instead of writing a book or having a side project, you may want to purely focus on accelerating your learning. If this is something you would like to do, then I recommend participating in a mentoring program.

There are different ways of gaining a mentorship or a mentoring opportunity within your own organisation. Mentoring can either be formally or informally arranged. By having an assigned mentor to coach you, provide guidance and take the time to explain all things HR to you, you will naturally gain exposure to aspects of HR that are beyond your early career days. You will also gain the insight of their own experiences. If your mentor has been in HR a long period of time, you also stand to gain information and to understand a different way of thinking when approaching HR.

Reaching a senior and strategic partnering level of HR takes years of experience, expertise and a certain political savviness. To secure an opportunity to be mentored, you may have to create the opportunity yourself. Most large and small organisations do not have a formalised mentoring program, and if they do it is primarily focused on mentoring the senior management succession pipeline. To create this opportunity, you may have to be bold and reach out to someone in your network, at your current place of work (direct or indirect manager) or someone you have grown to admire as a role model. You do not have to be acquainted with the person you choose to approach. You may have even been following a HR professional's career on LinkedIn. You can be bold and send this person a message over LinkedIn explaining to them how you admire them, and that you would love the opportunity to learn from them (it is a compliment after all!).

You can politely engage in conversation and ask for them to mentor you. A brave young lady once reached out to me in this manner over LinkedIn and that same afternoon we were chatting over the phone and have been in contact ever since. Be bold! You can take a similar approach with finding a mentor in your own organisation. If you are going to look for an internal mentor, it is a courtesy to have a conversation with your immediate manager before you have any other conversations. Not only is this a courtesy, but your manager may have other ideas, suggestions or take the opportunity to mentor you directly.

Building a personal brand, which reflects you, is key to you kick-starting your career into success. Apart from your online presence and other pieces of work you can publish and interact with your network; you must also focus simultaneously on building your own competency as a HR professional. If you have an excellent online presence and your portfolio of work is lacking, or you have unfortunately built a reputation that you're unsuitable for the role you're in, this will undo all your efforts. You must be dedicated and committed to becoming a high-performing professional as well as know what makes up your bread and butter. The other chapters in this book will assist you in understanding the pillars of the employee life cycle and beyond. However, your learning journey does not finish there. You need to have both technical HR skills and knowledge, along with business acumen, to become a stand-out HR professional.

Business Acumen

The pursuit of ongoing personal development is what will separate you from others in your career. Self-reflection and awareness in identifying what your gaps in knowledge, skills and experience are is necessary in your own personal growth. By reading this book, you have made the decision to invest in learning more about the technical aspects of HR and to absorb as much relevant information about corporate politics as you can to avoid making mistakes. However, the technical aspects of a HR role do not encompass everything you need to know. To become an effective business partner, and eventually a strategic business partner, you need to see the value in developing your business acumen. This type of investment is often overlooked by HR professionals as it is deemed unnecessary or for people in more "technical" functions such as finance or payroll. This is not the case. Developing your business acumen will allow you to stand out and build your commercial savviness. This is what you need to excel in and use to differentiate your personal brand.

In short, business acumen is your ability to comprehend and understand the levers in a business that can be pulled or pushed to achieve certain outcomes. Understanding what makes a business money and other factors that impact the likes of revenue, gross profit and asset management are all parts of business acumen. From how I've characterised business acumen, you can see that this is completely unrelated to how much you know about human resources nor how much experience you have.

Business acumen is about speaking the same language as those providing commercial advice and making business decisions in an organisation and communicating in such a way that demonstrates you understand the bigger picture. Acquiring business acumen is also incredibly useful in gaining buy-in from stakeholders, raising your internal reputation, demonstrating an affinity to solve problems beyond the HR remit and contributing on a higher level than what is dictated by your position description. Business acumen is not an innate skill or trait people are born with. It is acquired by focusing and having a willingness to learn from others inside and outside the human resources function.

There are a few different approaches you can take to actively develop your business acumen. I found it especially useful in the first few years of my career to read widely. I read a variety of books in accounting with examples of profit and loss statements, holistic books on the importance of cash flow, people, assets, etc.; undertook courses in health and safety; and attended some payroll short courses. There is so much material available on the internet and captured in literary texts that there is no reason to not have a reasonable baseline of business acumen. If reading numerous texts is not your idea of fun, then try networking with people outside the HR profession and listen to how they speak and explain concepts they are working on. What lingo are they using? Why are they making a particular decision or have arrived at one solution over another? How does their function interact with others in a business? Is their function revenue-generating or revenue-neutral?

Networking in this way not only boosts your personal brand, but also awareness of what else is occurring in the business. At the same time, through this process, you will grow more comfortable using the business lingo in general conversation.

From this you will become more at ease conversing at a higher level or in front of a group of people when the time comes to demonstrate your new knowledge.

From reading widely and networking with different professionals, you want to know how to explain in simple terms how the income is earned by a business. From the beginning of prospective customers or receiving new business, providing the services or product, the supply chain or execution of the service and how the business then receives the money. You should also endeavour to become familiar with areas of business development, account management, creating a client pipeline and the technologies used to manage these relationships and revenue streams. Familiarity with these other functions of a business comes from immersing yourself in work outside the HR remit. Embracing projects that are not typically HR will expand your network and build upon your political and commercial savviness.

Leadership

As a HR professional, you will need to learn how to perform the juggling act; you're representing the employee's rights and entitlements as well as the stakeholders in your portfolio. At times, the agenda of the business and the employee's views can conflict with one another, and it is up to HR professionals to balance both needs, which is not easy. When this type of internal tension arises, it is an opportunity to exercise your "know-how" of the business and to lead by example. Having leadership qualities and experience will benefit you in your HR capacity and is conducive to building a well-rounded personal brand. To become an effective leader and a competent HR professional, there can be no room for you or any other HR professional to have Imposter Syndrome.

Having Imposter Syndrome is a sort of complex whereby the way someone perceives their own competency and skill set is incongruent to the way others perceive them. Their perspective on themselves is skewed – negatively. If this is something you are experiencing, you may at times feel that when you have setbacks or you make mistakes that you're not meant to be in this career and not worthy of promotion opportunities. Having this mindset and perception is a huge barrier to anyone's success regardless of their profession. Realigning a mindset like this is important, by first identifying your real competencies and familiarising yourself with a benchmark of quality versus poor work. You can establish a quality benchmark by seeking out work portfolio examples from senior executives, conducting your own research as to how projects are delivered, as well as seeking materials from your immediate manager, business network or the internet.

Another way to tackle this syndrome is to develop healthy coping mechanisms for when setbacks do occur. Self-awareness and reflection cannot be focused on self-talk, such as "I'm just not good at my job… this career isn't for me", but rather reflecting with "I made a mistake and will learn from this… this is all part of learning". Diarising your career experiences and times when you're feeling doubtful of your own abilities can help with this reflection. You can understand whether you have any specific triggers or people in your world who negatively impact your self-worth. By completing this exercise, you may start to see patterns that there are demands from your role that make you uncomfortable or trigger the negative self-talk. I have personally found this method useful and have diaries covering over ten years of my working life. By keeping yourself in check with these thoughts, it will allow your leadership capability to flourish and, in turn, make you more competent and suitable for your role.

Being a leader in a business is not necessarily connected to the position and title you hold. It would be foolish to hide behind the role of a HR representative and the esteem and respect this dictates from employees. New HR professionals are vulnerable to making this mistake without proper guidance. HR professionals that reflect this assumed esteem in their actions are deemed cold, unapproachable and fail to bridge the gap between employees and management. To become a true leader in a business, you need to earn the trust of your peers, employees, and others you work with. Leadership encompasses a variety of competencies, which can all be learnt. Leadership capability is not an innate attribute and can be nurtured over time with effort. These competencies include, but are not limited to, the following:

- Adaptability to changes in an organisation. Having the ability to embrace ambiguity and the changing nature of an industry, working environment and pressures.
- Understanding the importance of integrating new technologies and streamlining existing processes. Acting as a change agent to ensure a business remains competitive and productive and is not constrained by a lack of adequate systems.
- Having integrity by keeping your word. Leaders should steer clear of making promises or commitments they cannot deliver on or do not have the necessary approvals for.
- Be open and transparent in communication. As a leader you would be privy to more information than others in the organisation, which can be private and confidential. Leaders need to use their discretion in sharing business updates to keep their team informed, without divulging commercially sensitive information.

- Networking with other managers and leaders in the business outside the HR function. Understand how they have handled certain matters in the past to learn from their actions, regulate your own decision-making and apply consistency across the business.
- Understand the importance of being able to delegate work tasks and responsibilities fairly among the team. As a manager, it can at times be difficult to "relinquish control" and not be involved in the day-to-day operations. However, you need to have a level of trust with team members that they will complete the tasks correctly and to a high standard so that you are able to focus on more leadership-based tasks.
- Empower your team members and inspire them to contribute ideas, recommend solutions and implement actions to address challenges in the business.
- Do not take credit for your team members' contribution. If as the leader of a team you are presenting someone else's work or contribution to a project you have been overseeing, reference their contribution. Ensure they are thanked for their efforts and the team and relevant stakeholders in the business know what their contribution was to that piece of work.
- Publicly praise good work and privately give constructive criticism. Delivering constructive feedback can be difficult to provide correctly; the message can be poorly received by the recipient and viewed as a "personal attack". Give the recipient the opportunity to digest the feedback and explain their version of events and how they believe the situation or tasks could have occurred differently.
- Practise active listening. A leader who listens to their team members has a more productive and engaged team. Active listening is about acknowledging good and positive

feedback, confirming your own understanding of what has been communicated and adjusting your communication style accordingly. Active listening allows you to take appropriate action to the feedback you gather. It is also an important part of being a leader who genuinely cares for their team members.

The above is not an exhaustive list and is only a brief overview of the types of competencies you would need to demonstrate in your capacity as a HR professional. There are a lot of texts and resources available on the internet and published by authors who purely focus on leadership. I recommend conducting your own research and having a deep dive into this topic. Not only would this personally benefit your own career and personal brand, but it would equip you with the basic building blocks if you were required to develop a leadership development program for a business in the future. Becoming a leader will take years to practise and hone what works and does not work for you. There is no set mould of what a leader looks like and there are different leadership styles you can take on for different situations, as well as with the people you are interacting with. Please remember this when you are supporting a manager with their team during difficult times, or you yourself need to step up and lead by example. Having this mentality will ultimately benefit your reputation.

Your Reputation

There are quite a few expressions that exist today around the impact of someone's reputation on their success and perception by others. One such expression is "your reputation precedes you", which can have either negative or positive connotations, indicating that you really are what people say you are whether that is referring to bad or good things. This saying known widely by people is how an individual can be generally judged by others. If someone unfortunately has a poor personal brand and their reputation is tarnished, this will inhibit their career progression in a business or the career opportunities presented to them within their network. Establishing a healthy and well-known reputation is beneficial to you in a HR profession and to anyone else looking to build a strong personal brand.

The first pearl of wisdom I would like to cover is that your reputation is an asset you need to protect. In a corporate environment, your reputation in the business is critical in people recognising your talents and contributions. During your career, you will unfortunately come up against others who will purposely make efforts to tarnish your reputation to elevate their own. You need to take measures to ensure that your reputation remains intact, and refrain from retaliating in a similar manner. If your reputation is damaged, and it may not even be warranted, it is very hard to recover and restore trust among the ranks. Therefore, one strategy to employ is to avoid making corporate enemies, so that they do not perceive you as a threat or have reason to target your reputation. You may find yourself in the unfortunate situation that if you are out-performing your colleagues that they can become jealous and feel threatened by you. Without doing anything wrong on your part, they then may decide to undermine you (unconsciously or not), spread rumours in the business or even try to take credit for your work.

Identifying these types of people in the workplace is a part of developing political savviness, which is covered in detail in *Chapter 10: Business Politics*. For the purposes of your personal brand, you must take safeguarding your reputation seriously, as well as appreciate the power of having the right people know your name and what you stand for.

Having people of influence or high standing in the business know who you are, and understand your capabilities and show they truly appreciate you, will serve you wonders! Having senior leaders advocate on behalf of your reputation and mention in their own network that you're good to work with or "know your stuff" goes a long way with opening up promotion opportunities. When others speak well of you, it is a lot more impactful than boasting or you showing the quality of your work to others. Word of mouth is by far the most powerful networking tool and is very effective in boosting your personal brand. As a HR professional, having this type of reputation in the business will also make your job a lot easier, as managers and employees will trust you more easily with information they would not ordinarily share. On the flip side, if you were to develop a poor reputation in the business, it will likely become more difficult for you to build trust and gather information you may need to perform your role.

Another benefit of having your positive reputation spread among your network and in the business you support is that your opinion will naturally become more highly regarded. You will find that people will give you the time to explain your opinion, generally consider your opinions and advice, and learn to accept that this is coming from a well-informed source. You will find that you face less resistance from a business accepting your views and any recommendations you make by having a formidable personal brand. Inversely, having a terrible personal brand will encourage people to doubt your opinions and advice, and may even take a standing against what you have to say. And you won't get hired!

Keeping with the theme of learning how to boost your reputation, when you're faced with adversity and challenges it can be tempting to complain. It's a part of being human to complain and sometimes you can even bond with people over having mutual complaints and adversities. However, for the sake of your reputation and your personal brand, it is not a good idea to complain for the sake of complaining. When you're frustrated with something in the workplace, there is a certain way you need to approach this and voice your concerns. You should bring up your concerns in a respectful manner, first to your direct manager and without an audience.

Remain calm and pragmatically explain what your concerns are, what impact the issue is having on you in your role and suggest any ways of fixing this. By taking this approach, you will not be perceived as complaining, but rather informing your manager of your concerns and how you would like to work together to find a solution. People who complain often and without any intention to find a solution become known as whingers, and their reputation in the business becomes defined by this whingeing. People who regularly complain and have negative attitudes towards the business can be quite toxic and implicate your own perspective on the workplace.

As a HR professional, I have come across legitimate complaints from these types of people, but their concerns weren't taken seriously by the business and dismissed as "there is that person again... whinging as usual". If you're able to, limit your contact with these people as they will by association dampen your reputation and weaken your passion for the business. These people may also weaken your ability to be taken seriously if you need to raise genuine concerns in a business.

Part of being a leader is having the maturity to admit to your mistakes, take accountability for these and if appropriate apologise to others. This is necessary to protect your reputation and maintain your personal brand. Recognising when you should apologise and admit fault is not easy, but is necessary to build a reputation of having integrity. There is nothing worse than having someone you work with never take accountability for their actions or apologise when they make mistakes. Particularly when their mistakes have had a direct impact on you.

I have certainly known a few people over the course of my career who have refused to take accountability and will find any excuse to demonstrate why they are not at fault. Devoting more energy to finding excuses rather than taking accountability doesn't gain respect and doesn't allow the people involved to properly move on from the matter. Part of being a leader is having the maturity to know that when a mistake is made, you cannot shy away from this. Own up to the error, apologise to those who the mistake has inconvenienced and communicate how you're going to rectify the situation. Generally, people are receptive towards this approach as everyone, including leaders, will make mistakes from time to time.

Building a strong personal brand has a lot of benefits to your career and the opportunities that will come to you. Building a positive personal brand requires a lot of consistent effort over a period. If you follow the recommendations in this book by conducting a self-evaluation on your career goals and journalising them, developing your own business acumen and leadership capabilities, and ensuring you have a solid reputation across your network, you will reap the rewards of your labour. Mirror the actions taken by other successful people you would like to emulate and use this insight to develop your online footprint and brand. I have observed how senior HR professionals have conducted themselves in a business, and how they have built a strong personal brand through influence and networking. By making observations and understanding how a person is perceived by on-lookers, you can start to understand what leadership style and behaviour would best suit you. I have also observed what their digital footprint is like, and what extra projects or side businesses they have worked on to boost their career. Through these observations, I have been able to make well-informed decisions about my own branding and how I want to be represented through my work. Through your own trial and error, you can start to see what it really takes to build a strong personal brand and reputation. Just remember that as you continue this learning journey, you will make mistakes. When you do inevitably make these mistakes, own up to these, do your best to turn the situation around and use your learnings to your advantage.

2

RECRUITMENT

RECRUITMENT IS WHERE THE employee life cycle begins. Recruitment is what attracts talented candidates to a business – where future employees consider and accept a formal letter of offer from the business and then get on-boarded. I consider recruitment one of the most important pillars in an employee life cycle and one that HR needs to fully appreciate and understand.

The sole mission of recruitment is to hire the right person, in the right role at the right time. Companies that are successful at this have built and implemented a talent acquisition strategy and have reaped the benefits. Large companies such as Google have a comprehensive talent acquisition strategy that aligns to their core company values, employee value proposition, and offer new recruits a career and not just a job. From implementing rigorous tests and assessments, the candidates they recruit become advocates for the business. They report Google having a positive work culture; a challenging work environment for their development; and they consider the business one that they can see themselves staying at long-term. By reducing replacement costs and stabilising the turnover rate, companies like Google reap the rewards in increased productivity and engagement from their employees. In businesses where the recruitment is not executed effectively, a business can hire the wrong people, which can have significant financial and reputational impacts. Later in this chapter and in *Chapter 5: Employee Relations*, I refer to examples of how poor recruitment practices impact a business.

Having a talent acquisition strategy in place is a competitive advantage for any business trying to attract top talent in an industry or with a focus on specific professions. A comprehensive strategy would incorporate many facets, with set performance targets, standardised job descriptions and professional advertisements, with the hope of poaching top talent from competitors and building a pipeline of talent ready for job vacancies.

Some performance indicators a company may have is how long they have to recruit a vacancy, the number of female applicants interviewed or shortlisted (for gender diversity), and whether the employee placed passes their probationary period. These performance indicators are just a few examples of those assigned to internal talent acquisition consultants or recruitment consultants employed by a business. The primary role of these consultants is to ensure that they are supporting the hiring managers to fill vacancies and meet any company-wide initiatives for promoting gender diversity, company culture, as well as compliance requirements. Talent acquisition consultants have a difficult role in balancing the needs of the company and the hiring manager and managing expectations of multiple prospective employees at the same time. Let me now take you through how a talent acquisition consultant can contribute value to a business at the very start of the recruitment process.

When a vacancy becomes available, management will engage either with HR and/or their internal recruitment team to start working through a requisition process. If this happens to be a new role, then a job description would need to be drafted by HR in collaboration with the hiring manager. A job description (JD) or position description (PD) is a document that outlines the overall purpose and scope of the role, the responsibilities, degree of budget control (if applicable), the number of direct reports (if applicable), where the position fits within the organisational structure, the reporting line, required and/or preferential skills, knowledge, experience, qualifications for successful candidates, and any other relevant details. The more detailed a job description is, the more the business can rely on this document if performance expectations are not being met, or if the employee is performing very well or is due for a promotion; the JD can be used to analyse the performance, which would be helpful when determining whether a prospective or current employee has outgrown the position.

When you are helping the hiring manager draft a JD in a HR capacity, it's important to consider what the inherent requirements of the position are.

Humesware Pty Ltd is looking to recruit an accountant to join their business. This is a new position as the business no longer wants to outsource these activities, and, by completing this function in-house, they will reduce expenditure. The inherent requirements of this position is that the employee would need to maintain their relevant accreditations throughout the duration of employment as well as work in an office environment for a maximum of 38 hours per week. If a prospective employee cannot fulfil the inherent requirements of the role, you would be able to reject this applicant. These considerations are important so that the hiring manager understands what appropriate skills, experience and qualifications are required for the role, and what pre-employment checks are appropriate. From these initial discussions, the requirements of the position can be captured in a document. A starting place is to write an overview of the position description.

At the top of the document is the name of the position; the reporting line, which is to a role, and not the name of the current incumbent (Finance Manager); number of direct reports (if applicable); and the department this role is in. Underneath this section, the document can have the "Purpose of position" section, which should be one paragraph on the key areas of focus, why the position exists in the business and the main value-adding activities that need to be performed.

For the accountant position, this introductory paragraph could go like this:

This role is required to contribute to the provision of the basic day-to-day business operations by providing quality and accurate accounting and finance data produced by the collation, analysis and potency of data. This data must be reliable and applicable towards achieving Humesware's strategic objectives and maintaining business profitability. This role is the expert in processing orders in a timely manner as well as managing invoices, payroll and credit notes. This role is responsible for the end-to-end maintenance of data integrity in MYOB software, the inventory counts and notifying departments when stock levels need replenishing. As a people leader, this role is responsible for providing commercial advice to all management levels to support them to reach their operational targets.

Some organisations will provide HR with a template of how the position overview needs to be written. This may need to incorporate all the company values or which specific values are applicable to the accountant position. These introductory paragraphs need to provide an accurate snapshot of the position's overall duties and responsibilities so that this is transparent to prospective employees and the business.

Experienced talent acquisition consultants will send prospective employees a copy of the job description to ensure they know what the expectations are, and so there is no ambiguity as to the role they are being interviewed or being made an offer for. This is also why a detailed document is beneficial for all parties involved, as you do not want to be in a situation where a new employee has been on-boarded and after a few months it is not the role they believed they started.

Hiring a new employee who has different or unrealistic perceptions of what the role is leads to a lot of time, resources and money lost to the business, and it also inconveniences the new employee as they need to awkwardly resign and seek further employment.

For the bulk of the position description, there are different methods of capturing the key performance indicators and areas of focus. Some organisations choose to use a table format, with bullet points and others choose to write a few paragraphs. I personally have no preference as the formatting is dependent on the organisation's marketing layout. For the purposes of this example, I have included a short table to give you an idea of what this may look like.

Areas of Focus	Key Performance indicators:
Operational Excellence	• Collate and analyse necessary data effectively using accounting software. • Back-up all documents and ensure the business meets record-keeping requirements. • Provide managers and customers with invoices and notes of credit in a timely manner. Diligently follow-up with customers to ensure invoices are paid as per the terms of business. Escalate late accounts to senior management in the first week of each month. • Build cost-efficient freight calculations and aim to provide customers and dealers with the most competitive price, while maintaining the business' gross-margin targets. • Answer phones in a friendly and professional manner. • Meet all end-of-month and quarterly reporting requirements for Profit and Loss Statements, revenue and EBITDA reporting. • Provide commercial and accounting advice to all levels of management, to help them achieve their operational targets and recommend appropriate changes to their cost expenditure, overheads and asset management.

In a PD, if a table is used there are at least four areas of focus with a list of Key Performance Indicators (KPIs). This would provide the necessary detail for a PD to be used for selecting the right candidate. When you're building a PD, it needs enough detail to brief the recruitment team. This is necessary as the recruitment team are not across the details of this position and the daily responsibilities the role would incur. Therefore, having a detailed document allows them to fully understand the requirements of the position and hire the right person according to the business' specifications. The other attributes the business needs to know are what previous experience, skills and knowledge are required and preferred in the shortlisted applicants.

The next section of the PD can be "Skills, Knowledge and Qualifications". This section is where a business lists the essential and preferential attributes of the incumbent. Continuing on with our accountant, here is a drafted list:

Essential Criteria
• Relevant Accounting Degree and CPA/CA Qualified.
• Minimum five (5) years post qualification and multi-national company experience.
• Experience in full set of accounts and intercompany accounting.
• Experience with ERP systems such as Oracle, SAP and MYOB.
• Independent, high attention to detail and ability to prioritise tasks to ensure completion within timelines.

Preferred Attributes
• Previous experience in Supply Chain and Logistics, manufacturing industry.

- Previous management experience leading a small team.
- Previous merger and acquisition experience.

At the end of the position description, I recommend having a few sentences around how the PD does not capture all the requirements of the role. A suggested sentence is '*From time to time, the role may be required to perform ad hoc duties*'. Having this sentence allows the business to reasonably request the employee to perform tasks that may not normally be in their role remit. I also recommend at the bottom of the document to have an area where the employee signs and dates the document, to acknowledge their understanding of the position description.

New starter employees would sign this document once they have been issued a written employment contract and are being on-boarded into the business. Having employees sign-off on the PD can be relied upon if any performance-based issues occur in the future.

With the hiring manager satisfied with the finalised position description, the business needs to now understand what the appropriate remuneration package or monetary arrangement is to compensate an incumbent. Providing compensation recommendations falls into HR's remit or, if you're working in a large organisation, there may be a remuneration and benefits function that performs this task. Let's assume that a HR representative needs to conduct this exercise. The first step is to grade the role. Questions for you to consider are below.

- Is the role governed by a modern award or enterprise agreement? If no, the role would be covered by a common-law contract (non-award employee).
- What is the scope and breadth of the role?

- Does this role sit at the strategic end of a managerial level or is it more operational?
- How experienced would a suitable incumbent need to be and what is the market range in salary for this type of candidate?
- What is the industry standard offering for this role?
- What have previous incumbents been paid if the position is not new?
- What are similar roles in seniority paid in the business?
- Would the role be eligible for any type of short-term incentive scheme or bonus scheme related to business performance?
- Will the business be offering only the superannuation guarantee?
- Are there any other benefits on offer in terms of leave loading, additional annual leave per year or any other perk?
- Would this role be eligible for any type of allowance?

These are just some questions HR need to consider prior to recommending a remuneration amount. In large organisations, they would have a compensation framework built to ensure all new employees are offered remuneration within a designated bandwidth.

The compensation framework would also standardise any eligible allowances, perks or additional benefits attached to roles to ensure employees are remunerated fairly and compensated according to their level of experience and the contribution they bring. When an offer amount has been recommended by human resources, this amount is included in the job requisition, which is then subject to an approval process. A job requisition approval process is used by large organisations so they can track how many additional overheads are being added to their business and can manage this expenditure closely. A requisition number is allocated to all vacancies so that the length of time to fill a role can be tracked, and the maximum offer that could be made to an incumbent is set.

Good news. Humesware's senior management has approved the accountant job requisition. It is time to now start finding quality candidates! For a talent acquisition consultant, this is where their fun begins as they have many methods they can draw upon to find stand-out recruits. One method is to place an online advertisement on well-known platforms to allow candidates to apply with their CV, a cover letter (if requested) and to confirm their working rights. The advertisement should be professionally written with no grammatical or spelling errors; use the business' logo and marketing format; and make reference to any pre-employment checks, which will be conducted during the recruitment process.

For an accountant role, a background check would be deemed relevant to the inherent requirements of the role; you would need to understand whether the accountant has been deemed bankrupt in the last five years. There are a range of other pre-employment checks a business could conduct, such as two reference checks, a pre-employment medical and a criminal check.

If a check is deemed relevant to the role, then they can be conducted, and the applicants notified that this is a requirement of the recruitment process. The advertisement would also incorporate aspects of the JD; it could leverage the overview paragraph and include the essential and preferred criteria. The advertisement needs to sell to the candidate why they would want to work for Humesware and what the company can offer (e.g., a dynamic work environment and a work-life balance).

Making the advertisement appealing and stand-out among others is a recruitment consultant's speciality.

Another method consultants use is to try and poach suitable candidates from competitors or approach candidates who have not directly applied to the job advertisement. Organisations use technology such as LinkedIn Recruiter to message candidates with a suitable skillset who have profiles on this platform.

From this initial correspondence, consultants can understand whether they have targeted candidates open to new opportunities, or if they are content in their current roles. Recruiters like to target talent from similar industries using this method, as they are familiar with the pressures of the workplace environment and so the learning curve is reduced if they were to join Humesware Pty Ltd.

Talent acquisition consultants need to exercise caution when trying to poach employees from competitors as candidates want to maintain confidentiality so that their current employer is not aware that they are entertaining the prospect of departing the business. Also, Humesware does not want the competitor to know of a new role or a vacancy that has been created that could give Humesware Pty Ltd a competitive advantage in the marketplace above the candidate's current employer (the competitor).

The final method a talent acquisition consultant may use is to outsource the hiring activities to a recruitment agency. Jobs can be outsourced to recruitment agencies when a role is niche, difficult to fill or the internal recruitment team is under-resourced and is unable to dedicate the necessary time and effort to effectively recruit for the position. Engaging recruitment agencies can be quite costly based on their placement fees. However, recruitment agencies provide an invaluable service when there is a critical talent gap in a business.

The level of service provided by an agency is highly influenced upon the agency's hiring philosophy and the individual consultants' expertise and morale in finding suitable candidates for a role. Since a consultant's pay is heavily dependent upon the successful placement of candidates, this can unfortunately lead to some careless placements – when the placements are made so that the job is finalised rather than achieving the best outcome for the client (Humesware) and the candidate.

When a recruitment consultant becomes fixated on commissions and making placements quickly, they jeopardise the quality of recruitment. Although the majority of recruitment consultants I have encountered over the course of my career have been lovely, customer-service driven individuals, you can also understand how a consultant may act in a way that is not in the best interests of the client and the candidate.

Some organisations may have built long-lasting relationships with specific recruitment agencies, and have established personal connections between the business' hiring managers. For HR representatives, these relationships can be very beneficial. However, they can also have negative ramifications as the business may be paying extravagant placement fees. The business may also be exclusively using the agency for all recruitment needs, despite the agency not being a specialist in the areas required. In these circumstances, HR may need to advise hiring managers of what the market standard is for recruitment fees, as well as the level of service they could reasonably expect from an agency. From my own experiences, long-standing relationships can work really well or the agency may become complacent in their level of service and supply the most convenient candidates for vacancies instead of the best ones. Here is an example of when a recruitment agency viewed HR as a threat to their long-standing income stream via the working relationship with Humesware Pty Ltd.

Lola Felts Recruitment (LFR) had established a long-standing relationship with Humesware for over ten years. This relationship was established and maintained by Mr Max Millo, the managing director of LFR. As Ms Smith, the HR Manager for Humesware, had commenced her new role in the business, Humesware did not know what a quality recruitment service looked like. Over the course of two months, Ms Smith had recognised Mr Millo's scheming nature and his potential to seriously impact the business' stability. Mr Millo had built close working relationships with a lot of hiring managers due to him placing them at Humesware himself. Therefore, transitioning the hiring managers away from using Mr Millo's services was going to be a huge undertaking.

The low quality of service became apparent to Ms Smith very quickly, as Mr Millo had been assigned a vacancy to fill and he had instantly sent through several "suitable options" without a job description. When Mr Millo was questioned about this, his reasoning was that he was very familiar with how the business operated and knew the job specifications well enough as he had worked with Humesware for a long period of time. At first, this sounded reasonable. However, Ms Smith advised Mr Millo that the company had recently updated their job descriptions and specifications, and changes had been made to the organisational structure. Going forward, Mr Millo could no longer rely on assumptions, as what may have worked in the past may not work in the future. Mr Millo also didn't adjust well to the recruitment activities being centralised through HR, as he was accustomed to dealing directly with the hiring managers. Breaking this habit was difficult and the hiring managers needed to also embrace this change.

Ms Smith's first meeting with Mr Millo was incredibly awkward, as the phone calls and conversations leading up to the meeting were already quite intense and confronting. Mr Millo did not welcome the change in expectations and the ways of working with Humesware. As the client, Ms Smith was requesting that all shortlisted candidates were sent directly to her first for screening prior to them being forwarded through to the hiring manager. Ms Smith also reasonably requested that all shortlisted candidates already have their working rights verified along with their CVs. Despite Ms Smith explaining the reason for this, Mr Millo was not pleased and responded with *"I can tell if they are Australian or not based on their accent, so I shouldn't have to ask for their passport details"*. How ridiculous is that as a response? This is just another example of the type of service provider Mr Millo was. Regardless of the poor level of service and difficult interactions, Ms Smith knew she had to continue working with Mr Millo in the future. Due to his relationships within the business, he had the potential to poach the hiring managers whom he had placed at Humesware for other open positions he had with other clients. His hold over middle management made him a threat to the business' talent and stability.

Keeping this in mind, Ms Smith was stuck having to nurture the existing relationship while resetting expectations up until the internal recruitment team was finally established.

With the implementation of the internal talent acquisition team at Humesware, all job vacancies had to be allocated to the recruitment team in the first instance. External agencies could only be engaged by the recruitment team and once the recruitment team had made attempts to fill the position in the first instance. Business approval would be required to engage a recruitment agency and their placement fees would need to align with the market standard. The decision to run recruitment activities internally was justified as it reduced company costs associated with placement fees. Having an internal recruitment team would also help Humesware work towards building an employment brand. Mr Millo and his agency's involvement with Humesware eventually came to a crashing holt with the implementation of the recruitment team, and his influence over the hiring managers came to an end.

From this one example, I don't want you to think that all recruitment agencies have malicious intentions, as they don't! They provide a valuable service to organisations when they are unable to keep up with their recruitment needs themselves. Many recruitment companies are highly ethical and have a proven reputation for placing high calibre candidates. Large recruitment agencies have their own internal performance targets, with consultants being measured and held accountable according to the level of client satisfaction. To ensure positive recruitment experiences for a business you're supporting, you need to find reputable consultants who are specialists in filling the vacancies your business has open.

A talent acquisition consultant has the expertise to decide how they will best fill a role, whether this will be through advertisements, poaching or engaging a recruitment agency. When an applicant applies for a position, they should be initially screened by the talent acquisition consultant using the information available on their CVs. Once some candidates have been deemed initially suitable, they should be contacted for a phone conversation, to understand what role they are looking for; confirm their current working arrangements, as sometimes their CVs are not up to date; confirm where they live, so that the proximity to the primary place of work can be calculated; and confirm whether they are currently being interviewed for any other role. Once you have narrowed down your short list, the consultant may then forward the candidates' CVs to HR or the hiring manager for their initial thoughts prior to locking in a face-to-face or online based interview.

Another variant to this process is that, after the initial conversation, the recruitment consultant may hold the first face-to-face or online interview. Once the candidate successfully passes this phase, they may then be referred onto HR and/or the hiring manager for feedback.

Organisations have different processes and may modify their processes according to the seniority of the position. Multiple rounds of interviews are common practice for large organisations, as a business tries to gain a lot of buy-in prior to hiring a candidate. Depending on the role, HR may also support the hiring manager by attending interviews during a recruitment phase for a role that has high turnover, or the role is deemed particularly important to the business.

Once all the interview phases have been finalised and the preferred candidate has been identified, the candidate should then undergo and complete any required pre-employment checks. Once these have been satisfactorily passed, the business would then be in the position to make an initial verbal offer. The verbal offer would outline the remuneration package or arrangement on offer, and the candidate can indicate whether they accept, decline or may try to negotiate the offer. When an arrangement is agreed in principle (verbally), the business can then draft a letter of offer outlining the terms and conditions of employment in writing.

New Starters

Once a candidate has satisfactorily passed all the necessary pre-employment checks, an initial verbal offer is made to the candidate. If this is verbally accepted by the candidate, the offer is then made in writing by way of a written employment contract. Assuming all the details of the contract are agreeable, this would be signed by the new starter and a signed copy returned to the employer. A detailed explanation of employment contracts is provided later in this book. For the purposes of your learning now, you just need to know that the employment contract is just one document of many that need to be completed by a new starter joining a business.

For a business to properly on-board a new starter into the business and be entered correctly into payroll, the new starter needs to complete and return a variety of documents. I will start with the tax file number (TFN) form. The TFN form is a statutory document that needs to be filled by new starters indicating their tax file number, full name, full address, and working rights to indicate whether they would like to claim the tax-free threshold, and whether any deductions need to be made on their behalf to contribute their income towards any HECS/FEE-Help.

New starters should claim the tax-free threshold if the new job will act as their primary source of income. If they don't claim this and the new role is their primary source of income, the business will need to tax them at a significantly higher rate and they would need to individually contact the Australian Tax Office in order to claw back the over-charged tax. In Australia, if a new starter has accrued a debt in relation to studies at a university, TAFE or college, and are above the minimum threshold to contribute their income towards their debt, this needs to be selected on the TFN form. For more information on the deduction thresholds, please refer to the Payroll section in this book. Once the TFN form has been correctly completed, payroll will complete the bottom half of the form, store the form for record-keeping and enter the required details into the payroll system.

Another required form is the superannuation choice form. This requires the new starter to indicate what superannuation fund they would like the business to make contributions to or they are able to select for them to use the default fund of the organisation (which would be pre-filled on the form sent through if a default fund exists). To accompany the completed form, the new starter should also attach the compliance letter of the chosen super fund, which can be downloaded from their super fund's website.

The compliance letter notifies payroll that the chosen super fund is an approved Australian product and meets the legislative compliance requirements. Most businesses will not on-board a new employee onto payroll without the compliance letter, and this would be a reasonable response from payroll officers.

An Employee Details Form is not a standardised form provided by the Australian Tax Office, but rather the title given to a document for employees to provide the required information to on-board them. An Employee Details Form requires an employees' full name, full address, contact phone number, personal email address (to send them payslips), as well as the contact details of their next of kin. The next of kin information is reserved for emergency situations, so that the business has other people to contact if anything happens in the workplace, or for whatever reason the business is unable to get in contact with the employee after numerous attempts. There should also be a section on this form for the new starter to provide their banking details so that they can receive their wages or salary as per the payroll cycle.

If an employee returns this form and the banking numbers are illegible, it is very helpful for a HR representative to reconfirm the numbers to the employee so that the payments are deposited into the correct bank account. This will save a lot of angst from the employee's, payroll's, and your perspective. If necessary, HR should instruct the employee to fill out a new form so that the banking details will not be mistaken.

One of my recommendations is to have new starter employees sign-off and acknowledge that they understand and agree to abide by specific company policies and procedures prior to them commencing employment. When the above documents are sent to the new starter, businesses can also attach policies such as the Code of Conduct Policy, Information Technology Policy, Drug and Alcohol Policy, and any other appropriate policies related to their position to read and sign-off.

The sign-off form itself can be a one-page checklist, requiring the new starter's signature and date of completion. This can be relied on in the event any of these policies are breached during their employment and as evidence to support that they were made aware of the business's expectations. It is evidence to support that they had agreed to abide by all the signed policies and procedures. During disciplinary matters or in matters where the business is considering terminating employment, one important consideration is whether the business can prove that the employee was reasonably aware of policies and procedures to which they are accountable. Having this covered in the new starter on-boarding process is incredibly beneficial for any business.

A legislative requirement that all businesses must comply with when a new employee commences is to provide a copy of the Fair Work Information Statement. The Statement is a document that outlines the eleven National Employment Standards (NES). These are the minimum employment conditions employees have a right to, and one of the NES is for new employees to get a copy of this document. To ensure all employees are issued this document, a lot of organisations include this in the new starter pack. This ensures there is a record of them being issued and this is not accidentally missed by the business in the rush to on-board the new starter. *Chapter 4: Employee Entitlements* covers the NES at length, as you need to be familiar with these as a HR representative.

Another legislative requirement is for the business to retain records of these private and sensitive documentation for up to seven years. The information must be kept in a secure and safe place, where there is a minimised risk of a privacy breach occurring.

Depending upon the requirements of an organisation, other forms may need to be completed to properly prepare for the new starter's first day. These documents may be internal forms such as a New Starter IT form, requesting the IT department set up a new customer email address for the employee and provide them a certain level of access to systems in the business.

Another internal form may be a request to procurement for a laptop and phone. These processes vary between businesses and should be documented so that the on-boarding of the new employee is a smooth one and everything is ready for them on their first day.

On-boarding Programs

Starting a new role can be a very exciting time, and it's natural to want to delve straight into the complexities and challenges of a new role. However, the first few months should be a balance between structured learning and on-the-job learning. A structured on-boarding program aims to provide a guide and insight into a new company and help broaden your understanding of the business in your early stages of employment. An effective on-boarding program involves indoctrinating a new starter in the organisational culture; explaining how their role interacts with different functions; providing networking opportunities; and providing opportunities for the new starter to receive feedback from their direct manager on how they are progressing. The new starter should have the proper support to go through the various on-boarding stages.

From my own experience, I have surmised that there are four on-boarding phases all new starters go through. The first phase is called Discovery and goes for the first two weeks of employment. Discovery is characterised by an intensive learning period while a new starter is settling into their new role, getting to know their colleagues, manager, navigating the office, online portals and discovering who to speak to regarding specific information queries.

Navigating available systems and understanding current processes within the context of their role is the main focus within this two-week period. New starters are also relying on their first impressions of the business and can only rely on how they are feeling at this stage regarding their decision to continue their employment. Until the new starter progresses through the other phases, they have limited information to make a pragmatic and well-informed decision as to whether they will remain in the business for a long period of time.

I have labelled the second phase as Assessment. The Assessment phase lasts for a period between the third and six-week mark. In these weeks, the new starters will be trying to understand their new role in depth and forming views about the alignment of the company values, culture, and their career with the business. New starters also begin to formulate views on the senior management team or direct management team and how they lead strategy, team meetings, the existing processes and system in place and identify areas of improvement. During this phase, the direct manager is also formulating their views on how suitable the new starter is for the business' culture and in performing the role.

The Awareness phase occurs during week six to ten of employment. During this period new starters develop their own awareness of how their role contributes to the bigger picture and the business' success. Developing this type of awareness is critical in the employee becoming invested in their role, so that they aim to achieve goals and perform. If this sense of direction is not achieved and the new starter does not get a sense of how they fit into the broader team, employees can become disillusioned with why they have been hired or what the purpose of their role is. During this phase, it is important for managers to ensure that they are providing this meaningful context so the new starter remains engaged throughout their on-boarding journey.

The final phase brings the new starter to a total of three months in the business. During this phase, a new starter would be able to confidently articulate the direction and strategy of the business, or the team that they are a part of, and how their own individual contributions fit within this strategy. Having this degree of clarity in their own direction and the direction of the business is a positive sign that the on-boarding journey is a positive experience for the new starter.

With the four phases of an on-boarding program covered, I would like for you to now understand how a business can implement a successful program so that the overall experience is positive for new starters. So that the new starter can reflect on their experiences and thoughts during their on-boarding journey, I recommend the business organise a work-diary to be given to the new starter. The work-dairy would be business branded, part of their induction kit and would likely be well-received by the new starter. Diary entries would record the new starter's impressions, questions they may have, notes on discussions or learnings and feedback they have received from their direct manager. New starters can also make regular references to their Key Result Areas (KRAs) specified in the job description or by their manager. Keeping this at the forefront of their mind will help them to understand what commercial and business specific knowledge they need to know to perform their role effectively.

New starters should also reflect on the conversations they have with other teams in different departments, or the information provided during on-boarding meetings – meetings organised for a new starter in their first few weeks so they understand key contacts and information required to perform their role. In an on-boarding program document, a general overview of each department may be provided, with an organisational structure to show who is the head of each function. Another useful method to help the new starter along their on-boarding journey is to integrate a buddy system into the program. An assigned buddy assigned to the new starter on their first day would act as the person they can turn to for guidance and ask any questions. The buddy may be a colleague in the new starter's team or an experienced member of that team. The buddy should also assist the new starter in navigating business systems and sourcing information. The on-boarding program needs to emphasise that the success of the new starter's on-boarding does not rest with the assigned buddy. How successful a new starter will be in the company is their own responsibility, and they are accountable for ensuring they progress through the program as it has been intended.

During the three-month on-boarding program, the document should set-up reminders for the new starter and their direct manager to have one-on-one meetings. During these meetings, the employee would have the opportunity to ask for direct feedback on their progress, ask questions, and for the manager to provide any positive and constructive comments. The purpose of these meetings is to be a building capability exercise and to support the new starter's development.

This should not be used by managers to make negative comments, as this period of time is all about learning and making initial mistakes so that they become proficient in their roles.

At the successful completion of an on-boarding program, the business should have a process in place to gather the new starter's feedback on the program's structure, content, and delivery. The feedback mechanism needs to welcome open and honest feedback. The mechanism may be a brief online survey sent by HR to the new starter, so that the feedback remains private and confidential. With this feedback, the business can continue to improve and modify the existing program and ensure it is meeting the needs of employees performing various roles. Variants of the program may need building to cater for junior to senior roles in the business.

Apart from giving employees a positive first three months at a business, what are the other benefits of having a comprehensive on-boarding program? There is a strong business case that employees who are effectively on-boarded into the business have a higher and faster trajectory of performing in their role and a reduced percentage of turnover in the first twelve months of employment. There are various other benefits attributed to an effective on-boarding program, which could be integrated into the strategic objectives of the program. These objectives could be the following: effective knowledge transfer, a quantifiable measure of how the new starter remains engaged throughout the on-boarding and in the first twelve months of employment, level of performance at six-month and twelve-month milestones, and the degree of understanding of the business' brand, company culture and values. These objectives will help a business measure the return on investment (ROI) of the program, and how it has directly impacted on the bottom line. Another key component of an effective program is that they need to meet the needs of the new starter.

When a new starter joins an organisation, they can experience a lot of different emotions. These can be excitement, a degree of nervousness or indifference. Understanding the emotional journey that can occur, the on-boarding programs needs to try and influence this so that new starters feel as though they "fit in" to the culture, are well connected, and begin building a support network of their choosing. Along with the buddy system and the organised functional overviews, the business should try and facilitate networking opportunities. This may be through a monthly meeting where new starters are introduced to one another or among a broader team, or a communications platform where all new starters are welcomed to the business so people know that they are there! Making new starters feel welcome and good is critical in retaining them.

An important strategic objective of effective on-boarding programs is educating new starters on company culture. How could a business define and characterise their culture in a way that can be understood within a three-month period, when it can take years to fully understand? This is certainly not an easy enterprise!

A business should start with outlining what type of behaviours are expected and what is deemed high performance. For example, some organisations value an entrepreneurial mindset and ability to put forward new ideas, whereas others promote operational excellence. Is the workplace environment fast-paced or more informal and relaxed? Does the business expect all the numbers and figures to be analysed so that all the information is accurate, or would the business prefer to make fast decisions with as much information that can be gathered at the time as over-analysis of scenarios is discouraged?

In some organisations, working long hours is an expectation, whereas other organisations promote work-life balance; how can this be summarised to a new starter? What are the business' performance priorities and how does the business want to be positioned in the market and industry? Does the business focus on inorganic growth (mergers and acquisitions) or organic growth (growing market share, revenue, profit)? By answering these questions, the business would be able to characterise what the company culture is, but also address the main challenges a new starter will face.

When a new starter joins a business, they bring with them a set of habits or ways of working from previous organisations and their own experience during their career. Sometimes their ways of working from previous businesses does not align to their current venture. This can apply to how a new starter may seek permission to take an action or seek approval for a decision to be made in a business. How decisions are made and who makes certain decisions varies between businesses. By removing the element of guessing, the business is supporting the new starter's learning curve. Another consideration is how project updates, information, documentation and announcements are communicated to work groups; are these done with emails, through noticeboards, toolboxes? Does the communication style change for the targeted audience?

Having managers cover this during the fortnightly meetings and providing some examples of previous communications will really help the new starter understand the lingo used and how to communicate effectively.

For a business to have an effective on-boarding program, the business needs to establish strategic objectives; feedback points for the manager and new starter; considerations for the business' and new starter's needs; and how to best support their learning curve. The benefits and ROI to a business is supported by research and allows a business to build a strong employment brand and competitive advantage in its industry. Having an on-boarding program is becoming the benchmark for organisations being pro-active in maintaining healthy retention rates and leveraging the existing workplace culture to properly induct new recruits.

3

SAFETY

PART OF A HR professional's role is looking after the wellbeing of your employees. This overlaps with the safety function in organisations. The *Workers Health and Safety Act 2011* (WHS Act 2011) is an important piece of legislation that all HR professionals should be very familiar, to the extent that you should be familiar with the *Fair Work Act 2009*.

HR professionals, managers and supervisors alike have inherent workers health and safety responsibilities to take care of their own health and safety, as well as the additional responsibility to oversee the health and safety of team members in the workplace. Safety is a shared responsibility, and everyone has a role to play in ensuring their own wellbeing in a workplace. This is prescribed as such in the relevant legislation.

As a worker and as a HR professional, you have legislative obligations under the *Workers Health and Safety Act 2011*. This piece of legislation provides employers with instructions on what is required under law to meet compliance requirements and ensure all workers remain safe and healthy in the workplace. In this Chapter you will be taken through the various definitions and what it means to have a "duty of care" to employees in the business. As a duty holder in the business, you will need to understand what this means and what impact this will have on your day-to-day responsibilities. You will also need to understand why it is incredibly important to encourage all levels of management and employees to report safety incidents in a timely manner, and what specific processes should be undertaken when an employee has injured themselves.

The main purpose of having work health and safety practices in a business is to provide a safe workplace for all workers, whereby they can all return home safely every day. This encompasses protecting all workers against harm to their health, safety and welfare by way of eliminating risks arising from the workplace; providing mechanisms for fair consultation and representations of WHS concerns; promoting the information and training; and maintaining legislative compliance.

As a HR professional, you need to familiarise yourself with these mechanisms and the frameworks currently in place, as you will be involved in creating these and/or ensuring that they are abided to by all employees. Disciplinary issues can arise with employees when safety processes are not followed by employees and can result in HR becoming involved to support fair and equitable management of these matters.

If a business was to provide an unsafe workplace or environment for workers, this would have serious repercussions. An unsafe workplace has a domino effect of creating an atmosphere and environment where people do not care about safety and do not report safety concerns. This transforms into an unhealthy safety culture, which then cultivates into a place where safety incidents are more likely to occur. The higher the frequency of hazards and near misses in the workplace, the greater chance of employees getting injured. This is not the type of safety culture any business would want to have or nurture in the future.

As a HR professional, you must be committed to embedding a healthy safety culture in the business you support, acting as a leader in this space and ensuring any non-compliances are dealt with consistently.

Legislative Obligations

The objective of the *Workers Health and Safety Act 2011* is built upon the principle that employees and employers must act together to ensure a healthy and safe workplace environment. This means in principle that workers and other persons need to be provided the highest level of protection against harm to their health, safety and welfare from hazards and risks arising in the workplace as is reasonably practicable.

This is a shared responsibility and does not rely on just a few people in a business to be accountable. All levels of management share this responsibility and can contribute towards a healthy safety culture and practices in the business. It is often the case that HR are the go-to point of contact for safety related questions. Therefore, it is absolutely critical to understand your obligations under the *WHS Act 2011* so that you understand how you, employees and the business at large can meet obligations under the Act.

The legislation is very explicit around different types of roles and their associated responsibilities. The first type of a role is called an "officer", which refers to the term Officer under the *Corporations Act 2001*, with someone that holds public authority to make decisions on behalf of the business. A snippet of this is "a director or secretary of the corporation or a person which makes or participates in making decisions that affect the whole or substantial part of the business of the corporation".

In most business' cases, the officer/s of the business would be the CEO, company secretary and other senior leaders entrusted with looking after safety. An officer and duty holders have the responsibility to demonstrate leadership and governance in safety.

As a HR presentative, you are often recognised as a duty holder.

Another component of this role includes acting with due diligence to meet your duty of care requirements. What this essentially means is that you, along with senior management, need to make decisions that do not negatively impact the health and safety of workers. You also have the responsibility to ensure decisions have considered employees' overall health and wellbeing.

Another definition that you need to understand is what a PCBU is. Managers, supervisors, safety and HR professionals are often all considered PCBUs under the *WHS Act 2011*.

A PCBU stands for a "Person Conducting a Business or Undertaking".

In the *WHS Act 2011*, the definition refers to "the entity that operates the business or undertaking – corporate or natural person". In this case, as a HR professional you're a natural person.

It also applies to corporations, association, self-employed, contractors, sub-contractors, partnerships, labour hire business, and franchisees. As a PCBU, you need to understand that there are requirements for you to consult with workers on safety, health and welfare matters on a regular basis. It is recommended that managers, HR, and safety professionals consult with other PCBUs in a business when trying to implement new or different ways of working across an area, so that ideas can be leveraged and shared. This Chapter really is all about sharing!

As a HR PCBU, you're also responsible for resolving WHS issues at a local level and having a mix of management worker representatives to support this process. If a workplace dispute is raised regarding a safety manager, human resources should be involved to try and reach a resolution without an external body becoming involved. All resolutions and frameworks put in place must comply with the WHS Regulations, which are applicable to the business you are supporting. (These regulations can be downloaded from Work Safe Australia website.)

In the spirit of sharing responsibility, workers in a business also have health and safety responsibilities. The responsibilities do not solely rely on the management, safety and HR representatives in the business. Each "worker" or team member in a workplace must take reasonable care of their own health and safety. They must not act in an unsafe way whereby they are jeopardising their own safety and the safety of those around them. They must take reasonable care that their actions do not adversely impact others. They must also follow reasonable instructions and co-operate with the business' policies and procedures in place. It is important to note that all employees can refuse to perform work and stop work, if they believe that they would put them in harm's way, potentially cause them injury or a serious injury. They need to have a reasonable belief or concern that the instructions provided by the business are not reasonable, and by following the instructions they are not meeting their obligations and would thereby be acting in a way that could adversely harm others. You would be involved in trying to address any scenario where a worker or workers have stopped work due to them feeling unsafe in the workplace.

WHS Legislation Overview

As per Section 19 of the *WHS Act 2011*, a primary duty of care is defined as this: "PCBU or person must so far as reasonably practicable, ensure that the health and safety of other persons is not put at risk from work carried out as a part of the business undertakings."

This applies to maintaining the work environment, ensuring the plant structures are safe; safe systems of work exist; there is safe use, handling and storage of equipment and substances; the provision of relevant training; and the conditions of the workplace are monitored for the purpose of preventing illness and injury.

As a HR representative in the business, your overarching "duty of care" applies to three key focus areas: managing risks, monitoring/maintaining and reviewing our safe work systems and practices, and the need to consult/represent and participate in relevant safety discussions and dispute resolution.

To manage existing risks in the business, they first need to be identified. Identification of safety risks can be done by regular and timely incident reporting, safety risk assessments, regular auditing and site inspections. These are a just a few mechanisms that can assist your business to identify the risks, evaluate the risks and create appropriate action plans to mitigate or eliminate the risks.

Management of risk is often referred to as the hierarchy of control. The hierarchy of control is a system that ranks the most effective to the least effective controls to minimise and manage workplace safety risks. The first and most ineffective level a business can use as a first line of defence is Personal Protective Equipment (PPE). Examples of PPE are steel cap boots to prevent injury to the toes from falling objects and a hard hat on construction sites to prevent head injuries. PPE is used where a risk can't be eliminated but the risk of an injury can be prevented through the use of PPE. The next level of control is administrative, whereby procedures and safe working procedures are implemented to control the level of risk in completing a certain task or an environmental factor for example.

The third level is engineering controls such as a lock-out tag out procedure where an engineering measure prevents the risk from occurring. The next level is substitution, whereby you substitute a factor or part of the environment that would ultimately decrease the probability of an incident occurring. And then we go to the highest level of control when the business can completely eliminate a risk. An example of this may be changing a chemical that could be hazardous to a 100% safe alternative and the chemical is still able to meet the business requirements of the original substance. These controls are all about managing risk.

The second pillar of monitoring/maintaining and reviewing risks is about constantly monitoring safe work systems and ensuring they not only work but are being followed. For example, if there is a requirement for employees to wear safety boots at all times and the business notices that some employees are now wearing sneakers to the workplace, this needs to be monitored and the behaviours of workers changed. HR are instrumental in developing and implementing company policies that allow the business to enforce these safety requirements.

This then leads into the maintenance of safe work systems, which applies to procedures, policies and behaviours. Safe work practices need to be maintained and are critical in ensuring compliance and the workplace remaining safe. It is also imperative that the business continues to challenge working practices to understand if there is a safer way to do things. The business cannot rely on "this is the way we have always done it, so it is fine" mentality. The business needs to constantly review and improve on ways of working so that we can improve the safety and wellbeing standards of our employees.

The last pillar is focused on ensuring worker consultation, representation and participation in the workplace. This refers to a business' obligations to work together, discuss, consult and try and resolve issues and concerns in the workplace. When the business makes decisions that would significantly impact workers, the business is obligated to consult, and ensure there is adequate representation of the working groups. There needs to be genuine consultation whereby employees are given the opportunity to provide feedback and the business considers this feedback prior to making or implementing the final decision. These consultation requirements mirror the consultation clauses captured in modern awards. Consultation must be genuine and conducted with the sole objective to resolve any type of workplace disputes, work through issues or if the business is looking to introduce major changes in the workplace. If obligations such as the need to consult is not met by a business, the business and certain individuals can be prosecuted and heavily fined.

Offences and Penalties

There are penalties if individuals who hold an officer position, duty holders and the business do not meet their duty of care obligations. As a HR representative, you need to be informed as to what is at stake for the business if safety is not treated seriously. If an incident were to occur and a worker/s was seriously injured or even killed in the workplace and the business was found to have directly contributed to this incident, there can be serious repercussions for the business and duty holders. Ensuring the safety of the people that work for or in a business is always serious and needs to be treated seriously.

The worst type of penalty in the *WHS Act 2011* is classified as a Category 1 breach, whereby the business or person who had a duty of care to an individual, by way of their conduct jeopardised the safety of an individual, causing a risk of death or serious illness. This conduct is deemed "reckless conduct" and means that the behaviour demonstrated a blatant disregard for the health and safety of that impacted individual.

There are many types of penalties that apply to different types of breaches and I won't go through all of them. The key point of this section in the chapter is to provide you awareness of the consequences and why safety is such an important matter for you to understand and uphold in business.

Now that you're familiar with the consequences of breaches and if serious incidents occur, we need to return to the legislation. There is an overarching national legislation and regulations that impact responsibilities. It is also important to understand that there is also state-based legislation, which influences these. You need to refer to the state-based legislation in which you reside. If the employees you support are national, you need to take into account the applicable state-based legislation. The first place to look to familiarise yourself with the legislative framework is to look at the Safe Work Australia website. Safe Work Australia is an Australian Government agency governed by the *Safe Work Australia Act 2008*. The primary responsibility and function of this body is to improve the workers' health and safety as well as workers' compensation arrangements nationally. Putting this simply, they are the national policy body responsible for the development and evaluation of the WHS laws, which are comprised of:

- Model WHS Act;
- Model WHS Regulations;
- Model Codes of Practice.

I have covered in detail the *WHS Act 2011*, which is the first bullet point above. The regulations and codes of practice are not legal documents, but provide best practice for employers to apply in their business. It also provides employers a national consistency on how to apply the requirements in the *WHS Act 2011*.

Then, in each State, there are individual pieces of legislation and regulations that the employer must abide with. It is important to remember that the umbrella legislation is the *WHS Act 2011*, with the WHS regulations acting as a supporting document to the legislation. The regulations have no legal effect and provide industry guidelines and instructions on various topics. Other documents include International Standardised Organisation (ISO) accredited risk management instructions and guides, along with the codes of practice. If you have a grasp of this framework, you will be in a solid position as a HR representative to provide advice. Also, if you don't have all the answers and need to gather additional information, you now have reference points in the relevant legislation, codes of practice and regulations.

All the core theoretical components have now been covered so that you can now start to absorb how a business can go about practically meeting these requirements. Before I get into the meat of this, here are some critical questions to consider as a HR professional:

- Why should workers report incidences?
- When should a worker report an incident?
- How do we report incidences?
- What should you do if you are injured or someone is injured in the workplace?

Hopefully, you have had a go at answering these questions. I'm going to work through each question, starting with the why: why should workers report incidences? Why is it necessary?

I've just covered that you and the business you're supporting have obligations under the *WHS Act 2011*, but there is more to this. Reporting incidents, near misses and hazards gives the business the opportunity to learn from what has happened in the past and prevent it from happening again. Reporting incidents also helps the business to identify future hazards and maintain a safe work environment. Incident reporting also is part of an integrated management system of safety. The purpose of reporting incidents is not so that individuals in the business are apportioned with blame. For a business, the purpose of reporting incidents is to keep their people safe. If an incident has occurred that involves a worker being injured, you need to work with management to immediately facilitate the appropriate medical care for the injured employees as a priority.

The next question is when should a worker report an incident? Before you can answer this question, you need to understand the various definitions of the types of incidents and their categories. The distinctions between each category are important for reporting processes, as well as ensuring the action taken matches the type of incident that has occurred.

A "near miss" is the term used to describe a "near hit", a "close call" or "nearly collision". What this translates to is that a near miss is something that could have been an incident but was not one. It is an unplanned event that had the potential to cause harm, but did not actually result in human injury, damage to equipment or disrupt the normal business operation. It is important to report near misses so that the business can learn from these occurrences and prevent an incident or incidents from occurring.

A "Hazard" is a potential source of harm. These can be substances, events or circumstances that may all constitute a hazard as their nature has the potential to cause harm to workers, the environment or business property. A First Aid Injury or FAI is when an employee has been injured and had to be treated using supplies in the first aid kit in the workplace or by the appointed first aid officer in the department. This type of incident may be a cut, abrasions to the skin, a sprain… These are all minor injuries and need only require a follow-up or subsequent observation by a medical practitioner. These minor injuries do not ordinarily require medical care.

Medical Treatment Injuries or MTI are an injury or disease that has resulted in a certain level of treatment given by a physician and more care was required than just first aid.

A Lost Time Injury or LTI is something that results in time lost from work, a permanent disability, or a fatality. The lost time could be as little as a day from work or not being able to attend one shift. Environmental incidents are when an incident occurs that could have a significant impact on the environment, such as an oil spill going down the drains, or pollution in the air. A damage incident is when something that has occurred has damaged the business' property or equipment.

With you having an understanding of the different types of incidences, you need to now be able to apply this knowledge practically in your own workplaces. So how do you go about reporting incidences?

How each business requires their workers to report incidences can widely vary in terms of incident form templates and whether they are available in an online platform, as a carbon-based copy form or a combination of both. If there is a consistent methodology where the form is used by all workers, levels of management and can be analysed and quantified for reporting purposes. The important components of a safety incident report form are the following:

- The report date of the incident needs to be accurate particularly with establishing the date of an injury for workers comp and treatment matters.
- The location of the incident; the nature of the incident. If there was an injury, where had it occurred? Where is the injury on the body? Were there any witnesses to the incident?
- What is the recommended course of action and when will the action be finalised?
- There should be an option to include photos of the incident or injury, as photos can be especially useful in providing insight to people reviewing the form that may not be familiar with the working environment in which the incident occurred.

Employee Injuries

So, what if you have injured yourself or one of the workers in your client group has become injured? Absolute priority should always be given to the adequate treatment of an injury and/or illness. Should injured employees require treatment, a supervisor/manager are required to arrange to transport them ta medical facility. This may involve the supervisor/manager or another employee to accompany the injured employee to seek medical treatment and ensure they are being taken care of while waiting for or undergoing medical treatment. Once the injury has been addressed and the worker's wellbeing has been taken care of, the business can then return its focus to reporting the injury.

It is essential to report injuries to not only protect everyone, but also to meet your legal obligations. It is also important that injured employees understand their obligations to participate in suitable duties when on a return-to-work plan and that they must comply with these requirements.

The key takeaways from this chapter section as a HR professional are the following:

- It is everyone's responsibility in a business to report safety incidents, near misses and hazards.
- A business' and individual's obligations are governed by a comprehensive legislative framework and its sole objective is to ensure that all workers remain safe and healthy in their places of work.
- Championing the reporting of safety incident reports in the business you support is helpful, so that the business can learn from near misses and hazards, as prevention is better than a cure.
- To develop and implement prevention measures in a business, all workers need to participate in reporting near misses, hazards and incidents on site.
- As a HR representative you need to lead by example and be a Safety Champion.

Becoming a Safety Champion

As a HR professional, you are by default expected to lead by example in how you behave in the workplace. You are also expected to be a positive advocate for change and upholding safety as a number one priority.

One of the fundamental ways you can become more involved in leading the safety agenda is by becoming a member of your local safety committee at the site you are based on or any other site that is suitable. If local safety committees do not yet exist, there is now an opportunity to lead the implementation of these in your business.

The function of local safety committees is to provide a formal mechanism by which the business can consult with employees at a local level. The primary purpose of the committee is to manage risks that are present in the workplace, which may be reoccurring, new or emergent risks. By having local safety committees, risk is no longer managed in a top-down way, but rather through consultation and working together to create ways to improve the performance and implementation of risk management. This meets the business' legislative requirements to consult with our employees and is also a great way to communicate major changes when a decision has been made by management.

All safety committees must comprise of an even mix of management and employee representatives. Employee representatives can comprise nominated Health and Safety Representatives (HSRs) and elected employees; employees must be elected by way of a work group vote.

Management can nominate their own representatives to be present, which can include HR. Once the committee members have been selected, the roles need to be defined and allocated.

The Chairperson is usually a management representative responsible for organising the safety committee meetings and ensuring that the agenda is followed. The chairperson is also responsible for the following:

- Organising the date, time, and place of the meeting with members.
- Leading the safety discussion and ensuring that the meeting follows the agenda.
- Ensuring that all members can speak without being interrupted by other committee members.
- Communicating with senior management and HR when concerns are raised that may have implications for the business.

There is another key role in local safety committees, which is the record keeper. Meeting minutes are taken at each meeting, then distributed to all members after the meeting has finished during tool-boxes and pinned on noticeboards. If there are any follow-up actions due between each meeting, the record keeper is accountable for following up so that the minutes are adjusted to reflect any updates. The chairperson and the record keeper would work closely together to ensure each meeting discusses only relevant topics related to the meeting minutes, as well as ensuring that blame is not apportioned to individuals.

As a safety committee member, it is expected that you and all other members represent the areas that you work in, perform the allocated action items assigned to you (if any), provide any relevant safety guidance as per the legislation, and engage and actively participate in discussions. Being an active member of a committee provides you with an insight into the key challenges your client group face; it makes employees more familiar and comfortable with you as a HR representative and also builds your reputation in the business. You will be seen as genuinely caring for the needs of your employees and it will help break any type of perception of HR as sitting in an ivory tower, disconnected from the business and the employees' real issues and concerns. Being a safety champion means you have a real understanding of what the business needs; you can help implement practical safety programs and how these would work once implemented.

Another component of being a Safety Champion is leveraging the existing safety culture and developing ways of lifting the benchmark. One method that HR can contribute to is training managers and supervisors in how to properly investigate safety incidents, so that they are able to write a safety report and release a safety alert (if required). Building safety as a priority into workplace culture is essential.

There are specialist safety investigation courses available in Australia, which may be an appropriate option for your business, but can be quite expensive. If you don't have the assigned budget for this, you could develop internal guidelines for managers to use on how to conduct an investigation. The guidelines you provide would be like the process outlined in *Chapter 5: Employee Relations*, for conducting workplace investigations.

The benefit of managers being able to conduct these investigations themselves is that they can get to the root cause of the incident, why it occurred and what are the key learnings from the incident. What managers are looking for during the investigation is what were the chain of events that caused the incident. Was it the state of mind of the individual/s involved? Was there a system of work being carried out that did not suit the tasks performed? Was a safety mechanism bypassed or incorrectly implemented? Were there any type of faults in the safety equipment or the equipment used? Was adequate supervision provided for the work performed?

This is the first level of enquiry.

The next level of enquiry is understanding the critical factors and causes in the design components of the equipment used (if applicable), environmental components of the workplace and the processes that were followed or not followed, and the behavioural contributions of the employees involved in the incident. These factors involve looking at the existing procedures and whether the actions taken by the individual/s involved complied with this procedure, or perhaps the actions taken are the normal practice on site even though it may deviate from the procedure. One consideration is that there may be a lack of procedure/s in place, which outlines a safe method of performing this work. With the absence of this procedure, employees have performed the work unsafely, which may have caused an incident to occur. Another consideration is if there has been an improper use of safeguards, failure to wear personal protective equipment (PPE), or there may have been inadequate training provided to the individual/s involved. All these factors are necessary to establish the facts: what exactly happened that led to the incident occurring?

To establish the facts of an incident, a lot of organisations employ the methodology of the five *Whys*. This methodology starts with the problem. For example, the problem may be that a vehicle was dropped from a vehicle lift in a service centre, narrowly missing the automotive mechanic. The consequences of this incident would have been severe or fatal. The first why here is "Why did the car drop from the vehicle lift?" with the possible answer being the hydraulic lifting tubes failed.

The next why might be "Why did the hydraulic lifting tubes fail?" with the possible answer being "The hydraulic fluid has been slowly leaking from the tubing for a few days now."

The next why might be "Why has the hydraulic fluid been leaking for a few days?" with the possible answer being "The vehicle lift is overdue for a service and the hydraulic fluid was listed as a maintenance task a few weeks ago".

The fourth why might be "Why wasn't the vehicle lift fixed immediately when hydraulic fluid was leaking from the tubes?" with a possible answer being the company, which usually does the maintenance on all of the vehicle lifts, recently went into liquidation. The business has been searching for an alternative service provider for the last few days.

The fifth why might be "Why did the automotive technician continue to use the vehicle lift, knowing that hydraulic fluid was leaking?" with the possible answer being "There were no alternative lifts available and, if the lift wasn't used, cars wouldn't be serviced and the business would fall behind on KPIs".

From this example and lines of questioning, the investigator now has a good understanding of the motivations of the business and behaviour of the technician, which led to this near miss. As the reader, you're able to understand the facts that occurred and contributed towards the near miss and the serious consequences of the decision to continue using the lift, despite apparent safety issues.

With your professional human resources guidance, the manager has finalised her investigation and fully understands the events leading up to the near miss occurring. To prevent this from occurring again in the workplace, the key learnings should be shared with all other employees in the business. This can be done through a safety alert.

A safety alert should be a one-page proforma or a succinct means of communication like a memo to provide context to the incident:

- the nature of the injury (if applicable);
- the severity/seriousness of the incident;
- what action was taken and needs completing;
- and most importantly, what are the key learnings?

The safety alert can include any photos of the incident or site of the incident to provide employees, who are unfamiliar with that specific working environment, the relevant context to understand what had transpired.

I do not recommend having any references to individual names and any type of photograph of an injury, as these can upset employees.

With your joint role of acting as both a HR representative and a Safety Champion, you need to ensure that all HR related advice aligns to best practice safety procedures, methods and legislative requirements. This is why, at the beginning of this chapter, I made you aware you should be just as comfortable with the legislation and day-to-day requirements of safety as you are with providing human resources advice.

I am not saying you need to be a safety expert, but it is expected that you understand the basics included in this chapter so you can perform your role as effectively as possible and you're seen by the business as a credible source of knowledge and insight. If you want to be considered a high performer and kick-start your HR career, you cannot neglect safety with the mindset that it is separate to HR.

HR and safety overlap and you must be an advocate for safety, health, and the wellbeing of employees in your client group.

Workers Compensation

As a HR professional, it is a requirement as a safety champion to understand a business' obligations to manage and prevent workplace injury and support the rehabilitation of injured workers. These responsibilities stem from the *Workplace Injury Management and Workers Compensation Act 1998* ("**the Act**").

The Act's purpose is to establish a workplace injury management and workers compensation system for the prompt treatment of injuries, providing the necessary medical and vocational rehabilitation for workers injured in the workplace.

The Act instructs businesses on how to provide injured workers with income support while they have no or reduced capacity to perform their duties, or in the unfortunate event that they are permanently impaired or a death occurs.

So how does a business manage injured workers? When a business reaches a certain size, it becomes a legislative requirement to have resources assigned to managing injured workers. Dedicated roles have the titles of workers compensation advisors, injury management advisors and/or return to work co-ordinators.

Research indicates that the best way to rehabilitate the majority of injured workers is in the workplace; by providing suitable light or alternative duties to perform while they are undergoing treatment, with the aim for them to return to pre-injury duties. Therefore, having an effective Return to Work (RTW) plan is so critical, as well as a resource dedicated to overseeing this plan. Employers are also obligated to have documented processes and systems outlining how they will manage the RTW of an injured worker, which also needs to be consistent with the employer's insurer.

71

Having a dedicated RTW co-ordinator will help the employer to comply with these processes, and meet the key underlying principles for an effective return to work plan. These principles include:

- Having processes in place that all workers and managers understand and know what needs to be done in the event of a workplace injury.
- Safety and HR representatives, all management levels and workers understand the importance of early reporting of injuries to prevent exacerbating an injury, as well as meeting legislative and insurer requirements.
- Safety and HR representatives, all management levels and workers understand that the workplace has been supported to be the most effective means of rehabilitating an injured worker to pre-injury duties and a full recovery.
- All parties need to work together to support the RTW and full recovery of the injured worker.

These principles are important, but they do not adequately highlight how an employer and workers both have obligations under the Act to comply with return-to-work requirements.

As a HR representative, it will fall on your shoulders to raise awareness and educate managers that injured employees also have obligations when they are covered by a workers compensation claim. Workers are obligated to cooperate with the business to prevent work-related injuries to themselves and others, comply with the RTW plan set out to them by the business and the RTW co-ordinator; also workers cannot unreasonably refuse to comply with their injury management plan. If an employee is demonstrating consistent non-compliance with the RTW plan, the business can take disciplinary action and the insurer may decide to suspend weekly benefits. A lot of managers feel uncomfortable performance managing an injured worker or are under the presumption that once a worker goes on workers compensation they become "untouchable". This is very wrong!

This is a fallacy and workers need to do everything they can to ensure that they fully rehabilitate into their role and work towards assuming pre-injury duties; pre-injury duties and capacity is what they were performing prior to their injury, as well as the total working hours.

With the expectations of the RTW co-ordinator and the injured worker covered, I now need to touch on how the insurer, nominated treating doctor and workplace rehabilitator/s fit into the picture.

When a worker is injured and sees their own personal doctor, with the technical term being "nominated treating doctor", the doctor is required to complete the initial WorkCover medical certificate.

This is called a certificate of capacity and would initially assess the type of injury, what treatment is required and what the current working capacity is. This may be reduced working hours, recommendations for alternative duties and arrangements, or even no capacity for duties for a period.

The certificate of capacity is then provided to the employer to process and pass onto the insurer, so that a claim is opened and a claim number generated. The nominated treating doctor is also required to arrange and monitor the appropriate treatment of the injured worker, by referring the worker to specialists, and liaising with the employer on the progress of recovery.

When an employer would like to liaise directly with the nominated treating doctor regarding the treatment and recovery of the injured worker, the employer is required to gain written consent from the worker to do this. When contact is made by the employer, it is best practice to have a list of questions prepared or even a formal letter with questions so that you can best understand what the diagnosis, prognosis is and what other accommodations (if any) can be made to support rehabilitation.

The role of a workplace rehabilitator is to promote the early and safe return of the worker by providing adequate and appropriate assessment of the worker's needs, and identifying barriers to their recovery. This role is instrumental in designing suitable duties to assist the employer to meet their obligations in providing suitable employment, and if this is not possible to then arrange retraining, or alternative employment when the worker is not able to return to pre-injury duties. How successful a worker's return to pre-injury duties is hinges on the co-operation of the rehabilitator, along with all the other involved parties, and how they implement the RTW program.

A RTW plan program is a document that outlines the agreed management systems and processes to follow when any worker is injured in the workplace. A worker must notify the employer as soon as possible about their work-related injury, so that the worker can then consult with a medical practitioner for treatment and obtain a WorkCover medical certificate.

Once the employer receives this certificate, they are then required to notify the insurer within 48 hours of becoming aware that a worker has sustained an injury. When the insurer contacts the worker, the employer can contact the nominated treating doctor to ascertain the treatment, and workplace rehabilitation needs so that an injury management plan can be developed.

When required, provisional weekly payments may commence within seven days of the initial injury, and the employer will be informed by the insurer if payments have been approved, as well as any type of reimbursement for medical expenses. Once the insurance and claim side has commenced, the business needs to then focus on developing a RTW plan.

The RTW plan would need to identify suitable duties, establish a timeline for these suitable duties and when the worker and the business could aim for a full recovery, as well as create a document for all parties to monitor progression.

The suitable duties offered in a RTW plan cannot be randomly assigned or duties the manager believes the worker can perform without further injury. The assigned suitable duties or any accommodations must be made with consideration of the special needs of the worker, any special circumstances such as the worker's carer responsibilities, impact of the workload on other team members, and whether the worker would require additional training in order to perform the suitable duties. No suitable duties can be offered without medical advice being provided from the nominated treating doctor, to ensure they will not exacerbate the injury and is appropriate for the current working capacity. Suitable duties can also be provided in a variety of ways, such as offering duties at a different work site, different working hours, modified duties, performing a different role entirely or a combination of these arrangements.

For suitable duties to be an effective method of rehabilitation, they need to be time-limited and upgraded towards pre-injury duties and hours when progress has been made. In the event the employer cannot accommodate suitable duties or they are not available, another host employer will be found by WorkCover or the rehabilitation provider.

While a worker is undergoing rehabilitation and participating in a RTW plan, they cannot be disadvantaged. The Act emphasises that the main priority for all parties involved is for a successful return of the injured worker to the workplace. There needs to be collaboration so that all arrangements are discussed, and the injured worker is familiar with their obligations under the Act.

Employers cannot dismiss an injured worker for six months (or the period specified in the governing award or enterprise agreement) after the worker has become unfit to perform duties due to a work-related injury. If an employer dismisses a worker on these grounds, unlike other unfair dismissal claims whereby the applicant must make a claim within 21 days, the dismissed worker can make a claim for reinstatement for up to two years from the dismissal date.

An employer may also permit injured workers to use their accrued personal leave on the basis that they are able to supply medical certificates. If any disagreements do arise during the RTW plan, in my experience I have found having the involvement of the rehabilitation provider is very useful in these discussions.

If the employer does have concerns regarding the treatment of the injured worker or requires additional information regarding their ability to return to pre-injury duties, independent medical consultants can be engaged to conduct relevant assessments.

When a RTW plan is going well and an injured worker is demonstrating the expected progression, this is every HR's happy place. However, when an injured worker is unco-operative or showing a reduced ability to return to pre-injury duties, the business becomes frustrated and seeks out human resources' intervention. Therefore, it is important you understand the end-to-end process that businesses must follow and the inherent legislative obligations.

If you're also assigned the RTW co-ordinator duties in your capacity as a HR representative, you would be incredibly involved in the day-to-day management of the claim. If you need to support the business in managing an injured employee's exit, a proper and fair process needs to be undertaken while also conducting an appropriate risk assessment for the termination. Chapter 5 covers how to do this in detail with multiple examples. On the assumption you have already conducted a risk assessment and you have the business' approval to commence proceedings to terminate an injured worker, below is some guidance on how this could be done using a fictitious example.

Ms Melanie Harper was a long-term Humesware Pty Ltd employee based in Victoria Australia, who had suffered a work-related back injury on 4 January 2017 and had submitted a worker's compensation claim on 18 January 2017. The business had continued to support Ms Harper's rehabilitation throughout the claim and provided suitable duties in excess of a 52-week period. During her claim, she had seen several medical specialists and on medical consensus further surgery was not recommended. The conservative treatment had included physiotherapy and vocational rehabilitation. The insurer had organised for an independent medical examination, which demonstrated that no further progress had been made over a six-month period. It was determined that no amount of non-invasive medical care would make a meaningful difference to the lower back dysfunction. As the business had exceeded its obligation to provide suitable duties, the business had the intention to work through a process of withdrawing suitable duties.

A meeting was organised between Ms Harper, her manager and Ms Smith (HR Manager) to discuss the business' intention to withdraw suitable duties and for a fitness for duties assessment to be undertaken. During this meeting, a formal letter was issued on the company's letterhead outlining the history of the claim and that the business had fulfilled its obligation to provide suitable duties or pre-injury employment for a period of 52 weeks of a worker's incapacity. Based on the review of the claim, the business is formally advising Ms Harper that the business is unable to provide ongoing suitable duties and is withdrawing these duties.

I recommended reiterating in the letter that Ms Harper's employment remains ongoing. However, to review Ms Harper's ongoing employment, she is required to undertake a fitness for duties assessment to help the business make a decision. During this meeting, the appointment time, date and confirmation of attendance should be discussed and locked-in.

I also recommended that Ms Harper provide a copy of the letter to her doctor.

As a HR professional, it is a reasonable expectation that you would write the first letter issued during the meeting, as well as the letter sent to Ms Harper's doctor. The purpose of the letter to the doctor is to request a medical examination for a comprehensive medical report, so that her fitness for duties can be assessed. In saying this, it is best practice to provide the doctor with a history of the claim, what the business would like the assessment on and provide a list of questions you would like the doctor to address. In the letter, you could write that you would like the below questions specifically addressed in the report:

1. To provide the current diagnosis of Ms Harper's medical condition/s.
2. To provide the prognosis of Ms Harper's medical condition/s.
3. An assessment as to whether Ms Harper would be able to perform the full range of duties (pre-injury duties) without restriction.

4. If Ms Harper is not currently fit to perform the inherent requirements of her pre-injury position, what job modifications or steps would need to be taken by Humesware Pty Ltd in order for Ms Harper to be able to do so?

5. How long would any modifications need to be in place for?

6. Are there any considerations Humesware Pty Ltd need to make to ensure a safe working environment for Ms Harper?

7. Any other relevant information.

Once the fitness for duties assessment has been completed, a medical report is forwarded through to HR, then a meeting should be organised with Ms Harper and her support person to discuss the results of the report.

During this meeting, the findings of the report would be discussed along with the business' concerns. Ms Harper would have the opportunity to provide her feedback and suggest any workable solutions regarding any other type of accommodation that had not been previously considered. After this meeting, the business would then take away any comments and make the required preparations to gain approval to terminate Ms Harper's employment on the grounds of her being unable to fulfil the inherent requirements of the role.

The example involving Ms Harper is an unfortunate one and is an example of how a business may wish to manage employees on long-term workers compensation. When determining the appropriate course of action, HR should make enquiries as to whether termination of employment would impact the insurance premiums and what the associated risks are with terminating their employment. For more information on how to conduct a risk assessment and conduct termination processes in a procedurally fair manner, please refer to the Employee Relations Chapter.

4

EMPLOYEE ENTITLEMENTS

As a HR PROFESSIONAL in a business, you're seen as the go-to person when managers, supervisors and employees have questions regarding employee entitlements. "Employee Entitlements" is a broad term used to describe how people are paid, which can be either wages or salary, annual leave, personal leave, long service leave, superannuation and any other type of benefit. How these employee entitlements are paid, what rate of pay, applicable allowances and the details of each benefit are dependent upon whether an employee is an award covered or non-award-based employee.

When an employee is classed as an award-based employee, this is referring to the modern awards released by the Fair Work Commission.

A modern award is a document that covers a specific group of employees in an industry, and outlines in detail the minimum terms and conditions of employment for those employees. The terms and conditions will either match or go above the conditions outlined in the National Employment Standards (NES). Unlike the NES, which will be covered in detail in the next section, modern awards provide specificity on entitlements such as breaks, applicable allowances, penalty rates, over-time, base rate of pay for different classifications, rostering, definitions on various roles in scope, hours of work and payment of wages.

Non-award employees can be referred to as common-law contract employees, as the terms are used interchangeably. As these employees are not covered by conditions stipulated in a modern award, their entitlements and payment details are contained within an employment agreement. Regardless of what different terms are entered into in an employment agreement, they need to be equal to or better than NES conditions.

National Employment Standards (NES)

When employees start a new job, the employer is obligated to provide them with a copy of the Fair Work Information Sheet, which includes the 11 NES conditions listed below:

1. Maximum Weekly Hours

This first NES establishes the maximum weekly hours for employees, as well as the circumstances in which an employee may refuse a request or requirement to work additional hours. The maximum weekly hours of work are deemed as 38 hours per week for a full-time employee. For a part-time employee, the employee needs to work less than 38 hours per week.

The 38 hours per week is inclusive of any planned or unplanned leave, which may be annual leave, personal leave or a combination of paid and unpaid leave. Employees have the right to refuse any additional hours of work if the request from the employer is deemed unreasonable. It is quite common for employment contracts to have a clause stipulating that the "maximum weekly hours to be worked are 38 hours per week, but you may be requested to work reasonable additional hours".

The term "reasonable additional hours" may seem quite ambiguous or subjective upon initial review. However, there is clarification provided in the FWA and other resources such as the Fair Work Ombudsman website. Examples are provided of when the request to work reasonable additional hours may be rejected by employee, such as when the additional hours would pose a threat to the worker's health and safety or there are extenuating personal circumstances.

It is also important to note that some employment contracts, modern awards and enterprise agreements stipulated averaging the maximum weekly hours. These same employment conditions apply in this respect, that full-time employees cannot work more than 38 hours per week and an employee that is not full-time would need to work the lesser of 38 hours, or their ordinary hours of work.

2. Flexible Working Arrangements

Section 65 of the *Fair Work Act 2009* outlines the right for employees to request flexible working arrangements. This section of the Act forms a part of the NES, whereby an employee who has worked for the same employer for greater than 12 months can request flexible working arrangements. True casuals are excluded from making flexible working arrangement requests due to the nature of their contractual engagement. Please note that casuals who are deemed to be regular and systematic and have been with the same employer for greater than 12 months can make a flexible working arrangement request.

A flexible work arrangement may include changes to the employee's ordinary hours of work, shift pattern, reduction in total hours of work, or location of work. Examples of this could be a change to start and finish times, reducing from full-time to part-time hours per week for an ongoing period or on a trial basis.

So how do employees make a request for flexible working arrangements and how can an employer respond to these types of requests? It is best practice for employers to ask employees to submit their requests to the appropriate manager in writing. Most large organisations have a policy and form, which can be completed and signed by the employee to submit their flexible working arrangement application. Once an employee has submitted their request, the employer must respond within 21 days, which outlines in writing whether their request has been approved or rejected, and the reasons for the decision made.

Within the 21 daytime period, it is recommended that the employer and the employee have a discussion to understand the reasons for the flexible working arrangement request and any hesitations that the employer would have in granting the request. After having an open and transparent conversation, the employer must determine whether there are any reasonable grounds to refuse the request. These may be that, due to the employee's role and the nature of the role, a change in the working pattern or hours of work would impact the operational requirements of the business. It is important to note that the employer must genuinely consider the needs of the employee. After due consideration, the employer may grant the request subject to a trial period of three or six months, to understand how the change in working conditions impacts the business directly and whether the business could accommodate the change on a more permanent basis.

This is a good option particularly if the business has reservations for approving the application, but also wants to support the employee with their personal circumstances.

As a HR professional, we would be expected to support the business in reviewing these types of applications, as well as supporting these discussions. HR professionals are expected to provide neutral guidance and advice so that all minimum employment conditions are met, but also so that the business is not negatively impacted.

3. Parental Leave and Related Entitlements

As per Section 70 of the *Fair Work Act 2009*, there are provisions for employees to have access to maternity and parental leave when a child is born or a child is adopted. Parental leave is the general term used to describe the entitlements for employees to take 12 months of unpaid leave when an employee gives birth, a partner or a de facto partner gives birth, or a child under the age of 16 years of age is adopted.

Please note that employees can apply to their employer for an additional 12 months of parental leave, but this is at the discretion of the employer to approve this. Parental leave also covers different types of leave: maternity leave, paternity and partner leave, adoption leave, special maternity leave, a right to return to the previous job and "no safe job" leave.

We are not going to cover all these types of scenarios in the book and will primarily focus on the most common example, which is when the mother of an unborn child notifies her employer that she is pregnant and applies for maternity leave closer to the due date.

There are eligibility requirements for employees to apply for and have access to parental leave. All employees in Australia are entitled to 12 months of unpaid parental leave, if they have worked for their employer for at least 12 months: before the date or expected date of birth of the child if the employee is pregnant, before the date of the adoption, or when the leave starts, and have or will have responsibility for care of the child.

Casual employees are also eligible to access unpaid parental leave if they have worked for their respective employer for at least 12 months and are deemed to be regular and systematic, and if it is a reasonable expectation that they would have had ongoing work.

Employees who have just taken parental leave do not have to work another 12 months to be eligible for their next period of parental leave with the same employer. However, if they have changed jobs, the requirement to be with the new employer for at least 12 months would apply again. Different circumstances would apply if an employee transfers between different business entities within the same business group or when a business is acquired by another.

As a HR representative, you are often the first point of contact for employees looking for information on parental leave and what application they need to make. You should be familiar with this NES principle and act to communicate the leave arrangements with payroll for processing the leave of absence. The internal processes for these applications would significantly vary between organisations, as some organisations have sophisticated maternity and parental leave policies whereby, they pay above the NES requirements. Some large businesses pay employees while they are on parental leave – this may be through a top-up scheme, where the business makes up the gap between what they would ordinarily get paid and the minimum wage processed by Human Services (Centrelink).

Other organisations may have a tiered payment system where for the first few months of leave, employees would receive 100 % pay of normal salary and as the leave progresses, the per centage decreases. Exceptional maternity and parental leave policies do exist for large organisations where they provide full pay to all employees throughout the entire 12-month period.

As a HR professional, you're also expected to understand that businesses cannot discriminate against employees or adversely impact them in any way for making an application for parental leave. An example of adversely impacting an employee due to their parental leave requirements would be to make their position redundant on the sole basis that they are pregnant, and the business still genuinely requires that position to meet operational demands.

Other examples may be to demote a pregnant employee and replace their role with another internal candidate. This type of treatment is not acceptable from an ethical standpoint, but also from a legislative one. If an employee is dismissed on the basis of them being pregnant, they can make a genuine application for unfair dismissal, and could also lodge a general protections claim as they had been adversely impacted due to a proscribed reason.

4. Annual Leave

As per Section 87 of the *Fair Work Act 2009*, for each year of service with the same employer, an employee is entitled to four weeks of paid annual leave, or five weeks of paid annual leave if the employee is classified as a shift worker.

Annual leave is colloquially referred to as "holiday pay" and refers to when an employee is paid for their time off from work. Please note that modern awards, employment contracts and enterprise agreements cannot offer fewer annual entitlements than those proscribed in the NES.

All employees are eligible for annual entitlements except for casual employees. However, this eligibility criteria only strictly applies to true casuals. When a casual has been regular and systematic for at least 12 months and has an expectation of continuance work, they may have the ability to make a claim for annual leave entitlements.

HR professionals need to understand the nuances of these type of scenarios, and I encourage you to read widely. You need to understand what is going on in the industrial environment, what cases are currently being tested in the Federal Court or Federal Circuit Court, as well as what determinations have been made and have become precedent. These types of matters become highly technical and as a HR professional, understanding the basics of what annual leave is, how it's paid and how it accrues is a bare minimum.

As soon as an eligible employee commences their employment, their entitlement to annual leave begins and starts to accrue. Leave accrues gradually throughout the year so that you accrue four weeks (20 days) of leave within a 12-month period. Any unused annual leave entitlements are not wiped from the employee's entitlement bucket, but are carried over into the next year or 12-month period. There are circumstances when the accrual of annual leave becomes frozen. These include when an employee takes a period of absence (unpaid leave), which may be unpaid personal leave or unpaid annual leave, unpaid parental leave and unpaid family and domestic violence leave. You'll need to familiarise yourself with these types of leave, as you need to equally understand them and how they can impact the provision of other entitlements.

5. Personal/Carer's Leave, Compassionate Leave and Unpaid Family and Domestic Violence Leave

This NES has a combination of different types of leave. We will start with personal/carer's leave, which is well known as "sick pay" or "personal leave" and is a statutory entitlement for all full-time and part-time employees.

This entitlement is paid time away from work for when an employee is sick or injured (non-work related) and has caring responsibilities for an immediate family member/s and family emergencies. Casuals do not accrue paid personal leave/carer's leave, but are able to take unpaid personal/carer's leave days from work.

Carer's leave and personal leave are recorded differently from a payroll perspective. Employees accrue up to 10 personal/carer's leave in a 12-month period, and when time is taken off for carer's leave or personal leave, the days taken are from this 10-day balance.

Employees need to know what the definition of immediate family members or household members are, as employees cannot have access to this leave when it applies outside of this list. The list of immediate family members and household members can be found on the Fair Work Ombudsman website.

Compassionate leave is very different to Personal/Carer's leave and is referred to as "bereavement leave". All employees including casuals are entitled to take this leave. (Please note that when casuals take this leave, it will be unpaid.)

Compassionate leave can be taken when an immediate member of the family or household member dies or contracts a life-threatening illness/injury. The definition of what an immediate family member and household member is consistent across Personal/Carer's leave and Compassionate leave. Unlike with Personal/Carer's leave, employees are entitled to two days Compassionate leave on each occasion an immediate family member or household member dies or contracts a life-threatening condition.

The Compassionate leave also needs to be taken as one single continuous period; as two days consecutively or two separate periods of one day each, or any separate period that the employer and employee agree upon.

A common misconception is that Compassionate leave is taken from the Personal/Carer's leave balance. However, Compassionate leave is not accrued and is available to full-time and part-time employees on pay, and casuals can take Compassionate leave unpaid.

Employers can request evidence or supporting documentation for the reason for Compassionate leave, such as a funeral notice, death certificate or for the employee to sign and date a statutory declaration.

In July 2018, amendments to the *Fair Work Act 2009* allowed all employees, including part-time and casual employees, to have access to up to five days of unpaid family domestic violence leave within a 12-month period. As per Section 106A of the *Fair Work Act 2009*, this leave does not accumulate year to year like Annual Leave or Personal/Carer's Leave. Domestic Violence leave is available in one single period of five days – separate periods of one or more days each or any separate periods agreed between the employer and the employee.

It is at an employer's discretion if an employee is to be paid for these five days of leave and whether the employee is granted more than five days within a 12-month period, paid or unpaid. Unpaid family and domestic violence leave are to only be used when an employee's close relative seeks to coerce, control or cause harm and fear to the employee. Please refer to the definition of what a close relative is on the Fair Work Ombudsman website.

6. Community Service Leave

Community Service leave is characterised as leave taken when an employee is acting in the interests of the community, which is inclusive of volunteer emergency management activities, and jury service. All employees including casuals are entitled to take Community Service leave and this is all unpaid except for jury service. It is important to understand that Jury service leave is paid according to each state-based legislation and have varying arrangements across the different states.

Referring to Section 109 of the *Fair Work Act 2009*, voluntary emergency management activities are listed as when an employee engages in activities dealing with an emergency or natural disaster, activities on a voluntary basis, and is a member of a recognised emergency management body such as the State Emergency Services. Community Service leave is unique as it does not accrue and is unlimited; an employee can take as much community service leave while they are engaged in the activity and to allow for a reasonable amount of rest time and travel. The employee in turn must notify their employer of their absence and the expected period of absence as soon as possible. In some circumstances, the employer may be notified after the employee has already started engaging in their community service activity.

As a HR professional, it is important to understand how employers are obliged to support community service volunteers, those summoned for jury service and employees serving as defence reservists.

It is recommended that when a new employee starts with their employer, the employer has a form or document that requests new employees to declare their involvement in community emergency services and/or if they are a reservist so there are no surprises!

7. Long Service Leave

The accrual and payment of long service leave is dependent upon the governing state-based legislation. Employees become entitled to long service leave when they have been employed by the same employer for a long period of time. The length of service required without a break is determined by the state you live in Australia. There are also strict eligibility criteria as to whether you can access your long service leave while you're on parental leave, when you resign and whether you can access pro-rated accruals. Or if you're terminated by way of initiative of the employer, and how you take the leave in single periods or blocks.

HR professionals are often asked to provide advice to employees and managers on accessing long service leave accruals – whether entitlements could be cashed out or accessed early due to pressing circumstances?

It is critical to understand the nuances within each state and what an employer can and cannot legally approve. The payment of long service accruals when an employee departs a company must be processed within seven days of departure, as in some states late processing of payment could be deemed a criminal offence. Overall, you need to know the legislative requirements. Conduct your own research and if necessary, obtain legal advice.

8. Public Holidays

Gazetted public holidays are dependent upon the state your employees live in and can differ year to year on what date they fall. HR professionals need to be aware when these days occur so that employees are paid accordingly, but also so that the payroll department can adjust their payroll cycle to accommodate days out of the office.

Employees are only entitled to public holiday pay if they would have ordinarily worked on that day as per their roster or ordinary hours/days of work, then they are able to have the day off and be paid.

Employees are not entitled to be paid for gazetted public holidays without working on that day if they are part-time employees and the public holiday falls on a day that they would not have ordinarily worked, or for casual employees.

All employees are entitled to be paid for all work performed on the gazetted public holiday as per the rates stipulated in either their employment contracts and/or the governing modern award conditions. This applies to all types of employees, full-time, part-time and casual employees.

In Australia, penalty rates apply when an employee is required to work on a gazetted public holiday. For an updated list of the calendar year gazetted public holidays in your state, refer to the Fair Work Ombudsman website for information.

9. Notice of Termination and Redundancy Pay

When an employee is terminated by way of initiative of the employer or the employer has made the decision to make an employee's role redundant, the reason for the departure must be made in writing to the impacted employee. This formal notification is delivered to the employee during a meeting, emailed to the employee directly or mailed to the employee's personal address.

When an employee is terminated or made redundant, the employer is obligated to pay out a minimum notice period based on the employees' years of service with the company, unless they are required to work through their notice period. Employees who are over the age of 45 years and have completed at least two years of continuous service with the business, are entitled to an additional one week's notice.

Notice can either be worked by the departing employee or paid in lieu by the employer. Not all employees are entitled to be paid their notice period; employees terminated for serious misconduct, daily hire workers or true casuals are not entitled to a notice period.

The same with a notice period, the severance portion of a redundancy payment is based on the years of service with a business. When an employee has reached ten years of continuous service, the number of weeks an employee is entitled to is dropped from 16 weeks (at least nine years but less than ten years' service) to 12 weeks. The reason for the reduction in weeks when 10 years' service has been completed is due to the state-based long service leave legislation coming into play at this time. After 10 years of service, departing employees would have access to their long service leave accruals being paid out at redundancy. Only employees who have completed a period of 12 months service are eligible for redundancy pay. For further information on how redundancy pays are calculated, please refer to the Genuine Redundancies section in this book.

10. Fair Work Information Statement & Casual Employment

When a new employee commences their employment with a business, every employer is obligated to provide the new employee with a copy of the Fair Work Information Statement. In my humble opinion, best practice is to include a copy of the Fair Work Information Sheet with the employment contract and other on-boarding documents. This can be distributed via mail, email, in person or any other mode the business distributes these types of documents.

The Fair Work Information Sheet includes information on all the National employment standards, the right for an employee to apply for flexible work arrangements, and a range of other topics such as right of entry and the role of the Fair Work Commission. In 2021, The Fair Work Commission has introduced a specific information sheet for casuals that also needs to be issued to new employees. This means that there is an information sheet for permanent employees and a different information sheet for casuals. The Casual Employment information sheet is listed as the eleventh NES.

As a HR professional, you are expected to understand all the information contained on these information sheets so that if any new employee has questions, you're able to answer them without hesitation. I would classify this type of knowledge as fundamental and incredibly important for all HR practitioners to grasp.

Employment Contracts

Prior to new employees joining an enterprise, it is commercial practice for them to be issued an employment contract from the business owner, talent acquisition or human resources team.

An employment contract is a document that outlines the terms and conditions of employment and must be signed and returned to the employer prior to starting work.

When an employee signs the contract it indicates their acceptance of the terms and that they abide by these terms throughout the duration of their employment. Employment contracts can be issued to any type of employee, regardless of whether they are on a salary, earn wages and/or are covered by an industrial instrument. Employment contracts can provide terms above and beyond the NES, and applicable modern award conditions. Despite this ability, employment contracts cannot override legislative requirements and employee rights protected by state and federal based legislation. Therefore, I recommend that organisations use standardised employment contracts for different positions and arrangements, so the probability of errors are reduced.

It is common practice that an employment contract on the first page includes the date of issue and a welcome page. The first may read like "we are pleased to confirm our offer of employment to you with Humesware Pty Ltd ("**the Company**") on the terms and conditions set out in this employment contract".

The standard terms and conditions would then be covered outlining the position, the commencement date of employment, and the employment status. The employment status would indicate whether the employment terms are for a casual, full-time or part-time permanent position, and what the duration of the contract may be. The duration of the contract may stipulate an end date if the role is employed on a fixed-term basis. If in the event the role is permanent, then an end date will not be specified and the employment will continue until terminated in accordance with the provisions of the employment agreement. The conditions on which a permanent contract can be terminated by any party is specific to each contract and is referred to as providing notice. The primary place of work should also be stipulated with the physical address location. The business may also like to stipulate that from time to time the Company may require the employee to work in other locations on a temporary or permanent basis. Travel may also be a requirement on an ad hoc basis and travelling would be expected as a part of their duties.

Moving onto the bulk of the employment contract, the employment contract should refer to any relevant and applicable industrial instruments, such as a modern award or an enterprise agreement. Another clause included in the beginning of a contract or in a contract schedule is the probationary period. A probationary clause from an employment law perspective is very interesting.

The reason why organisations include probationary periods in employment contracts is so that the business has a set period to decide whether the employee is suitable for long-term employment. During the "probationary period" the employer is able to end employment giving only one week's notice and with little associated risk. The premise of this period stems from the qualifying period or minimum employment period covered in the *Fair Work Act 2009*.

Section 383 of the FWA defines the meaning of the minimum employment period as six months of employment ending at the time of dismissal or before the dismissal for large organisations, and a period of 12 months for small businesses. As this definition is quite stringent this can present some challenges for a business when they would like to rely on how a probationary period has been defined in a contract of employment. It is important to note that the contractual conditions cannot override what is stipulated in federal level legislation.

I'll explain what I mean by using a fictious example, involving Mr Matt Barron an employee working at Humesware Pty Ltd as a pastry chef. Mr Barron's manager, Mr Munro decided to offer a permanent contract to Mr Barron as he had performed well as a casual chef for a nine-month period already in the business. Rejoiced with the opportunity, Mr Barron signed the new contract of employment despite it stipulating that he was to enter a probationary period of six months from the date of conversion. Since his conversion, Mr Barron has had some personal circumstances that have detrimentally impacted his performance. Mr Barron has on repeated occasions been late to his shifts, called in sick with little to no notice and has produced dishes from the kitchen that were not quality. Mr Munro was very frustrated and felt as though now that he had been made permanent, Mr Barron was taking advantage of the business. It is for this reason he now wanted to rely on the probationary period in his new contract and terminate Mr Barron's employment giving one week's notice. The difficulty with this is that Mr Barron's length of service when he converted from casual to permanent was unbroken and had been honoured. Mr Barron's length of service is what dictates the qualifying period (legislative component) or "probationary period" and cannot be overwritten by any type of contractual term. In this example, Mr Munro is unable to rely on the probationary clause in Mr Barron's employment contact, and the clause in actuality is defunct.

The probationary period never truly applied and should not have been included in his new employment contract. It was an administrative error for including this in his contract of employment. When any employee who has been with the company already in a role, particularly casuals it can be often misunderstood that when they are made permanent or transition into a different role that a probationary period can apply. As per the Fair Work Act, a "probationary period" does not exist and is a commercial term used widely for the first six months of employment. Unfortunately, the term "probationary period" has been synonymously misunderstood as the qualifying period; whereby an employer can dismiss an employee without a comprehensive process and providing one week's notice in lieu. Only the qualifying period is governed by the FWA and cannot be superseded by an erroneous term issued in a common law contract. The qualifying period can only apply to the first six months of employment, which in Mr Barron's case is six months post his original hire date on 23 October 2019. Even if Mr Barron was converted from casual to permanent in an identical role as a pastry chef, a probationary period/qualifying period would not have applied. Unfortunately, only performance management is an option for this matter, as there is no legal work around the employment clause.

With reference to Mr Munro's challenge, a business may question what the point of having an employment contract in place is, particularly when you need to rely on the contract to take action.

As a HR representative, it is an important aspect of your role to understand how each clause in a contract of employment should be drafted and can be used by the business in different scenarios. Clauses need to be drafted correctly and only include clauses that the business can confidently rely on when circumstances dictate this.

Other clauses I would deem mandatory in an employment contract are the hours of work, general duties of the position, references to company policies and procedures such as the Code of Conduct and the Information Technology policies. A clause should also be dedicated to the remuneration; how the employee will be paid; the rate of pay and if the employee is paid using a salary; how the base salary will compensate for overtime; any applicable loading under the award, and whether superannuation is included in the package or in addition to the base salary.

How much notice is required if an employee decides to resign or the business decides to terminate or make the employee redundant should also be covered in a stand-alone clause. The conditions in an "Ending Employment" clause could refer strictly to NES or the conditions could be above the NES conditions. A clause that is not included in a lot of contracts I have seen throughout my career and would solve a lot of problems if it was, is the deduction of amounts owed.

Occasionally, employees can be erroneously overpaid by the business and thereby owe the company money. Having a clause in the employment contract that outlines how monies owed will be deducted to the extent permitted by law is a useful clause, especially when a business can rely on this clause in the unfortunate circumstance when an overpayment has occurred.

When an employee departs the business, they may have had access to commercially sensitive information and intellectual property. Having a clause that outlines their obligation when employed with the business and after they depart will help in the event ownership of intellectual property is challenged and intellectual property is stolen by the departed employee.

A clause covering workplace surveillance ensures that the employee has been adequately notified that they may be monitored while in the workplace and informed on how this surveillance will be used during the course of their employment. As a part of an employer's privacy obligations, they cannot monitor an employee's presence in the workplace in an inappropriate manner. Employers also need written consent from employees when collecting their private and sensitive information. This privacy collection consent extends to collecting information that needs to be submitted to the Australian Tax Office (ATO).

Towards the end of the contract, if it is appropriate for the type of role and seniority level, there may be a "Restraint of Trade" clause or a "Restricted Area" clause in the contract.

A Restraint of Trade clause outlines how the employee cannot work directly for a competitor or work within a certain distance of the primary place of work. The restraint of trade cannot be unreasonable, and it is quite difficult to enforce once an employee has left the business for a number of reasons. The first reason being that an employee is not obligated to tell their current employer where they will be working next. The employer would also need to commence legal action and acquire a court injunction to enforce the contractual conditions. As legal fees can be costly, the business would need to decide whether pursuing an injunction is worth the desired outcome.

Most employees and businesses would believe that the only enforceable conditions of employment are those explicitly laid out in each clause of the employment contract. However, many cases have gone before the Fair Work Commission and the Federal Court to argue the basis of an implied term, which can exist in employment contracts.

An implied term is a condition that is not explicitly addressed in an employment contract, but what is expected to be implied by the nature of the agreement. For example, it is an implied term that an employee can always reasonably expect to be safe in the workplace. This may not have been included in the contract, but that may be an implied term of the employment agreement. There have been multiple cases of an employer arguing that an implied term exists, such as good faith and reasonableness between the employer and employee. This argument is not a common occurrence and as a HR representative you would unlikely have to deal with this type of matter in your career on more than one occasion.

The key take away from this chapter section is that drafting employment contracts need to be done correctly. Attention to detail is essential in your role as a HR representative when drafting employment contracts so that the nature of employment is clear, it would be difficult to dispute the terms of the agreement and the document safeguards the business from future conflicts.

Employees are most concerned with how much money will be going into their pockets, and so having an extra zero on the end of a base salary is an unfortunate error to ever make. Always double-check the details of the employment contract before it is released to a new starter to sign. The nature of the contract also needs to reflect the nature of the role and the work to be performed, or the business may run the risk of issuing sham contracts. One scenario when this can arise is when someone is engaged as an independent contractor when they are acting as an employee.

Independent Contractor vs. Employee

In some cases, an independent contractor may be considered an employee due to the nature of the engagement being in all actuality an employment-based relationship. The basis of an employment relationship is when a worker provides labour in exchange for remuneration provided by the employer. The name given to the nature of a relationship is an important consideration of the FWC when ruling on matters of contract. However, if a contract is labelled as an independent contractual arrangement, but the nature of the relationship is different and one of employment, then the FWC in this respect may ignore the label given. This is why the FWC or the federal court would look at the genuine substance of the relationship in question when making a determination as to whether someone is an independent contractor or an employee.

The FWC uses a test to assess whether a person is an independent contractor or an employee. The factors assessed are whether the person performs work as an independent entrepreneur or business owner operating a separate entity, and if in performing the work is the person operating as a representative of the business and not as a person receiving the work.

If these considerations are confirmed, it is highly likely that the person is engaged genuinely as an independent contractor. There are a multitude of other factors that can help the FWC to determine the nature of the working relationship. These are the following:

- The worker is not excluded to perform work only for a specific business and is genuinely entitled to work with other businesses.
- The worker can advertise their services to other businesses, as there is not an exclusive relationship, and the services can be offered to multiple businesses at the one time.
- The worker provides their own clothes, tools of trade and equipment and maintains this equipment without the

involvement of any other party. The worker wears their own uniform of choice and has their own business cards.

- The worker is responsible for lodging their own statements with the ATO and is not reliant on other businesses to do this for them.
- At the completion of work, the worker invoices the business for their services directly.

When the FWC is considering what a genuine employee relationship looks like, they look at the reverse of the above factors. For example, an employee would be provided their business cards from an entity, as well as the place of work and the uniform they need to wear when performing their duties. The above points are not all the factors the FWC may consider. For additional information on what considerations may be made by the FWC, you can refer to the downloadable bench books from the FWC website.

If in the event the FWC deems that a worker is in fact not an independent contractor and has satisfied the criteria to be recognised as an employee, then the employer would need to treat the worker as an employee going forward. This would require the business to provide employee entitlements and make any appropriate back-pay of entitlements and superannuation contributions. If in the event the worker is no longer required due to the operational requirements of the business, the worker would now be entitled to notice and a redundancy payment appropriate for the length of service they have engaged with the business. There have been many cases that the FWC has made determinations on in unfair dismissal claims and when an industrial dispute has arisen.

As a HR representative, I encourage you to research these cases and see if you can identify any of these types of risks in your current business. Regular and systematic casuals present a similar risk to businesses pertaining to claims of entitlements that have been traditionally reserved only for permanent employees.

Payroll

The payroll department performs a critical function that keeps a business moving and operational. As the team ensures employees are paid on time, in full and correctly every pay cycle, they are very important in ensuring employees are treated fairly and paid for the work they contribute towards the business. Despite how much employees may enjoy their role, the primary purpose of working for most employees is to receive an income.

It is a reasonable expectation for employees to receive payment on a roster, whether the payroll cycle is weekly, fortnightly or monthly so that they can anticipate the payment and that the amount paid into their account and superannuation fund is correct.

Payroll performs a variety of functions that support the business to meet reporting and compliance requirements. These include reports submitted to the ATO, paying the appropriate amount of payroll tax and PAY-G, submitting payment summaries, reporting on workers compensation payments, and co-ordinating child support and garnishee payments. Garnishee payments are instructions provided by a government body to a business to deduct a specified amount of money from an employee's pay, for a period of time to satisfy a debt. Garnishee orders can be handed down from bodies such as Human Services (Centrelink) when child support payments have been missed or avoided.

As a HR representative, there are a lot of overlaps and interactions you will have with payroll throughout your career. If there is one key takeaway from this chapter section, it's that you should always strive to maintain a positive working relationship with payroll, despite the challenges and internal tensions that may arise. Unfortunately, HR and payroll teams can clash as they have different priorities, different skill sets, and there can be a miscommunication between what each team is trying to achieve. From my experience, these internal tensions can be avoided if HR representatives and payroll make a joint effort to understand one another, collaborate on any projects and always focus on solving problems rather than apportioning blame.

A lot of questions come from employees to HR querying their pay and entitlements, which HR won't always have the answers to. This could be due to segregation of duties HR have limited or no access to the payroll system and are unable to view employee payment details.

In this case, HR would need to request the specific information from payroll and confirm their understanding of the information prior to relaying directly with the employee. Another scenario may be that HR and payroll could have a contrasting interpretation of a current Enterprise Agreement (EA) and would need to collaborate as to what is the correct way to pay the employees according to the EA conditions.

Payroll can often ask for HR's approval or assistance with a matter when an employee is querying their pay and have become quite agitated or do not understand their entitlements correctly.

When employees become aggressive, upset or do not fully understand an aspect of their pay, payroll may redirect this query to HR so that a respectful conversation occurs. Another consideration is that payroll bear the brunt of complaints when employees are unhappy or there is a cultural issue in the organisation. Payroll can be sworn at over the phone, yelled at for matters unrelated to payroll as their contact details are accessible and they are a direct line to the company. HR representatives need to appreciate the pressure and challenges faced by payroll on this front. HR also need to understand the pressure associated with stringent payroll deadlines that cannot be moved. These include processing pay on time and as per the payroll cycle, submitting required reports to finance at the end of the quarter, month and end of financial year, as well as government bodies when required.

Having a full appreciation of the duties performed by payroll will allow you to perform your role in HR effectively when you need to work closely with payroll. During my career, there have been multiple payroll transformation projects that have involved an overhaul of current systems and processes. These projects have many moving parts and can involve various exercises requiring collaboration such as leave accrual reconciliations; verification of employee data; adjusting employee service dates; and workshopping downstream system workflows or live feeds of data information so that payroll becomes the one source of truth.

Whatever the scope of work may be, you must appreciate that working with payroll with mutual respect is important and should not be negotiable. Although this might sound a little preachy, internal tensions between HR and payroll is a well-known phenomenon for seasoned HR professionals. Preventing these conflicts and tensions stems from understanding payroll pressures and the demands of their function. To help you gain an understanding of what a payroll officer or manager needs to do, I'll take you through some of their important tasks.

Every year payroll is required to stay abreast with any announcements released by the Australian government pertaining to the federal budget, Medicare levy, superannuation guarantee, concessional limits, payment thresholds and any new reporting requirements to the ATO.

The introduction of Single Touch Payroll (STP) in 2019 has streamlined how quickly and easily the ATO receive payroll reports and information on how much each employee has been paid. The reason for the government introducing STP was due to the amount of double dipping into Centrelink (Human Services) payments or employees not meeting their Child Support obligations as they were hiding their yearly earnings.

STP has meant that every pay period, businesses are directly reporting to the ATO the monies paid to each employee as well as the super contributions made. Reporting on superannuation does not need to be every pay period. Inversely, this also means that the ATO can more readily monitor and audit organisations that are not meeting their obligations or providing the required information. One requirement that the ATO checks is whether a business is correctly applying the marginal income tax and Medicare levy that is released annually with the federal budget announcements.

When the personal income tax rates and any changes occur to the Medicare levy, these need to be updated in PAYG schedules, as well as incorporating the thresholds for Higher Education Loan Program (HELP) and Student Financial Supplement Scheme (SFSS) components. Any changes to the tax offset to a group of income earnings has no impact to payroll, as the offset is lodged by the individuals in their tax returns. Payroll also needs to adjust the system to ensure that the concessional limit for superannuation contributions made quarterly are abided by. Some superannuation funds will not accept contributions due to the employee's age or if they are on salary sacrifice arrangements, and so this needs to be checked by payroll prior to making any contributions to a new employee's fund.

Another change payroll needs to be across are those made to Pay As You Go (PAY-G) withholdings, starting with the updates to the tax-free limit for genuine redundancies. The updated tax-free limit thresholds apply on the date the redundancy is paid and not on the termination date. Employee termination caps and their thresholds are reviewed, along with the preservation age. The preservation age is not changed by law, but moves according to what year we are in, and impacts whether the concessional tax rate is applied to termination payments in lieu of 32 per cent. The downloadable separation certificate form and the process to submit these online through Human Services is another change payroll need to adapt to, and any changes to the payment summary disclosures.

I hope this is giving you a picture of how many updates payroll need to be across and this is not even covering the changes to minimum base rate of pay for any applicable modern awards!

HR can work effectively with payroll by addressing questions raised internally by employees and management regarding payroll, entitlements, and timesheet and attendance (if applicable). An example of a question that may come to HR is regarding long service leave accruals: a NSW employee asks you why they can see their long service leave accruals on their payslip but have not reached the ten years length of service.

Answering these technical questions on behalf of payroll builds rapport with the employees and fosters a good working relationship, so that payroll do not have the opinion that any payroll-related questions that come HR's way will be palmed off to them.

Another example may be around June-July, employees will ask how they can access their payment summaries in order to lodge their tax return. Sending out a broad communication prior to the financial year ending and including payroll in this communication can help reduce these types of questions coming through.

If the relationship between payroll and HR in a business is strained, payroll may be less willing to process urgent payments on your behalf. These may be requests to process termination payments or ex-gratia payments as a component of a deed of release urgently and outside of the normal payroll cycle. If payroll do not feel respected or that they are not treated as equals to HR, then they may not make as much effort to assist you or any other HR representative when the pressure is on you. Keep this in mind when you need to work with payroll if there are some challenging interactions there.

Being in HR, you also need a basic understanding or awareness of how Human Resource Information Systems (HRIS) interact with payroll products, and how the data feedback loop is dependent on how well these systems have been integrated.

In an ideal world, data entry pertaining to talent acquisition activities, on-boarding of new employees, contract variations and any other changes are first entered into a HRIS system and this information feeds into the payroll system. There may be further interactions between a time and attendance software (T&A) with the payroll system. The purpose of this set-up is to ensure that the source of truth is payroll and the business can confidently rely on the data produced from payroll as being accurate. If these systems are disjointed, then the data feeding into payroll may require manual intervention introducing the prospect of human error or a delay in the data reaching payroll. System integration issues is another potential source of conflict between HR and payroll, and should be a priority for any business.

If you're unable to pay people correctly, the business will find that their employees do not stay happy for too long! To help you along with your journey to building a good relationship with any payroll function you come into contact with, I have built some questions you need to know the answer to, as I consider these questions essential to being a solid HR practitioner:

1. If an award-based employee resigns from their position and is not working out their notice period, how long does the business have to process their final payment?

   The answer to this is seven days. It is a requirement for the business to process any outstanding monies to the departed employee within seven days of their last working day. If the employee happens to be based in Victoria, Australia and they have access to long service leave accruals, failure to make this deadline is considered a criminal offence under the state-based long service leave legislation.

2. If an employee has requested to sacrifice all their termination payments or redundancy payment towards their superannuation fund, what is the response that should be provided by HR?

   Employees are unable to salary sacrifice any type of termination or redundancy payment. Only normal earnings that are already set to a salary sacrifice arrangement and are outstanding can be salary sacrificed.

3. Does my accrued RDO's count towards the tax-free limit portion of the redundancy payment?

In a redundancy, the employee may receive a combination of payments that can be classified as Employment Termination Payments (ETPs), but only some of them may contribute towards the tax-free limit. Typically, only the following payments would contribute towards the tax-free limit or a redundancy: redundancy/severance payment, payment in lieu of notice and gratuity payments. Accrued RDOs do not contribute towards the tax-free limit.

4. What impact does my age have on the tax paid on my redundancy payment?

Preservation age is determined by the age the employee is at the end of an income year that the ETP is paid in. This may differ from the income year that the employee is terminated in. if an employee is at or above their preservation age the tax will be charged at a lower tax rate.

If the employee is below the preservation age at the time the ETP is paid, the tax will be charged normally at 32 per cent. Overall, the actual preservation age is dictated by the year the employee is born in. For an updated preservation table, you can visit the ATO Website.

5. When I am being paid workers' compensation and I'm not working, will the business still be making superannuation contributions?

No. Employees will only be paid superannuation when an excess has been paid by the business. Superannuation is payable on any days worked whether that is only part hours per day or part hours in a week. Superannuation is also paid when an employee performs light duties.

These are a few examples of questions that would help you in your role as a HR representative. Understanding this level of detail will not only impress payroll, but your HR colleagues and management. For a HR representative to understand payroll in this level of detail is not a frequent occurrence and may separate you as a reliable and highly competent professional. To continue this uplifting section, HR representatives also need to be aware of the importance of record-keeping and data security with payroll information.

Payroll is the epicentre of private and sensitive information in any business. Payroll has access to each employee's identity details, which an external scammer or someone with bad intentions is well aware of. Therefore, payroll can be the target of illegal scams and phishing attempts to gain access to company data or steal monies.

Here is a fictious example of a scam that could have gone horribly wrong, if it wasn't for the payroll officer being alert and cautious. A scammer chose Humesware Pty Ltd and conducted research on the names of the business' senior executives. Using LinkedIn, the scammer targeted the Chief Financial Officer to scam. The scammer then created a fake personal email address resembling his name, Mr Bob Jackson to bob.jackson@gmail.com. The scammer then used LinkedIn to find the contact details of the HR Manager, Ms Smith. The scammer, using the fake email address, sent correspondence to Ms Smith asking for an urgent change of banking details for the upcoming payroll cycle, which is to be paid the following day. Ms Smith, wanting to please a senior executive, immediately actioned this email and sent back the "change banking details form" for Mr Jackson (the scammer) to complete so it could be forwarded through to payroll. Within minutes the scammer forwarded through the completed pdf and Ms Smith forwarded this through to payroll in an email, marked "Action Urgently". The payroll officer noticed that the personal email address bob.jackson@gmail.com did not match the email address on the employee file. To verify that this was a legitimate change in banking details, the payroll officer called Mr Jackson (the actual employee). Mr Jackson said that he had not requested the banking details change. The payroll officer alerted Ms Smith to the scam and the police were contacted.

This is just one way payroll and other functions in a business can unintentionally release personal information, money or have a data breach. If personal information had been released to an unauthorised person or someone that the business did not intend on sending the information to, this is classified as a data breach. If the scammer was after Mr Jackson's personal information and had been successful in gathering this, Humesware Pty Ltd would have been obligated to take action in response to this data breach.

The business would have had to notify Mr Jackson that his personal information had been released – what information had been disclosed and what steps were being taken to safeguard the use and distribution of the information. The business would need to make attempts to contact the scammer in writing, and request that they delete the information and not use it. Within a 30-day period, the business would need to then formally notify the Office of the Australian Information Commissioner. Formal notification to this government body is required when there has been a notifiable incident, as the information lost or disclosed without authorisation is likely to result in serious harm to the impacted individual/s.

5

EMPLOYEE RELATIONS

THIS CHAPTER IS ABOUT the bread and butter of being a HR professional, managing employee relations (ER) in the business you support.

I define employee relations as when issues or concerns are raised by workers and/or managers in the business. This is a wide casted net and can include examples such as when a manager approaches HR for support with an underperforming employee; a formal complaint is lodged by an employee to HR or an employee has breached a company policy and procedure, which is deemed unacceptable by the business. These are just a few examples.

When a business undertakes any sort of disciplinary action with an employee, in the disciplinary action itself it is imperative to refer to the type of breach that has occurred. As an example, this could have been a breach of the code of conduct policy or a safety procedure. In disciplinary matters, it is important to have policies and procedures implemented, accessible to employees and to have them trained or signed off on them, so that they can be referred to later when required.

For most large corporate organisations, they will already have established policies and procedures, which are reviewed on a regular basis by the document owners. As these need to be internally accessible to employees, they are often on the business' intranet or included in new starter packs for sign-off before the employee commences their employment.

If you've been tasked with reviewing or creating a new policy, this can become a complex task. Particularly if the policy is considered an important item or would have financial implications for employees such as the parental leave policy. To get you kick-started on creating a policy, which you may need to rely on in the future for disciplinary matters, you can consider the following:

1. Why do you need the policy? Consider from a management and employee level why the policy is necessary and what value it will bring to employees. Is there any monetary benefit to employees? Will the policy be ongoing and reviewed on an annual basis? What employees are covered or in scope of the policy? Will this be a blanket policy or only apply to a specific group of employees? How would the policy be enforced and by whom? All these considerations are necessary as it will guide what functions and people in the business you need to engage with prior to launching a policy. If there are monetary implications then payroll would by default need to be involved, as well as the relevant finance heads so that the additional costs to the business are accrued for and included in the budget.

2. What content should you include in the policy? How are you going to format and present the information to the targeted audience? Policies need to be clearly written so

there is little ambiguity in the way it is applied. If a breach to the policy could result in potential disciplinary action up to and including termination of employment, this needs to be clearly stipulated in the document. This clause of the policy can then be referenced in the future during the management of any related ER matter.

3. Create your first draft. Organise to have your colleagues and the relevant stakeholders review this initial draft. Gain stakeholders buy-in and invite them to comment and workshop through the document. As they are approaching the policy from a different perspective, they may provide insights that you haven't considered and aspects of the policy that may not work for the covered employees.

4. Once you're in a final draft of the document, you need to start communicating with your client group or the relevant management level that the policy is going to be released. In this communication, it would be good to provide them with a briefing; when the policy comes into effect; the impact to employees; where the policy will be found; and the benefit of the policy to them and their employees. You may even want to provide them with talking points if the policy is going to be workshopped at an employee level. The briefing materials you supply are dependent on how you plan on distributing the policy to employees.

5. And lastly, you need to distribute the final document that has been approved and endorsed by the business and is now in effect. Ensure the correct version is available for the applicable employees.

Those are some brief points on how to develop and implement a policy so you understand the general picture. Once policies and procedures are in place, employees know that they exist and are held accountable to them, only then can they get used in disciplinary matters.

So that you gain some exposure on how HR professional is involved in these matters, I'll create an example. Ms Leah McMurray has been working for Humesware Pty Ltd for just over seven years in a call centre operator role. She is 51 years of age and has demonstrated performance shortfalls on an ongoing basis for over three years. Her performance shortfalls have been summarised as excessive absenteeism, sleeping while at work, and providing little to no notice when leaving work early, arriving to work late or not attending for work.

Since 2017, multiple HR business partners have tried to support Ms McMurray's wellbeing and to address the performance issues in the workplace. With Ms McMurray's written consent and permission, the business contacted her doctor by way of a letter to understand her current medical conditions, and to see if any adjustments could be made to the working environment to accommodate her conditions. The letter also specifically addressed her:

- Excessive absenteeism, often with little or no notice of non-attendance to the workplace.
- Unplanned early departures from the workplace.
- Sleeping in the workplace on multiple occasions.
- Ms McMurray's emotional state in the workplace, discussing committing suicide with her colleagues.
- Ms McMurray's capacity to work full-time hours in her current capacity.

After correspondence with Mc McMurray's doctor, she was then asked to participate in a company paid Fitness to Continue Medical Assessment. Based on the result of this assessment, Ms

McMurray was deemed unfit for work and was subsequently stood down for a three-month period to allow her time to rehabilitate and get the medical attention she needed.

Ms McMurray was also instructed by the company during this time to comply with the medical regime provided and engage with the mental health service for active treatment. At the conclusion of the three-month period, she would be required to undertake another medical assessment and be deemed fit to return to work. Letters were also submitted to her doctor and treating psychiatrist, whereby the company was informed that she had a three-year recurrent period of depression and anxiety. As Ms McMurray was given clearance from her treating medical practitioners, she was issued directions to return to work.

Since Ms Murray's return to work in August 2017, she had continued to demonstrate performance shortfalls in her role. She had subsequently received a written warning for the below issues:

- Lateness and absenteeism without adequate notice.
- She had put multiple customers on hold while falling asleep in her chair in the customer service centre.

After this written warning had been issued, she had continued to demonstrate the same behaviours, but the business was fatigued in addressing these issues. The previous HR business partner overseeing this matter with the manager had left the business, and it is now up to you to support the management of this matter.

As the current HR representative supporting the manager, your first step is to go through Ms McMurray's employee file to understand the history and context of what is happening now. Understanding that it is has now been six months since the first written warning was issued and that her behaviour has not changed, you recommend that the appropriate course of action is to issue a final written warning coupled with a performance improvement plan (PIP).

The final written warning letter and PIP is issued in a meeting with you, Mr Marick and Ms McMurray on 10 January 2018. Ms McMurray was offered the opportunity to have a support person present during this meeting and was given 24 hours' notice of the meeting, what the agenda of the meeting was and who would attendance.

The final written warning letter also offered Ms McMurray the opportunity to use the company's Employee Assistance Program (EAP). The detailed PIP outlined an action plan that would last for a duration of four weeks, with weekly reviews with Mr Marick and with the below performance expectations:

1. Attend a full week's work without any unplanned leave days. This will be reviewed each Friday at 1pm at a weekly Performance Improvement Plan. This will be measured by the clock-in timesheet entries for the week.
2. Arrive at work on time, and ready to take calls in the call centre at 9am each morning, and finish work at your correct shift time as per the roster/clock-in system.
3. Leave work at the correct time every shift as per the rostered shift times.
4. Notify Mr Marick if Ms McMurray will not attended work that day at least two hours prior to work starting via text message, followed up with a phone call.
5. Ms McMurray needs to remain alert throughout the entire duration of the shift and always comply with the company's policies and procedures while in the workplace.

At the conclusion of the four weeks period, Ms McMurray's performance was reviewed in consultation with human resources. It was then objectively determined that she had not demonstrated sustained improvement and, in some respects, her performance had further declined. Based on these circumstances, you recommend to Mr Marick that the business could now issue a show cause letter with the view to potentially terminate her employment, subject to her response and no mitigating circumstances. Mitigating circumstances refers to any new information that has been discovered that could have impacted Ms McMurray's ability to improve her performance. This could be that Ms McMurray has been privately suffering with an undeclared medical condition physically impacting her ability to perform the role, or that one of her children has recently passed away. Any type of information shared by the employee during this show cause process that would have reasonably impacted Ms McMurray's performance and was not originally factored into the business' decision to issue a show cause letter would be classified as a mitigating circumstance.

This advice should be accompanied by a risk profile of the matter for both unfair dismissal and general protections. You will be taken through this in detail later in the chapter. For the purposes of this example, let's assume you have crafted a risk assessment; it is also best practice to draft an investigation/ ER report so that the decision-makers in the business are fully informed prior to supporting your recommendation. There are many different formats and structures you can adopt, and some large organisations have internal forms and templates available. In the spirit of this book's kick-starter mission, here is what an investigation could look like for this fictitious example:

In large corporate environments, you may be in a circumstance where senior management and/or the relevant decision-makers who determine whether an employee will be terminated or not, are not familiar with the employee and may have never met them before. Therefore, it is important that the briefing provides them enough context and information to make an objective decision on the correct course of action, while considering the risk profile of the matter.

At the beginning of your ER report, you can have an employee profile of Ms McMurray. I like to use a table format so that this is neatly arranged. In the table you can include the full name of the employee, hire date, age, grade/ salary arrangement, union involvement (yes/no), name of the one-up manager from the employee, your name as the HR representative managing this matter, and a list of any prior disciplinary action. The name of the report should give an indication of what type of matter this is. Using this example, the report title could be "Ms Leah McMurray underperformance and excessive absenteeism – Recommendation to terminate employment".

The next section of the report would be a summary. This paragraph would provide a history of when the matter started being managed, the steps taken by management to address this complaint and what the recommended course of action is.

Here is an example of the summary section of your report:

Within a 12-month period, Ms Leah McMurray was granted a three-month period away from work whereby she could seek psychiatric assistance and engage a mental health provider. This provided her the opportunity to be reassessed and return to work once she was deemed fit by independent medical experts.

Ms McMurray had consistent support from her direct manager Mr Marick, as well as previous management in approving her early departures from work to attend medical appointments. Multiple HR representatives were involved in the management of this matter and Ms McMurray was offered access to the company's EAP service on multiple occasions. Despite being medically cleared to perform a full-time role, her performance had not improved since a first and final warning was issued and throughout the duration of her four-week performance improvement plan. It is for this reason the business is recommending issuing her a show cause letter, with the view to terminate her employment subject to no presented mitigating circumstances.

After a review of your fantastic report submitted to senior management and the relevant decision-makers, your recommendation to issue a show cause letter has been approved. You'll now need to inform Mr Marick of the business' decision and you can request Mr Marick to organise a meeting with Ms McMurray, himself and yourself present.

Mr Marick should verbally inform Ms McMurrary of the meeting providing a minimum 24 hours' notice of when the meeting will take place; that the purpose of the meeting is a follow-up in relation to her performance and that she is welcome to have a support person present.

Mr Marick should then follow-up this conversation with an email, reiterating the time, date, and location of the meeting and that a support person can be present. You are cc'd into this email and can accept a calendar invite. Ms McMurray informs you she would like a support person present (her mother), but her mother is not available until a day after the scheduled meeting, and has requested an extension. As this is a reasonable request and will afford her the opportunity to have someone present, you or Mr Marick accept the request for an extension and the meeting is pushed back a further 24 hours.

Ms McMurray and her mother have arrived at the workplace for the meeting. You and Mr Marick have printed copies of the show cause letter with the signatory being Mr Marick. You welcome Ms McMurray and her mother to the meeting. You would then ask Ms McMurray to confirm that she understands the reasons for today's meeting and what will be discussed.

Before the meeting begins, you would explain what the role of a support person is to the mother and note down her full name for your meeting records. Once the mother has acknowledged that she is only present to observe and not advocate on behalf of Ms McMurray, you would officially open the meeting and use the letter to guide the discussion. Reference to previous performance discussions, the finalisation of the performance improvement plan and prior disciplinary action issues is a good summary to lead into the letter here to be issued on the day.

You would issue Ms McMurray a copy of the letter, which you would use to help guide the remainder of the discussion. If the show cause letter is written properly, it would include background information on the procedural fairness followed to date, and the reasons for issuing the show cause. In this example, the letter may read as the following: "The business is not willing to tolerate your ongoing underperformance and absenteeism, and it is for this reason that you are being issued a show cause letter. You now have the opportunity to provide reasons to the business as to why your employment should not be terminated. You have the opportunity to provide those reasons verbally during today's meeting, or submit a written response to me, via email no later than 5PM [specific date]".

Once you have read through the letter together, you should pause and ask Ms McMurray if she understands the letter and if she has any questions. This is a good opportunity to clarify the process going forward and, once the business has considered her response and all available information, the business will determine what the appropriate outcome may be.

Ms McMurray opted to provide a response to the show cause letter in writing and indicated she would be sending this through to Mr Marick's email address before the specified deadline. The meeting would then officially close and, once this has been done, the mother would then be able to ask any questions or raise any concerns she may have.

In this instance, the meeting formally ended and both Ms McMurray and her mother left the workplace. Although this is an example, show cause meetings can really vary in how emotional the employee's reaction can be. Sometimes they may cry, get quite angry and upset during the process and feel as though the business is being unfair and unreasonable. Some employees may also be indifferent as they believed the business was determined to pursue this course of action; and that the "writing was on the wall" that they would be departing the business... even though this isn't the case.

Regardless of what happens during the meeting, as the HR representative you need to ensure that the meeting remains clam, respectful and if the situation begins to escalate or you feel as though the employee may need a break, you can adjourn the meeting for five to ten minutes.

During an adjournment, the employee and their support person can step out of the meeting and go into another room or area to discuss the matter. An adjournment is also an opportunity for the employee to compose themselves if they have become emotional. If an employee is represented by a union official, they may request an adjournment of the meeting for as long as required to either provide advice to their union member or to give the employee the opportunity to collect themselves.

HR representatives need to become comfortable with these types of emotionally charged meetings. I like to think of HR professionals as being the calm in the storm, equipped to defuse situations and assist managers with difficult conversations. In saying this, HR always needs to maintain a neutral and objective approach, balancing the needs and requirements of employees, as well as the business. Sometimes the needs and requirements of the business conflict with those of employees, and HR must manage these difficult situations. As difficult and as unpleasant as show cause meetings can get, this is only one example of the multitude of different situations HR representatives will become involved in when supporting a business.

With McMurray's written response receipted and acknowledged by Mr Marick via email, the business now needs to consider if any new information or mitigating circumstances have been presented, which were unknown previously. In Ms McMurray's response, she had indicated a desire for the business to consider her changing from full-time to part-time hours to help with her absenteeism and performance issues, as well as giving her more time to attend medical appointments. On face value this is a reasonable request and would in most cases be considered a potential option. However, the business has previously offered this option to Ms McMurray on several occasions to work part-time hours and the independent medical assessment had cleared her to work in a full-time capacity. When the business had offered Ms McMurray the option to transition to part-time hours, she had refused this offer. It is based on these reasons that the business was able to proceed with terminating her performance. Ms McMurray was given notice of an outcome meeting, afforded the opportunity to have a support person present and given 24 hours' notice prior to the meeting occurring. During the meeting she was issued a termination notice, outlining the reason for the business' decision to proceed with termination and notified that her notice will be paid in lieu, along with her accrued statutory entitlements. This finalised the matter and the necessary details were forwarded through to payroll for processing. You should also request that payroll prepares a separation certificate for Ms McMurray.

The purpose of covering Ms McMurray's fictitious ER matter in detail is so that you can understand what best HR practice looks like. The business made accommodations to support her rehabilitation by providing her a three-month leave of absence, provided access to EAP, offered additional training and support regarding performance, was formally warned of the performance issues on multiple occasions, and was afforded the option to have a support person present during formal meetings. The timeline of events, the support provided by the business and facts presented in a matter like this are critical if a FWC claim was to ever arise from the management or mismanagement of an issue such as this in a workplace. With the view to kick-start your HR career, here are some more examples so that you can learn how to manage similar ER challenges in a business once they come across your desk.

Case Studies

To become a high-performing HR practitioner, you need to gain exposure to various ER matters throughout your career. These can vary from very simple matters, for example when an employee has breached a drug and alcohol policy where there are guidelines in place on how each breach is managed, to highly complex matters where you may be dealing with a sexual harassment case involving senior management. To try and give you as much exposure as possible, I have put together some case studies that I have personally been involved in or observed during my career. In these case studies, no real names or references have been made to organisations and individuals. These examples have been provided solely to help you understand how you could handle these types of matters in a human resources capacity.

To provide some context to the first example, the general manager of a wholesale distribution centre had terminated three warehouse/storeperson employees just before the Christmas period had begun.

In early January, once the business had resumed after the Christmas shutdown period, the HR representative was provided a list of positions that needed filling with the right candidates within three-weeks. The HR representative in this example had only two years of relevant experience and was in a standalone capacity due to internal changes.

The HR representative placed an advertisement on a job board and starting sieving through the long list of applicants and their CVs. During efforts made to short-list candidates, HR came across an interesting application by the name of Mr James Jerry. Mr Jerry had applied for the role of a storeperson, which significantly contrasted to his overall career history. Mr Jerry had not included recent positions he had in the last few years and had only listed several senior positions as a finance partner in banks. Mr Jerry had a bachelor's degree in commerce and accounting, and the closest role he had to warehousing would be as a foreman for a carpentry company. So why was he applying for an entry level warehouse/store person position?

The HR representative was intrigued and thought of all the added advantages of having someone that qualified and skilled to be in the business on the ground level. Mr Jerry could potentially help drive continuous improvement in the business and devise methods to reduce operational costs and increase efficiencies, which was a focus of the business at that time.

In saying this, HR gave Mr Jerry a phone call and asked the question "why do you want to work in warehousing when you are highly qualified and experienced in finance?"

Mr Jerry's response was quite simple. He wanted to change career paths and he was no longer interested in the stress and responsibility of being in a senior management position. He indicated he just wanted to work and be paid for the work he had performed, and then go home.

HR was satisfied with this response, and he was subsequently invited to a face-to-face interview in the office. Mr Jerry arrived to reception ten minutes early for his interview. He was asked to complete a pre-employment pack, which clarified details such as his full name, working rights, career goals, and whether he had a criminal history (yes or no). This form had required a signature and date and was seldomly reviewed until a formal offer was being considered. On this occasion, during the interview with HR and Mr Jerry, the HR representative reviewed the form and noticed that he had ticked "yes" to having a criminal history.

The interview continued with the HR representative going through the prepared questions, which were behavioural and situational based. As this is the first time the HR representative had come across someone selecting yes to criminal history, they were caught off guard and weren't sure how to adequately address this.

A lot of assumptions had been made about Mr Jerry as he had been well-mannered, well-groomed, educated. In other words, he didn't match any of the stereotypes associated with people charged with criminal activity.

The HR representative indicated that the form had been ticked and asked him to elaborate on this. Mr Jerry said that his transition from senior banking positions to warehousing was due to him having committed crimes.

Over the course of five years, Mr Jerry had stolen large sums of money from his previous employers, and as a senior banker he had forged documentation to hide his tracks from external auditors. Mr Jerry indicated that he had stolen money to buy a house and a new car, and to afford proper medical treatment for his autistic son. Mr Jerry had only been released three weeks prior and was on parole. Mr Jerry offered to provide the conditions of his parole if he was to progress further in the interview. The HR representative then made an error by pursuing another line of questioning by asking a personal question, "why did you start stealing?"

Mr Jerry's responses are irrelevant, as you cannot employ a candidate based on their criminal history if the convictions are relevant to the inherent requirements of the role. Why he did the crime and the details of the crimes convicted are irrelevant. In this example, as the role would be dealing directly with the handling of cash, credit card information and invoicing to customers, he would not be suitable for the position.

On this basis, a business could lawfully decide to not employ someone like Mr Jerry with a criminal conviction due to the inherent requirements of the role. If the role was not involved with money handling, the business would have to disregard his criminal history and decide whether he could progress through to the next round based on the merits of his application. The reasons for having to make a fair assessment of suitability regardless of criminal history is that criminal history is protected under discrimination legislation.

The key learnings from this as a junior HR representative is to understand the inherent requirements of a position, and if criminal background checks are performed or if you ask for confirmation of a criminal history, you need to understand how this information will be used by the business.

If the business had rejected Mr Jerry's application based on his lack of warehousing experience and not his criminal history, the business needs to understand that there is a risk. Mr Jerry may act and posit that the reason he was not employed was due to his criminal history and not due to the lack of his warehousing experience.

As the business asked the question regarding his criminal history, it provides an avenue for prospective employees to make claims of discrimination. If you're ever in doubt regarding employment law or how to manage matters involving criminal background checks or declarations, you have the option to seek legal advice.

Moving onto the second case study example, I would like to explain a performance management issue, which has the involvement of the Fair Work Ombudsman. The Fair Work Ombudsman is an advisory body that provides guidance and conciliatory services for employees and employers when there is a dispute or concern raised. Unlike the FWC, they cannot make determinations or orders, and try to resolve disputes through informal discussions with the parties involved.

This second case involves a lady called Ms Mandy Wu, a stock controller who organises deliveries and pick-ups of warehouse orders. Ms Wu had been employed by the company for over three years and reported directly to the operations manager, Ms Lisa Roman.

Ms Wu was seven-months pregnant and intended to start her parental leave within two months. For this example, the

HR representative Ms Melinda Smith had only three years of experience and again does not have a HR manager or mentor to guide her.

Ms Roman approached Ms Smith regarding Ms Wu's performance. Ms Roman indicated that Ms Wu had for a period been making a lot of mistakes. Ms Wu had continued to incorrectly book the delivery and pick-up times of orders, which had caused issues for the warehousing staff and infuriated multiple customers.

Ms Roman had informally addressed her concerns regarding Ms Wu's performance on multiple occasions, offering further training and support. Ms Roman had also coached her that communication is key; she needed to first understand how long an order takes to put together prior to organising a delivery and pick-up time. Despite these discussions, Ms Wu's performance had not improved, and these errors were starting to have significant reputational impacts on the business. It is for this reason that Ms Roman had now asked for the assistance of HR to address these issues formally and look at what disciplinary action is appropriate.

Ms Smith met with Ms Roman to discuss the performance issues. HR requested some specific examples of these errors; any copies of customer complaints, which have been received, and the volume of work being completed on a weekly basis; number of orders booked for pick-up and delivery; and any other ad hoc duties completed.

HR also wanted to understand if there was anyone we could compare her performance to in the business, to establish a baseline of performance. Unfortunately, Ms Wu was the only stock controller in the business and any type of formal performance expectations would need to be built from scratch. Once HR was comfortable with the level of detail and supporting examples, Ms Roman organised a meeting between Ms Wu, Ms Smith and herself to discuss her performance. Ms Smith recommended that Ms Wu was informed of the nature of the meeting, given 24 hours' notice and the opportunity to have a support person present.

Prior to undertaking any type of disciplinary process, it is important to understand what the focus of the investigation or discussions are and establish whether factual circumstances relate to poor performance or misconduct by an employee. Conducting an informal pre-liminary meeting allows the employee to respond and provide their version of events so that the business can consider any relevant information prior to deciding.

As this scenario was not a show cause or termination meeting, offering a support person to be present is not a requirement. However, it is considered best HR practice.

How closely a proper process is followed will determine whether a decision to dismiss or the issuing of any other type of disciplinary action has followed procedural fairness. It is important for HR to guide managers on how to implement procedural fairness. In this scenario, I would recommend these steps:

Step#1: Establish the facts of misconduct or poor performance. You may decide to suspend full pay if the alleged misconduct is serious and there is a reasonable threat to other workers, property or the business.

Step#2: Write a letter to the employee, in this case Ms Wu outlining the allegations and reference to any documents or correspondence as evidence of the underperformance. The letter needs to outline that Ms Wu is being given the opportunity to respond to the allegations so that the business can consider this before an outcome is determined. The letter also needs to indicate that once the business has considered all available information that she could be subject to disciplinary action up to and including termination of employment. The letter needs to also indicate that the matters discussed are to remain private and confidential. If Ms Wu elected to have a support person, Ms Wu has the right to discuss this matter with her support person in confidence.

Step#3: During the meeting, Ms Wu has the option to verbally respond to the performance issues raised or have the opportunity to submit her response in writing to the business within 24 hours, with a set time and date. The submission can be sent through to Ms Roman's email address.

Step #4: Once the business has decided, a follow-up meeting is organised giving Ms Wu another 24 hours' notice and the opportunity to have a support person present. During this meeting she would be issued an outcome letter. In this case study, she is issued a written warning for underperformance, and given instructions on how she needs to improve her performance. The written warning letter also indicates that she would need to improve her performance, as ongoing performance shortfalls may make her subject to further disciplinary action up to and including termination of her performance.

Within eight working days of the outcome meeting, Ms Smith had received a call from the Fair Work Ombudsman. Ms Smith was not surprised by the phone call, as Ms Wu during her verbal responses had strongly argued that she was being unfairly treated and was performing well in her role. She had also indicated during the meeting that she was being unfairly targeted as she was pregnant and was soon to go on parental leave. Ms Smith asked the Fair Work Ombudsman when the mediation would take place and let them know that she would be in attendance.

During the mediation, Ms Smith clarified what process had been undertaken to ensure that the business had a firm understanding of Ms Wu's perspective and if there were any contributing factors to her underperformance. It was argued that the reason she was issued a written warning was not due to her pregnancy. The reason for the disciplinary action was outlined in the disciplinary letter and discussed in detail in the first and second meeting in the presence of her chosen support person. It was also argued that her application for parental leave had been approved earlier in the year prior to any type of performance-based discussions and less than six months ago, she was given an increased salary while she was pregnant.

The reason for the salary increase was a pay parity exercise to align her to other people in the business performing an equivalent role. Ms Smith indicated that the increase was not linked to her performance in any way. Ms Wu agreed that this was in fact correct and acknowledged the salary increase. Ms Smith was able to finish her argument that if the business' intentions was to try and terminate her employment or discriminate against her on the basis of being pregnant, her salary would not have been increased while she was pregnant. The mediator was satisfied with the level of discussion and Ms Wu conceded with the business' position. No further involvement of the Fair Work Ombudsman or any other type of body was needed or occurred after this mediation.

So why the long story? I'd like for my readers to appreciate the necessity of processes and how important it is to not deviate from these processes. Management of employees requires fair and consistent leadership from those in decision-making positions, especially HR professionals. Preparation and the support of the operations manager and other upper management staff is key for employees to recognise that their poor performance and misconduct have repercussions. It also demonstrates that they can defend themselves and address any allegation, which they feel is unfair or incorrect.

You must also keep in mind that following these processes does not guarantee that staff will cooperate or improve their behaviour or performance.

The example involving Ms Wu's performance went relatively smoothly even though a mediation was held with the Fair Work Ombudsman. This can be attributed to the amount of information available to support examples of underperformance.

Now what if Ms Wu's role was not clearly defined and she had only recently taken on the duties of organising deliveries and pick-ups?

This would mean that perhaps the business had not done enough to support Ms Wu to ensure performance issues arise. Therefore, having a job description in place is important to outline performance expectations, responsibilities, and duties.

When a business has ambiguous job descriptions, employees can become confused and misunderstand their day-to-day activities, responsibilities and set targets. Miscommunication is almost guaranteed, and employees are bound to become frustrated and reprimanded by upper management for not performing or doing what "was expected".

Having a clear and accessible job description is vital to manage employee performance effectively. It is important to recognise that in small and medium-sized businesses, it is common for employees to perform "all-rounder" roles. These duties can be very ad hoc varying week to week, and because the teams can be small, they would need to perform duties not traditionally in their remit when other team members are away from work on holidays or have called in sick.

While this is advantageous as employees are developed to become multi-skilled and can have the capacity to work flexibly, an overlap of responsibilities between employees can occur. This can blur the line of accountability and leads to the question, who is responsible for the timely completion and quality of tasks when they are not assigned to a particular job title or person?

The problem in this type of scenario is that no one person is responsible. To avoid this issue, businesses can implement specific job descriptions. For further information on job descriptions, please refer to the Recruitment Chapter in this book.

The last case study for this chapter is a great example of a new employee who joined a medium-sized business and presented a lot of red flags in his first few weeks of employment. For the purposes of this fictitious example, the employee's name is Mr Bobby Facini and was employed as a full-time permanent administrative assistant.

Within three weeks of commencing his employment, it was evident that he was having a toxic impact on the office environment and atmosphere, and he had a negative attitude towards his work. The direct manager knew he had made a hiring mistake after one week of Mr Facini starting and the only reason he lasted up until the third week, is that his manager wanted to give him the benefit of the doubt.

During the interview stage, Mr Facini presented well and was able to answer each question with the appropriate level of detail. Mr Facini had relevant work experience and worked in a similar industry at his last position. As he had been the last candidate interviewed on the short-list, he stood out as the top candidate. Subject to satisfactory reference checks and one last interview with the managing director, he was issued a letter of offer by the HR representative, Ms Smith.

At this point, Mr Facini indicated that he had a pre-booked holiday for 6-9 September. Ms Smith indicated he would be put on unpaid leave for these days off as at that stage he would not have accrued enough leave to be paid for these two days. Mr Facini also liaised with Ms Smith directly as he had some questions regarding his letter of offer. Ms Smith indicated that she would address these questions with him on his first day, which was Monday the following week. Mr Facini had already agreed in principle to the terms of the offer and returned all other necessary documentation to Ms Smith.

On Monday, which was Mr Facini's first day, Mr Facini was half an hour late to work. He did not call his direct manager or the office to let the business know that he was running late as he had been stuck in peak hour traffic or that he had been lost coming to work. This was the first clue or red flag that Mr Facini may not be suitable; but it was too early to tell. However, the remaining office staff did make a complaint to their manager that they considered this rude and did not demonstrate courtesy as they had organised times in their diaries to start their training regime with Mr Facini that morning.

That afternoon, he was issued with his employment contract in writing to take home, sign, and date. Mr Facini made it clear that he was not happy with the nominated salary amount. The amount of $52,000 p.a. was in alignment with the job advertisement and had already been discussed with him prior to commencing his employment. This came as a surprise to Ms Smith, as he was trying to negotiate more money even though he had started his first day.

The key point to note here is that an employee should not commence their employment or even set foot into your workplace without a signed and returned letter of employment. This protects the business from employees stipulating that their agreed employment terms are different, negotiable, and ensures they are covered by insurance in the event that they injure themselves in the workplace.

The manager had a private discussion with Mr Facini regarding his salary and that $52,000 p.a. was reasonable and in line with the advertisement. This ended this negotiation discussion, and his letter of offer was subsequently returned to Ms Smith on Tuesday.

On Tuesday, Ms Smith then had to requested Mr Facini to return his signed superannuation form as this was filled out incorrectly in the first instance. Ms Smith requested this Wednesday morning, as this was payroll day, and she did not want to miss this in the payroll cycle.

Mr Facini had originally agreed to provide this to Ms Smith on Tuesday, but it was a week and a half later until she received the correct paperwork. Mr Facini had also had his pre-booked holiday, which fell over a Friday and Monday creating a long weekend. This was not an issue until he had called in sick on the Thursday morning.

This may sound like the business is nitpicking on these small details. However, they are tell-tale signs adding up to one thing... that Mr Facini is not suitable for the business. Ms Smith requested a doctor's certificate from Mr Facini on Thursday morning when he had notified the business of his absence, giving him the entire day to attend a medical appointment.

On Mr Facini's first day back in the office, on 10 September, Ms Smith followed-up with Mr Facini regarding his medical certificate. Mr Facini indicated he had gotten a medical certificate on Thursday and would provide that to Ms Smith on 11 September.

One week later, Mr Facini finally produced a medical certificate. The medical certificate was unsigned by the doctor, and looked as though it had been scanned and potentially tampered with. Ms Smith kept this on file and requested Mr Facini to get a copy of the medical certificate signed by his doctor. Mr Facini protested and said he would need to leave work early to reach his doctor in time. Ms Smith explained that as the medical certificate was unsigned by the doctor, this is a mistake on their end. She advised that Mr Facini should be able to call up the practitioner's office and ask for the signed medical certificate to be emailed to him directly. Mr Facini conceded to this explanation and agreed to send through a signed medical certificate.

Four business days later, Mr Facini emailed Ms Smith a highly pixelated doctor's medical certificate. With the image photographed from a distance, the dates on the medical certificate illegible. Most people would accept this as proof and move on with the matter, but Ms Smith knew from a "gut" feeling that this was likely a fake certificate or a certificate from another past absence.

Ms Smith chose to do some investigating, and copied and pasted the image into Microsoft's Paint, enlarged the image and saved the file as a jpg. Using a free online image enhancer, the contrast of the image was enhanced so that the dates became clear. The certificate was not dated for his absence on 5 September, but for 7 April, which was prior to Mr Facini commencing his employment with the business. A copy of the enhanced copy and Mr Facini's certificate submitted were placed on the managing director's desk.

These print-outs were immediately followed up by the managing director with Ms Smith. A meeting was shortly held, and the medical certificate incident swayed the managing director to terminate Mr Faccini's employment during his qualifying period. Four business days later, Mr Facini was subsequently terminated.

Although the business in this case study found out relatively quickly that Mr Facini was of questionable character, the resources and time lost with his turnover were significant. It had taken a whole month to recruit and select this position, and almost a whole month of training. These training efforts could have been devoted to a suitable candidate!

The key learnings you can take away from this case study is that finding the right candidate for any business is essential. In this example, it was obvious that Mr Facini was not a suitable candidate. In other circumstances, it is not as easy to spot when a new hire was a wrong choice. Making a recruitment and selection decision must always be made with the business' best interests in mind as making decisions in haste or out of convenience can be quite costly to a company in the long run: financially and reputationally.

Conducting Workplace Investigations

From reading the above case studies, you can appreciate the number of resources, time and effort taken by a business to manage employee relations. When employees behave in an unacceptable manner or are underperforming, this can have detrimental impacts to surrounding colleagues, the work group and the individual employee involved.

Unacceptable employee behaviour can lead to a number of negative impacts to a business including excessive absenteeism, low morale, increased staff turnover, increased costs in recruitment and training of replacement employees, devoted human resources attention, and potential financial and reputational damage to the business.

At all times, the business is responsible and liable for inappropriate workplace behaviour, which is why most companies have a Workplace Behaviours Standard in place. Another term commonly used to describe this type of document is a Code of Conduct Policy.

In a Workplace Behaviours Standard, it would need to firstly incorporate the legislative framework that underpins employer's obligations. An effective Workplace Behaviours Standard ("**Standard**") is built upon the most relevant Australian law on both federal and state-based levels.

On the federal level, the standard should incorporate the *Fair Work Act 2009*, *Racial Discrimination Act 1975* and the *Racial Hatred Act 1995*, *Age Discrimination Act 2004*, *Sex Discrimination Act 1984*, *Equal Opportunity for Women in the Workplace Act 1999*, *Disability Discrimination Act 1992*, and the *Human Rights and Equal Opportunity Commission Act 1986*.

As a HR practitioner, you need to understand how these legislative requirements need to be upheld by employers and employees, as well as provide relevant guidance when related matters arise. This includes being familiar with state-based legislation in your home state, as well as any other state in which a business operates from.

You will need to research the related state-based legislation, which are available to the public for a free download on Australian government websites. The most relevant parts of the legislation are how these are applied practically in the workplace, starting with what is and is not considered workplace bullying, harassment, and discrimination.

There is an important distinction between reasonable management direction and bullying and harassment in the workplace. Managers have the right to direct work to be done in a certain manner and to also performance manage employees when ongoing errors are made. A manager can provide feedback and monitor behaviour without this being classified as workplace bullying and harassment.

Other examples of reasonable management direction are informing an employee about unsatisfactory behaviour in the workplace, taking reasonable disciplinary action and deciding not to select an employee for a promotion opportunity – subject to a fair and equitable process. These are examples of what is not considered workplace bullying and harassment.

So, what is considered workplace bullying and harassment?

Well, I'm so glad you asked. Workplace bullying is defined as repeated unreasonable behaviour towards a person. Repeated behaviour refers to ongoing behaviour that is not isolated to an incident, and unreasonable behaviour refers to circumstances when a person is subject to humiliation, victimised, threatened or intimidated.

There are many different forms of bullying, which can be verbal or physical assault, using a person's position and status to bully another, or even subtle psychological tactics aimed to humiliate.

In some circumstances, the type of bullying may be a form of discrimination if the behaviour involves the characteristic of a person, such as an employee being bullied by their colleagues for their sexual orientation.

Bullying in general can either be quite explicit with yelling and inappropriate behaviour or can range to more subtle types with indirect forms of bullying. Indirect forms of bullying are substantially more difficult to investigate from a HR perspective, as they can be well hidden and not witnessed by other colleagues or management.

To give you a better understanding of what I mean by this, here are examples of indirect bullying in the workplace:

- Providing an employee an unreasonable amount of workload or not providing an even share or distribution of the workload resulting in a person being underutilised.
- Excluding a person from work-related activities causing them to feel isolated or done with the intention to humiliate them.
- Not sharing critical information that a person requires in order to perform their job effectively.
- Deliberately excluding a person from communications, meetings or events.
- Setting unrealistic timelines for a task, project or specific duty to be completed by or to frequently change deadlines.

This is not an exhaustive list as indirect bullying can take many different forms and may even compound with many types of indirect bullying or even combine with direct bullying. Direct bullying is a lot more explicit. Direct bullying can involve yelling, abusive and insulting language, interfering with a person's property, inappropriate behaviour that intimidates or threatens, as well as physical violence towards a person. Again, these are just a few of the examples to give you an idea and compare indirect bullying to direct forms of bullying.

A challenge HR professionals will encounter in their careers is trying to determine as to whether an ER matter is either workplace bullying or harassment. Harassment in the workplace is defined differently to bullying.

Workplace harassment is an incident/s when an uninvited or unwelcome behaviour causes someone or even a group of individuals to feel intimidated, humiliated or insulted. Harassment can be an individual event or a series of events in the workplace, and it can also apply to a person witnessing the event. Similar to bullying, there are different forms of harassment, expanding to sexual harassment and racial harassment.

Sexual harassment is a very specific and serious form of harassment, pertaining to uninvited behaviour of a sexual nature. Sexual harassment can be physical, written, verbal or visual material presented to a person that has made them feel humiliated, offended, or intimidated. Other examples of sexual harassment could be stalking, threatening communications via text message, email, phone, social media postings, sexual assault or indecent exposure.

As stated above, there is a specific piece of legislation that employees and employers must abide by in the workplace; sexual harassment is unlawful underneath the *Sex Discrimination Act 1984 (Cth)*. From this federal level of legislation, as well as the applicable state-based legislation, failing to object to the behaviour at the time the event occurred is not equivalent to consent.

Instances of sexual harassment can occur in the workplace, between colleagues outside of work and during work-organised events like a Christmas party.

Racial discrimination is characterised by unwelcomed conduct in relation to a person's nationality, race, colour of their skin, or social origin. This type of harassment can be verbal remarks or inappropriate behaviour that demonstrates racial prejudice against an employee.

An example of this is say an employee called Jeff who makes a comment regarding a group of employees, loudly saying over a walkie-talkie "those bloody curries don't know what they are doing". In this example, those of Indian descent who Jeff was referring to had experienced racial harassment, as the inappropriate comments referred to their ethnicity. Anyone else overhearing this racial slur from Jeff and may not even be of Indian descent but are offended by this comment also have grounds to make a complaint.

If an employee (complainant) was to make a complaint regarding bullying or harassment, the business and any other individuals cannot vilify the complainant. Vilification refers to when a person tries to incite hatred or make circumstances more difficult in the workplace for the complainant, as a result of them making a formal complaint.

Vilification can also occur without a formal complaint being made, and when a person tries to incite hatred, humiliation or severe ridicule by other individuals or a group of employees on grounds of their characteristics; this may be based on an individual's ethnicity, sexuality, HIV status, disability, religion or any other type of protected characteristic.

A company needs to have processes in place to ensure that employees are not vilified, and if they are that these matters are managed appropriately so that the behaviour ceases and any applicable disciplinary action is carried out.

HR professionals also need to understand the premise of victimisation. Victimisation in the workplace can occur when an employee is subjected to threats that they or other colleagues will be disadvantaged, or suffer a detriment if did any of the following:

- Exercise their right to make a workplace complaint or exercise any other type of right permitted by law.
- Have intentions to provide a witness statement or information to the business regarding inappropriate behaviour they have observed in the workplace.
- Refused to behave in a certain way as the behaviour in itself would be discriminatory, deemed harassment or bullying.

- Has assisted another employee to submit a grievance to the company or they themselves have submitted a grievance.

When an employee is notified of allegations made against them regarding a complaint, HR need to notify them that they are under no circumstances allowed to victimise or vilify anyone in the workplace. This is specifically aimed at ensuring that the complainant does not suffer any detriment as a result of exercising their workplace right to submit a complaint.

As a HR professional, you need to understand the importance of your role in the resolution of grievances in the workplace, as well as how an investigation should be conducted into complaints regarding bullying and harassment.

Managing employee grievances effectively is a large component of what a HR professional contributes towards a business. When a complaint is made or a grievance is raised by an employee, it is HR's responsibility to assess the nature of the allegations and then determine whether a formal investigation is required.

A formal investigation will typically be required if attempts have been made by the parties involved to previously resolve the matter and this has not led to a resolution. Another reason to formally investigate a matter is that the nature of the complaint is deemed serious. There may also be evidence that a breach to governing legislation has occurred; there has been a serious breach to company policies and/or procedures, or the facts of the matter need to be ascertained.

Some matters that are not serious, or the facts of the matter are not disputed, can be managed outside of a formal investigation process. If a mediation between parties involved is an option as the relationship between the parties does not involve personal conflict, then informal methods should be the preferred course of action.

To determine the correct course of action, a judgement call needs to be made and making these types of recommendations becomes easier over time as you become exposed to more ER matters throughout your HR career.

After a complaint has been evaluated by the HR professional handling the matter, the second step is to analyse and establish the allegations. I recommend interviewing the complainant to understand the allegations in detail, take extensive notes and ask questions so that you fully understand the context of what has occurred.

Once you have summarised the allegations, you can then put the list of allegations to the complainant to gain their written confirmation that the allegations are correct and are an accurate reflection of what they are trying to communicate.

Once you have this in writing, you can then inform the relevant manager or senior manager of the nature of the complaint, as you will need their involvement in issuing a statement of allegations letter to the respondent/s; the respondent/s are the individuals to whom the complaint and allegations have been raised against.

Before you issue the statement of allegations letter, gather as much evidence as you can pertaining to the allegations. You should also ask the complainant if there were any witnesses to the incident/s that occurred, and if they have any supporting documentation, they can provide you.

Once you have formulated an investigation plan that is when you and the relevant manager should organise a meeting with the respondent and issue a statement of allegations letter.

The allegations letter should outline the nature of the complaint, what the investigation process will be going forward, and when you anticipate the investigation will be finalised. The respondent will have an opportunity to respond to the findings before a final outcome is determined.

The statement of allegations letter may also include instructions to remain suspended until the investigation has been finalised. Paid suspension may be an appropriate response if the respondent's presence in the workplace could potentially jeopardise the integrity of the investigation, such as potential intimidation or vilification towards the complainant.

The suspension may also be appropriate due to the serious nature of the incident, such as having a safety concern for the respondent, complainant or any other employee in the workplace.

If an employee is suspended, the allegations letter should also include instructions that they need to always remain contactable during the investigation and must be available for any type of meetings or questions from the investigator (often HR representative).

The suspended employee is also not able to discuss this matter with another worker, unless that person is a chosen support person, as the matter is deemed to be private and confidential. If the business has serious concerns that the respondent may act out against individuals or the company, you may also choose to collect their company property, temporarily de-activate their email account and mobile service.

With the statement of allegations letter issued to the respondent, they have the option to provide a verbal response to the allegations during the meeting or could be given the opportunity to provide a written response to the allegations within 48 hours.

Which option you choose as the HR representative is at your discretion. If the nature of the allegation is serious, I recommend requesting a response in writing so that every step in the process is clearly documented with a paper trail.

The respondent's written statement can be submitted to you and the manager via email, or on a written document; hard copy written documents need to be signed and dated by the respondent. The responses to the allegations must be considered when determining findings. The respondent/s may also provide a list of witnesses you could speak to verify their version of events, which can be contrary to the complainant's allegations. Now that you have included this into your investigation plan, you need to start conducting interviews of any available and relevant witnesses.

Not all workplace investigations will have witnesses. When the investigation only involves the complainant's version of events versus the respondent's, it becomes very difficult for the investigator to ascertain the facts. In these instances, allegations may be deemed unsubstantiated based on the balance of probabilities, as there is not sufficient information or evidence for the investigator to understand what is more likely to have happened.

The "balance of probabilities" is the test or burden of proof used by HR and workplace investigators to understand what is more likely to have happened. Using this test, findings are made, and allegations are either substantiated, partially substantiated or unsubstantiated. It is important to note that when you as an investigator get to the stage when you are presenting the findings (not the outcome) to the complainant that you explain that although allegation/s may be unsubstantiated, the findings are not saying that the incident/s did not happen. The findings are not a reflection of the truth, but merely a summary of what facts could be substantiated based on all available information, including the respondent's feedback.

When you are leading an investigation that has witnesses, you will need to interview them in a consistent and structured manner. When you organise an interview with a witness, it is important to reaffirm to them that they are not in any way in trouble as it can be quite daunting to receive an unexpected phone call or email from HR. You should explain what the conversation will be about and that they too have the option to have a support person present.

When you first make contact, you must make it clear that this matter needs to be kept private and confidential, as you do not want the witnesses to start discussing this matter with their colleagues or anyone else that could potentially become involved in the investigation.

At the interview, you can request that the witnesses sign a confidentiality undertaking. A confidentiality undertaking can be a one-page document that outlines the process you are taking that they are to not discuss this matter with anyone else in the workplace and that if they are found to breach confidentiality, they themselves may be subject to disciplinary action.

Some witnesses may find that this document is quite formal. As a HR professional, it is up to you to explain to them that this is a standard process asked of all witnesses interviewed and ensures the integrity of the investigation. In some cases, you may try to organise an interview with a witness, and they are not willing to open up to you, as they do not wish to become involved in the matter. In these circumstances, you need to gain their trust and influence them to understand that providing information is important for the business to determine what has occurred. When this is not sufficient to gain a witness' co-operation, you then may need to rely on the conditions of their employment contract and any relevant company policy. Employment contracts and company policies can state that all employees are obligated to participate in workplace investigations as a condition of their employment.

Once you have the signed confidentiality undertaking, you can then commence the formal interview. I recommend having prepared questions that are open-ended and do not lead the witness to answer in a way that would validate the allegation. You are trying to probe and understand the extent to which each particular witness was involved or observed the allegations, and any other additional information that may not have been gathered from the complainant and respondent at this point in the investigation.

I like to refer to interviewing witnesses as following the breadcrumbs; you can start with an initial set of allegations, and as you continue with your interviews more allegations may arise, which will then need to be put to the respondent in writing.

When new allegations are raised the respondent/s can again provide their version of events so this is considered prior to making a determination. When you are interviewing witnesses, I like to try and type their responses as they talk underneath the prepared questions so that the final interview notes are written as a script.

I have this luxury as I am a fast typer. If you're not able to use this method, you can paraphrase their responses and the examples they provide in a word document or with handwritten notes in your workbook. In certain states in Australia, recording a conversation without someone's permission is a criminal offence, which is why I recommend steering clear of relying on any type of recording device. If you do insist on using one, you will need express permission from all parties you are recording before the recording starts, and once the recording is on you need to ask for their permission again. By asking permission twice and having this permission expressed on the recording itself will help protect you against any allegation that you recorded them illegally or without consent. Whatever method you choose, you need to be able to understand what each witness states and how many witnesses were able to support each allegation when you get to the end of the investigation.

When you have finished your interview with a witness, it is important to summarise the key points covered to ensure you fully comprehend what they have explained to you. At the end of the meeting, you should also remind them of their obligations to be honest in their responses and that they have just signed the confidentiality undertaking. If they have any questions or think of anything else that is relevant, they have the option to contact you as the investigator over the next few days so that this is considered.

Once the meeting has been formally closed, you can note the time the meeting has ended in your notes so you have a full record of how long the interview lasted, who was present and what was discussed. Once you have finished interviewing each witness, as the investigator you need to assess the credibility of each witness. You can do this in an objective manner by considering some key questions.

Starting with which story is more plausible to have happened and makes the most sense with all the information gathered? Were there any witnesses who provided a version of events that was quite different or even contradictory to that provided by the complainant? Is there a possibility that witnesses may be colluding and agreeing on the version of events prior to them meeting with HR? Was each witness someone who had with their own eyes and ears observed the event or can firsthand verify that the allegation is substantiated? Or is the witness recounting the event as told to them by the complainant? Were the witness statements specific with context, rough time and date of the event or events? Or were they very vague with their details and couldn't offer much information when pressed for details? These are all highly relevant questions to consider when you're trying to decipher the credibility of the witnesses you have interviewed.

After your credibility assessment, you will need to make findings based on the balance of probabilities. No findings can be made regarding any type of allegation unless the allegation/s have been put forward to the respondent/s and they have had the opportunity to respond.

Once you have compared your findings against each allegation, it is recommended that you draft an investigation report. This would include a summary of the allegations, and against each allegation the respondent's version of events versus the evidence provided by the witnesses. Under each allegation you can then state whether on the balance of probabilities the allegation is substantiated, un-substantiated or partially substantiated.

The aim of the report is so that anyone who is not familiar with the details and persons involved would have a thorough understanding of what the allegations were, the process followed by HR, evidence and reasons behind the findings. If the risk profile of this investigation is deemed high, my preference is to separate the recommendations from the investigation report especially if disciplinary action or termination forms a part of the recommendation.

Other recommendations that do not involve disciplinary action or termination of employment may be for the respondent/s to issue a written apology to the complainant for the harm, offence caused, or for them to undertake refresher training on workplace expectations and relevant company policies. Another alternative to disciplinary action may be to separate the complainant and respondent/s into different working areas when allegations have been substantiated, if the change does not disadvantage the complainant. These are informal recommendations and would suit investigations that have a lower risk profile.

As a HR professional, you may experience a scenario when you finalise an investigation and based on the findings and all other available information, you determine that the complainant made a vexatious complaint. When an employee has made a vexatious complaint, which could be false or misleading statements against the respondent/s with the intention to cause harm or vilify them, then this would need to be addressed by the company.

A business should not tolerate this type of behaviour as a formal investigation is quite stressful and tarnishes the internal reputation of the respondent/s and is not in alignment with most companies' values. It is for this reason that when an employee makes a vexatious complaint, they themselves may be subject to disciplinary action up to and including termination of employment.

When you commence an investigation, it is critical to inform the complainant of this and the definition of a vexatious complaint. This warning should be documented in your interview notes in the event you need to refer to this in the future.

As you can appreciate, each investigation you conduct throughout your career will be different and will take different twists and turns. As the investigator, you need to stay in control of how the investigation progresses and remain objective at all times. Although you may have previous knowledge or understanding of certain matters relevant to the investigation, these biases cannot cloud the investigation.

Findings made need to be purely based on the evidence gathered and whether something is more likely to have happened based on this evidence. As the investigator, you cannot get emotionally involved in the investigation and take any employee's side. Your interactions with employees can be emotionally charged and they can make you feel compassionate.

Compassion and empathy are key as a HR professional. However, when you're investigating a workplace complaint or grievance, it is absolutely essential to remain neutral.

Genuine Redundancies

At times, businesses can be confronted with challenging macro and micro-environmental factors, toughening markets, navigating a global pandemic like COVID-19 and how it will impact Australian industry, and managing the loss of large customer contracts, which can ultimately devastate the bottom line.

Whatever internal or market-driven changes are impacting an industry or business, it is common practice to re-evaluate the ongoing operational needs of a business. This analysis includes looking at the spans of control across an organisation, determining what roles are operationally critical and what roles are no longer required, or not necessary to keep the business afloat.

When an impact assessment has been finalised with the assistance of HR, roles can be identified as being genuinely redundant. The definition of a genuine redundancy under the *Fair Work Act 2009*, section 389, is when a person's employer no longer requires the person's job to be performed by anyone because of the operational requirements of the employer, and the employer has complied with the requirements in any governing modern award or enterprise agreement.

There are two distinct points made in this definition. The first being for the redundancy to be genuine. The position, once it has been made redundant, cannot be performed by anyone; the caveat on this is that the business is able to rehire the position if operational requirements change once a reasonable time has passed.

I recommend leaving at least 12 months after the redundancy has occurred, whereas other organisations use a three-month buffer due to the Australian Tax Office requirements on the departed employee. The second point is that employers must comply with the redundancy conditions stipulated in any applicable modern award and/or enterprise agreement.

When an employee's position has been identified as redundant and their employment conditions are governed by a modern award or an enterprise agreement, the process that needs to be followed can vary significantly to employees who are only covered by a common law contract. These provisions will dictate how an organisation would implement individual or bulk redundancies.

For learning purposes, I refer to a fictious example of a business called Humesware Pty Ltd that had finalised an impact assessment and identified 50 roles that could be made redundant across New South Wales and Queensland Australia.

To provide context to this example, Humesware Pty Ltd conducted a national review of its organisational structure, current systems and processes in place as well as operational expenditure. For the business to remain competitive in the market, the business needed to radically reduce overhead costs and streamline manual processes to deliver a higher level of customer service going forward. With the sole aim to support the future vitality of the business, the decision was made to identify impacted roles and assess which roles needed to remain.

The 50 employees to be made redundant are covered by a current enterprise agreement. The EA has a redundancy clause, which outlines that employees must first be given the opportunity to volunteer for redundancy. Therefore, a business must consider expressions of interests to be made redundant from those in the business prior to making a final decision on departures.

Expressions of interest (EOI) also do not need to be accepted. It is at the discretion of the business as to whether these are accepted or rejected. The way in which a voluntary redundancy process needs to occur and the selection method used for decision-making needs to be consistent, and in alignment with the relevant consultation clause.

Enterprise Agreements (EA) must have a consultation clause, which outlines what the employer must do when the employer has decided to make a major change; making employee positions redundant constitutes a major change.

Prior to releasing any communications with the impacted employees and initiating the consultation period, it is important to conduct a briefing session with the relevant managers. They need to become familiar with the reasons for the change (if they are not across the detail); how each position was identified and justified as not being required in the future; what documentation will be issued, and how this will be implemented across the two states. As a business would want all impacted employees to hear the news at the same time, you would organise information sessions with the employees at the same date and time in NSW and QLD.

Once your managers have been informed of the timeline, it would be beneficial to notify the relevant union official in each state – only if the union is covered in the enterprise agreement.

You would only want to provide them 24 to 48 hours' notice at most, so that they are available to support their members in the workplace and answer any questions they may have. You could present this information along with a senior manager during a teleconference or face-to-face meeting. I would recommend providing them some context to the decision-making, without revealing any commercially sensitive information. You can also email them a copy of the "Notice of Proposal to proceed with Significant Change" letter as a follow-up to the meeting, so they can see firsthand what letter will be issued to the impacted employees in the next few days.

The "Notice of Proposal to proceed with Significant Change" letter refers to the Consultation clause of the EA and/or the relevant modern award clause. This letter is to be issued at the first consultation meeting organised with the impacted employees. The purpose of this letter is to formally notify employees that the business, Humesware Pty Ltd (**"Humesware"**) has a proposal to proceed with significant change in accordance with the governing enterprise agreement (**"Agreement"**).

The next section of the letter should describe what the nature of the proposed changes are and what impact this will have on their position. With the distribution of the letter, this marks the commencement of the consultation period whereby all relevant employees and their representatives have the opportunity to discuss any ideas they may have about the proposed change, and put forward any workable solutions.

The letter needs to indicate when the consultation period will close, and I recommend that another session is organised to formally close the consultation period. The final consultation period session will also allow the business to communicate if any feasible solutions have been presented by employees that would mitigate the need for redundancies or reduce the number of redundancies required.

As this is a bulk redundancy session example, you are going to have multiple people in a room that management will need to address. To help guide the discussion and to ensure each session across the two states are consistent, I would recommend HR preparing a PowerPoint pack. The PowerPoint pack would outline the business' internal review, contributing factors towards the decision-making, which positions have been identified as redundant (no names) and in which areas, and the process to be followed with associated timelines.

The voluntary redundancy process would also be explained in this PowerPoint, along with the supporting documentation. In bulk redundancies, the paperwork issued will differ to the paperwork issued to employees in a one-on-one redundancy setting.

At an initial bulk consultation session, the business would not issue redundancy quotes as the individuals had not yet had the opportunity to volunteer for redundancy. The information pack would only include the formal notification letter, any EAP contact details and would request for them to sign-off that they attended the session. An expression of interest form would also need to be included, which requests the employee to fill-out, sign and date the form to then have sent through to HR.

Only when an EOI form is submitted to HR would they be provided with a redundancy quote prepared by payroll. HR would also reiterate that despite making an EOI, this does not mean that their application is by default accepted. The business may deem that their knowledge, skills and experience are an asset and the business is not willing for them to depart.

For employees covered by a common-law contract, consultation sessions can be conducted in both bulk and one-on-one discussion settings. For common-law contract employees, it is appropriate to provide a redundancy quote with the formal notification letter in the initial consultation session, as there is no voluntary redundancy process to undertake. I also recommend providing a script for managers for both common-law contract and enterprise/modern-award covered employees.

Developing a redundancy script for bulk consultation sessions or one-to-one conversations is an important part of providing HR support to a business. A lot of managers are not familiar with how a redundancy process works and are not comfortable holding these difficult conversations. A script can ensure that the message delivered is consistent, the correct and critical information is being delivered at the same time and that employees understand the steps being taken by the business. I recommend a redundancy script first being labelled as "For internal use only" as you do not want managers to print and issue this script to the employees.

The Script is purely to ease managers into the conversation. The opening paragraph of the script should welcome the impacted employee/s to the meeting or information session. This welcome could refer to that the fact that the manager is using notes to guide the meeting, so that they don't miss any details and that the message is delivered correctly. Once the employee/s are properly welcomed, the important part of the conversation needs to begin.

If previous discussions or communications have been released from the business regarding transformation or large-scale changes to the business, this can be referred to in the meeting to bring context to the discussion. References could also be made to the financial state of the business, industry, and market trends and how this relates to the employee's role. The script needs to set the tone and lead into how the background information is relevant to the employees listening.

The next section should refer to "what this means for you"; what do the market changes or the organisational review mean to the impacted employees in their current role? This would be the opportunity to formally notify them that their role has been identified as redundant, and the role may be one of many impacted across the organisation. The day of delivery of the formal notice would mark the commencement of the consultation period.

The consultation period can then be explained as a period of time whereby employees are provided all the necessary information to consider various redeployment opportunities in the business (if they exist). Employees would also be able to provide their feedback on any alternative arrangements that may not result in a redundancy. The script should also indicate how long the consultation period is for and when a final decision is to be made regarding either redundancy or redeployment.

Management should then start going through what information is currently available. I recommend referring to this as an information pack, and it should provide the notification of a redundancy letter, an initial quote of the redundancy payment (estimate), current list of internal vacancies with contact details, FAQ document, a redundancy guide (if available), as well as any employee assistance program (EAP) and outplacement services provided by the business.

Some businesses organise for redundant employees to have free access to an outplacement service for a limited period of time, so that they are supported in their career transition. Outplacement services provide a range of support options from CV writing, attending interviews and applying for jobs online. Again, these services provided are not a mandatory requirement and can form a part of the information pack.

In the final part of the script, the manager can explain what would occur if the business is unable to successfully redeploy them into a role. They would either be required to work out the full duration of their notice period, a portion of the notice period or would be paid out their notice in lieu. The script should also give an indication when their employment would likely cease if redeployment options are not available, and when they would be able to reasonably expect the redundancy payment to be processed.

As this is a lot of information for impacted employees to take in, it is important for the script to include notes to pause and allow employees to ask any questions. The HR representative's contact details should also be included in the issued paperwork as another point of contact.

Managers also need to be coached that an employee's reaction can vary widely, from being in denial, being upset and angry, to then also demonstrating indifference. Some employees may also be unsurprised by the decision or even welcome the redundancy as they are close to retiring. Managers just need to understand that each employee's circumstances are unique, and they cannot predict (even though they may believe that they can) what the reaction may be of their impacted team member. An emotional reaction may also be delayed, with team member's becoming upset after the first meeting and once the magnitude of the information has finally sunk in.

At the end of the meeting, the script should instruct the manager to reiterate that all matters discussed during the meeting are to remain private and confidential. You may also want to emphasise the importance of this, as other employees may be receiving similar news on the same day (bulk redundancies) and the manager would like the other employees to have the chance to hear the news from them first.

If a manager is required to hold these individual meetings in one day, and meetings are scheduled back-to-back, it is important to allow the manager to have a break between each one. These discussions can be particularly tough for managers who have built relationships with their team members. It is also good practice to allow buffers between each meeting, as some employees may need extra time to ask questions or compose themselves before leaving the meeting room.

Developing a tailored redundancy script for managers is just one important part of preparation. HR representatives should also develop a Frequently Asked Questions (FAQ) document, particularly when rolling out numerous one-to-one or bulk redundancies. Having a FAQ document can be very helpful for both managers and impacted employees. From my own experience in HR, I have collated a list of questions, and I recommend you have written responses prepared to support your managers with these difficult conversations.

1. How will the selection process be managed for impacted employees applying for different positions?

In managing redeployment opportunities for impacted individuals, businesses can choose to directly appoint, redeploy or offer positions to employees who express an interest in vacant positions. Each impacted employee will be assessed based on the merits of their application, and whether they have the suitable skills and knowledge to perform the new role. The role also needs to a be a "like for like" redeployment opportunity, if the business is to directly appoint an impacted individual into the vacant position. If the vacant role is vastly different or the employee is simply not suitable for the role, there is no obligation for the employer to then make this appointment.

2. What is a redundancy payment?

A redundancy payment is the final payment processed when an employee departs the company. A redundancy payment consists of the accrued statutory entitlements such as annual leave and long service leave (if applicable), as well as the calculated severance payment. The severance payment component of a redundancy is based on the length of continuous service at the business. An overall redundancy payment amount is determined by what is stipulated in the employee's common law contract and as per the National Employment Standards.

3. Will there be voluntary redundancies?

The answer to this question is solely reliant upon whether voluntary redundancy is a process stipulated in a governing industrial instrument, EA or forms a part of the company's policies and procedures. If voluntary redundancy is stipulated in a governing industrial instrument, a voluntary redundancy process must be followed.

If there is no specific process stipulated in an industrial instrument, a business has the discretion to apply what is covered in company policies or follow a contrary process. Businesses are not bound to follow any above and beyond conditions covered in company policies, as these can be changed or no longer adhered to at the company's discretion. The company is only obligated to ensure that they are meeting legislative requirements and the redundancy payments processed are in accordance with the NES.

4. If I find a redeployment opportunity within the business, will I still receive my redundancy package?

No. Employees are not able to double dip, by being redeployed into a suitable internal position in the business as well as receive a redundancy payment.

5. Can I elect to take a redundancy payment instead of being redeployed into the business?

There is a level of discretion a business can make when deciding what the answer to this question may be. Starting with what the legislative requirement is, businesses are obligated to offer redeployment opportunities to employees and employees need to accept the redeployment opportunity. Employers are not obligated to pay a redundancy payment in the event an employee does not wish to be redeployed into a like for like position. However, a business may decide to give the option to employees to elect in writing to be made redundant instead of being redeployed. The reasoning behind this "opt out" option is that if an employee is not willing to continue working in the business or is not receptive to the changes incurred from being redeployed, it may be more beneficial to allow the impacted employee to depart the business.

When an employee elects to be made redundant, they would not have the right to submit for an unfair dismissal claim – to make a claim on the basis that the redundancy was not genuine – as they have forfeited the opportunity to be redeployed.

6. There have been no issues raised regarding my performance in any performance appraisals and discussions. Why are you making me redundant?

The company's decision to make a position redundant is not a reflection of the individual's performance. The decision to make roles redundant is not based on the individual filling the chair but based on the operational requirements of the business going forward. If the function or duties of the role are no longer required to be performed in the future, then the role is redundant.

7. What if during my notice period I have a job interview I need to attend?

A business will need to accommodate any reasonable amount of time off that an impacted employee requests to secure future employment while they are working out their notice period. Sometimes, employees are not willing to work the entire duration of their notice period as they are disgruntled or upset from being made redundant. In these cases, employees may start to take the remainder of their personal leave accruals during this time, as personal leave is not paid out in a redundancy payment.

If an employee is excessively absent during their notice period and are not adding value to the business in wrapping matters up, the business may make the decision to pay the reminder of their notice period out so that the employee could depart the business immediately.

8. I had annual leave planned and booked into the future. What will happen to this leave?

If the leave was booked for after the finish date of the employee, any unused leave will be incorporated into the redundancy payment. If an impacted employee has booked leave during the notice period, this needs to be managed on a case-by-case basis between the manager and the employee to make any adjustments.

9. Can I salary sacrifice any component of my redundancy payment into my superannuation?

You would need to refer to the Australian Tax office requirements to ensure this answer is still up to date. At the time this book was written, only the current salary sacrifice arrangements in place at the time of the redundancy could be honoured. The Australian Tax office only allows normal wage/salary earnings to be salary sacrificed. In saying this the leave and severance component of the redundancy payment cannot be sacrificed towards a superannuation fund.

10. What happens to my novated lease now that I have been made redundant?

If you have a novated lease, employees will need to contact the lease provider and notify them of their employment ceasing with the company. Arrangements will need to be made to either cease the lease or personally continue the lease with the provider after departing the company. A final reconciliation of the account will occur and any variance in Fringe Benefit Tax payable by the employee will need to be made.

11. Will I be issued with a statement of service before I leave the business?

It is important that the business understands how and who will co-ordinate the administration of this for departing employees. The business may decide that these are provided to all departing employees, or it is organised on a request basis only along with separation certificates. The statement of service should be written on the company letterhead, outlining the role performed, reason for departure stating redundancy and the length of service with the business.

12. How will I be sent my payment summary next year when I need to lodge my tax return?

The payment summary will be sent directly to the employee's MyGov account when the business finalises the financial year. The payment summary will be downloadable by employees accessing their personal MyGov accounts.

13. What is the tax-free limit for the redundancy and how will it be paid?

Payments that meet the conditions of genuine redundancy are tax-free up to a limit based upon the years of service of the impacted employee in the company. The tax-free limit is calculated using a flat dollar amount plus an amount for each completed year of service. Any amount that is not included in the tax-free component of the redundancy payment, is then taxed as a termination payment (ETP).

If a total redundancy payment is less than the tax-free amount qualifier, than the entire redundancy payment will be processed as tax-free excluding any unused annual or long service leave (if applicable). Employees do not need to specifically include the tax-free portion of the redundancy payment in a lodged tax return.

The suggested questions and answers are a good starting point to building an FAQ document for your business, for managers to use when implementing redundancies. From the answers to each question, you can see that there is some flexibility in the responses, and this is indicative of the level of discretion employers have in the way that they manage their employees.

Some employers can be more generous in the redundancy severance payments made, whereas other employers have made the choice to pay strictly according to the NES.

Once the redundancies have been finalised, and the employees have departed the business or some may be working out their notice periods, the business may deem that it is appropriate to release an announcement. An announcement may be released if the redundancies are a result of a transformation program, significant down-turn in the industry or the loss of the contract.

If the organisation at large is aware of the need for changes to be made, it is important to notify them when these have been executed but also so that they are sensitive to what is happening within the business. For small scale redundancies, a company-wide announcement would not be necessary. However, the manager of the team should communicate with the remaining team members on the departures and how the changes may impact them in their day-to-day responsibilities.

Unfair Dismissal and General Protections Risk Assessment

When a business is considering terminating an employee's contract of employment, it is up to you as the HR professional to advise the business of any inherent risks associated with this course of action.

For corporate businesses, there may be a formal process where certain decision-makers need to sign-off on the termination before the employee is notified of the outcome, or even before the show cause letter has been issued. The sign-off process may require a few forms to be filled out with information on the employee, what the matter is pertaining to, etc.

If the business you are supporting doesn't have a formalised process or you are not sure how to advise on the risk profile of an employee, this section of the chapter will help you along.

I find scenarios are incredibly useful for learning purposes.

Let's say that a fictious employee named Mr James Mac has demonstrated consistent absenteeism since November 2019 and it is October 2020. Mr Mac has had a total of 365 hours of unexplained/unplanned sick leave. Mr Mac had previously been issued a written warning on 20 August 2020 due his excessive absenteeism. Mr Mac has continued to be excessively absent since this warning was issued to him, with no improvement. There has been no independent medical assessment undertaken to understand whether Mr Mac is or isn't medically fit to fulfil the inherent requirements of his role, as a florist.

Mr Mac is 27 years old and has been in his current role for over 12 months with a base salary of $60,000 per annum (exclusive of superannuation guarantee). Mr Mac's manager has come to you frustrated with Mr Mac's absenteeism and has indicated that he has had enough and would like Mr Mac terminated immediately.

As a HR professional, you will see that this would be problematic upon initial review as it has only been two months since the first written warning was issued. Your recommendation in this instance may be to issue Mr Mac a final written warning as a substitute to termination of his employment. Mr Mac's manager is not initially happy with this advice, so now is the opportunity to persuade and influence him so that he understands the risks associated with pursuing termination of Mr Mac's employment.

What I have built and implemented in my own role as a HR Manager for various organisations is a risk matrix, with the first column being the risk profile associated with unfair dismissal, and the right column associated with general protections.

So, what would I include in this risk assessment you may ask? Well, with everything, you should start with what the relevant legislation states about unfair dismissal and general protections.

The *Fair Work Act 2009* provides information on how the Fair Work Commission would assess these different types of applications. I'll start with the risk profile for unfair dismissal, as these applications are a lot more common than general protections claims.

The threshold test for unfair dismissal is determined by whether a termination is "harsh, unjust or unreasonable". This comes directly from the FWA. In the risk assessment, I would have this threshold statement at the very top, as well as the possible remedies and commission orders that could be made:

1. Capped monetary remedy up until six months of ordinary earnings. In Mr Mac's case, the maximum amount he would be eligible to receive, in the event his application was successful would be $30,000 (gross). This amount is on the assumption that his base salary is the only type of ordinary earnings he would ordinarily receive. When the Commissioner makes a determination on the appropriate remedy to be made, the Commissioner can consider a combination of monetary and non-monetary benefits, such as the private use of a company vehicle, and other types of benefits. It is important to understand that if a monetary remedy is awarded to an Applicant, this is not for damages of psychological distress or harm. The amount awarded is to compensate the Applicant for any lost earnings they would have received had they continued to have worked for the

employer and not been terminated. The Commissioner will often rely on the Sprigg's formula to calculate an appropriate amount, which considers the Applicant's future prospects of employment, transferable skills, age and other factors to understand how long it would take for the Applicant to find other employment. If the Applicant has found other employment at the time the claim is being heard by the Commission, the Commissioner will take this into account when determining an amount.

2. Re-instatement of employment. If the employer was deemed to have unfairly dismissed Mr Mac, the Commissioner may order re-instatement of Mr Mac's employment. It would be up to the employer to have made it clear during conciliation and the hearing that the relationship is untenable, and it is for this reason the Applicant should not be re-instated. However, if the business has unfairly treated the Applicant and the Applicant is seeking re-instatement over a monetary remedy, then the Commissioner prefers to order re-instatement of employment. This is an important consideration for a business when terminating employees; as there would be nothing more embarrassing for Mr Mac's manager to have James back in his team, and most likely sharing his victory against the company with his colleagues.

3. Statement of service. The Commission may also order for the employer to provide the Applicant with a statement of service if a remedy has been ordered, and reinstatement has been deemed an inappropriate option for both the employer and the Applicant.

These are the three factors I would have at the top of the risk assessment, with an estimate of the amount of compensation that could be awarded. You would then want to determine based on the facts gathered to date whether there is a low to high probability of a claim being made, and if there is a low to high severity if the claim was to be successful.

Now you need to start addressing the facts that are favourable and unfavourable to Mr Mac's potential claim. The first point you may want to address is that procedural fairness had been followed to date, as Mr Mac has been afforded the opportunity to respond and provide feedback to issued outcomes. Mr Mac was also afforded the opportunity to have a support person present prior to any formal meetings commencing. The confidentiality of matters discussed were upheld by management and human resources.

Mr Mac's prospects of future employment are positive as he is only 27. Mr Mac has also been issued a previous written warning less than two months prior for the same repeated behaviour of excessive absenteeism and his behaviour has not improved. Another bullet point you may want to add is that the business may consider whether Mr Mac has been provided a sufficient opportunity to address his absenteeism.

These are the overall facts of the case to date. So how would you use all these facts to assess as a HR professional whether this is a risky termination or not?

You should refer to the applicable section in the FWA. I would refer to section 387 of the *FWA 2009*, which lists out the criteria of what is deemed harsh termination. Please note that pieces of legislation are often reviewed, and this section was referenced in December 2020. Using Mr Mac as an example, you may list the following:

1. That there would be a valid reason for Mr Mac's dismissal, either based on Mr Mac's dishonesty with respect to his pre-

employment medical information that indicated that he was fully fit to complete his duties as a florist, or for his reasons for excessive absenteeism that have consistently changed even after he was issued a written warning letter.

2. Mr Mac would be notified in writing of his termination and the reason/s for the termination. If this decision was approved by the appropriate decision-makers.

3. Mr Mac was not unreasonably refused to have a support person present or representative (if award based) at formal discussions with HR and management when discussing his absenteeism.

4. Mr Mac had been issued a written warning letter and had had multiple discussions with his direct manager pertaining to his excessive absenteeism, as well as the insufficient notice he would provide the business when he was going to be absent from the workplace.

5. The business's workplace policies and procedures have been adhered to in addressing this behavioural issue with Mr Mac and consistently applied.

6. Human resources presence has been consistent across all discussions with Mr Mac and the management of this matter.

The above list is just an example of how you may address the alphabetical sub-sections in the FWA and would need to be tailored to each particular case you are assessing. You may also like to add any additional, but relevant, comments for the business to be aware of to consider the risk.

You should also include any company policies and procedures Mr Mac has breached, any relevant training provided to Mr Mac that is relevant and demonstrates that he was aware of expectations, and any other relevant correspondence. All these bullet points are sufficient information to give the business an idea of the risk profile for unfair dismissal.

You don't want a risk assessment to be too lengthy or else the decision-makers may skim through important details, but it also needs to ensure it covers the key points. This is why I like to use colour schemes to communicate the risk; low risk columns are green, medium risk are orange, and red is clearly flagging this is risky business!

So, I have covered unfair dismissal for you, and now comes general protections. As you're aware, general protections (GP) claims are vastly different to an unfair dismissal claim.

GP claims have a reverse onus of proof, which means that the Commission will assume that the employer has acted unlawfully and has adversely impacted an employee until the Respondent can prove otherwise. The onus would fall on the business to argue that the decision to terminate Mr Mac's employment was not based on a prohibited reason/s. I would often have a sentence or two explaining this, as well as the following three points:

1. The Commissioner may order an uncapped amount of monetary compensation to the Applicant. Unlike unfair dismissal matters where the monetary amount that can be ordered by the Commissioner is up to six months of ordinary earnings. For GP claims, there is no limit. Therefore, employers need to be so careful and ensure that the business would not terminate Mr Mac on the basis of a prohibited reason.

2. GP claims can be made public. GP claims get a lot of interest from the media and when they go to a hearing, the details pertaining to the matter are made publicly available. A detailed decision is also able to be downloaded

by the public once a determination has been made. The company does not want to have this type of attention, particularly if the business is a public listed company; this is bad for a company's reputation, and your reputation as a HR professional as your name will be included in the determination, and negative news for shareholders to receive.

3. The last point to include would be an elaboration on the reverse onus of proof. The business would be tasked with making submissions to the FWC asserting how the business did not unlawfully terminate Mr Mac.

With these three points covered, you would then also rate the likelihood of the claim being made and the severity if the claim was to be made. Based on the fictitious circumstances of Mr Mac, this column for GP would be a bright red as it related to his absenteeism, due to illness.

In the bulk of this column's risk assessment, you would refer to the relevant section of the Fair Work Act. In this scenario, it could be Section 352 of the *FWA 2009*, and cross-reference to the *Fair Work Regulation 2009* (3.09), where a prohibition exists on the dismissal of employees for a temporary absence because of illness or injury.

The decision-makers are not going to know what you mean by a temporary absence and how this is prohibited reason, which is why you may elaborate with the below points as an example:

1. Mr Mac has provided medical documentation from a specialist deeming him to be fit to perform full-time duties in his current capacity as a florist, and yet Mr Mac's absenteeism remains ongoing. There is a contradiction here.

As per section 107(3) (a), the employee has not provided sufficient medical documentation to satisfy a reasonable person that Mr Mac's personal illness or injury (which is non-work related) would result in the degree of absenteeism demonstrated.

2. Mr Mac has not yet been absent from the workplace for a three-month period or a total of three months over a 12-month period. Mr Mac would need to have been absent for a total of 456 working hours to satisfy this threshold in this section of the Act, which indicates Mr Mac has been absent more than a "temporary absence" from the workplace. Mr Mac has currently been absent for a total of 365 hours since November 2019.

3. Mr Mac has been dishonest on his pre-employment check where he has indicated that he had no pre-existing injuries that would impact his ability to perform his role. Mr Mac has on numerous occasions indicated that he suffers from severe vertigo as a result of a serious ear infection, and a subsequent operation he had to undergo five years ago. As Mr Mac was not employed by the company five years ago, this condition should have been declared on his pre-employment medical check as a medical condition would impact his ability to perform his duties as a florist. The business may interpret this non-disclosure as dishonesty on Mr Mac's part, as his vertigo is a main contributing factor to his absence from the workplace. Termination based on dishonesty is not a proscribed reason underneath GP.

4. An independent medical assessment has not been organised by the company to understand whether Mr Mac is or is not fit to fulfil the inherent requirements of this role. The only documents provided to date are the medical documents provided by Mr Mac.

As you can see from addressing each point, in this column the business may wish to consider either terminating Mr Mac's employment because of dishonesty or his absenteeism. Terminating his employment based on his absenteeism is risky, as he is deemed to have only been temporarily absent from the workplace until he satisfies the threshold as described above.

The alternative may be for the business to see if Mr Mac's absenteeism continues and he reaches the 456 working hours in a 12-month period. These options are up for discussion with the business. The last section you should also include in your risk profile document is any mitigation strategies available or what you would recommend as the HR support for this matter. I'll cover this in more detail in the next section of this chapter.

With your finished risk assessment, attach any other supporting documentation to an email and send through to Mr Mac's manager and any other managers required to consider the information. Providing a detailed risk assessment with the full background of the matter gives the necessary approvers enough of an understanding to make an informed, objective decision on the appropriate course of action. Based on the red and green columns, you have now convinced Mr Mac's manager that proceeding with termination is too risky and it would be more appropriate to issue Mr Mac with a final written warning letter instead.

Using these types of risk assessments can act as a very helpful tool when trying to influence your stakeholders and protect the business from making decisions with high-risk profiles. Often managers can be in a heightened emotional state when they first come to HR with their employee concerns. It is your job as a HR professional to approach these concerns in a measured way and understand your role is not only supporting the manager, but also protecting the business and ensuring that Mr Mac is treated fairly with due process.

If Mr Mac were within his qualifying period or within six months of the date of his commencement with the employer, then the risk profile overall would be reduced. Employees are only able to make an unfair dismissal claim if they have been employed for a period greater than six months from the date that they commenced employment with the business. This period of employment is colloquially known as the probationary period. The term "probationary period" does not exist underneath the *FWA 2009* and is technically called a qualifying period. The reason why the distinction is important is that contractual terms in employment contracts can stipulate a reduced period of time for a "probationary period" such as three months or even extend a probationary period to twelve months. This contractual term does not override an employee's right to submit an unfair dismissal claim if they have not passed probation but met the qualifying period criteria. Likewise, if an employee's probationary period is three months and they are dismissed prior to six months length of service this does not then give them access to make an unfair dismissal claim.

Another consideration is also the high-income threshold, which changes annually. If Mr Mac earned significantly more than $60,000 base salary per year and was over the high-income threshold, this would prevent Mr Mac being able to make an unfair dismissal claim. It is important to note that the high-income threshold does not include superannuation contributions or any other component of remuneration. This is based on ordinary earnings. This needs to be considered in your risk assessment when putting together the unfair dismissal column.

FWC Claims

For continuity, let's assume that Mr Mac's manager decided to proceed with termination despite the associated risks captured in your comprehensive and colourful risk assessment. Mr Mac was not happy with being terminated and has inevitably decided to pay a nominal fee of less than $100 AUD to the Fair Work Commission to lodge an unfair dismissal claim.

Mr Mac has gone to the Fair Work Commission website, downloaded an F2 form, completed the form and either lodged the form with the online portal or emailed the completed F2 form to the FWC email address in the respective state. With Mr Mac being the one to have lodged the application, he will be referred to as the "Applicant". The Applicant would have also had the opportunity to attach any supporting documentation relevant to the made claim.

Mr Mac's claim would have needed to have been lodged within 21 calendar days of his dismissal taking effect, or it would not have been within the required timeframe. If Mr Mac's application was submitted late, Mr Mac would need to make assertions to the Commission as to why there was a delay and how his circumstances reasonably impacted his ability to lodge the application with the 21 calendar period. The 21 calendar days does not include the day that the dismissal took effect.

If the final 21 calendar day happens to fall on a gazetted public holiday or a weekend, then the final day would be extended to the next business day. However, if a gazetted public holiday or weekend occurs with the 21 calendar day period, this does not extend the period that the Applicant has to lodge the application.

Before the F2 form is lodged, the Applicant has to complete the form by answering questions regarding the dismissal. In this case, Mr Mac would need to identify his former employer of Humesware Pty Ltd, the date he commenced employment with Humesware Pty Ltd and the date the dismissal took effect. Mr Mac would also need to outline the reasons provided by the employer for dismissal and the reasons as to why Mr Mac has deemed the dismissal to have been unfair. Mr Mac also needs to indicate on his Application what outcome he is seeking from the claim, which is either a remedy (dollar amount) for lost earnings or reinstatement.

Once the form has been successfully receipted by the Fair Work Commission, the completed F2 form, any supporting documents lodged by Mr Mac with the application and the details of the listed conciliation are sent to the employer.

As a business' representative, you are the designated individual responding to the Applicant. In FWC claims, the party who did not lodge the application and make the initial claim is referred to as the "Respondent". In these types of matters, the employer has within seven calendar days to respond once the F2 Form has been served by the FWC.

The FWC will send instructions on the requirements, information links as well as the form to be used to submit the employer's response. The employer is to use an F3 form to respond to the Applicant.

As a HR professional, you may be required to complete the F3 form on behalf of the respondent if there are no internal legal resources available; external resources are not engaged or it is an expectation of your role to be able to comfortably complete the applications.

Whatever the circumstance may be, you need to think about what type of information you should include in the application. Remember that the first step is only a conciliation, which is not a legally binding discussion, and it is the first step where the Commission is trying to resolve the claim without it having to progress to a formal hearing or decision on the papers made by a Commissioner. The number of facts and information included on the form needs to be a balance of communicating the main points regarding what occurred in relation to the dismissal and whether you want to keep your arguments to yourself so that the Applicant does not have access to this prior to the conciliation. This all needs to be considered, as when you go to lodge form FWC you need to immediately provide the Applicant a copy as well, along with any supporting documentation.

The F3 Form at first asks you to confirm the Commission matter number, Applicant's full name and the respondent's correct legal entity, contact details and industry of the employer. The form goes on to request information on date the employer notified the Applicant of the dismissal; for this example, let's say it was 10 December 2020.

You will need to confirm Mr Mac's salary, being $60,000 base salary plus superannuation guarantee (SG). Now, in the event that an application was lodged by the Applicant and the employee was not dismissed, the employer can make another jurisdictional argument to object the claim and indicate this on the form.

The F3 form allows for the following types of jurisdictional objections that the Respondent can make:

1. The application was lodged outside of the 21 calendar days period. The application was lodged more than 21 calendar days after the dismissal had taken effect. This objection would hold if the Commission does not deem the reason

for the delay provided by the Applicant as a reasonable excuse.

2. The Applicant was not an employee. Sometimes applications are made against an employer when the Applicant is not directly employed by the Respondent. One example of this may be when a labour hire employee, who has been working on a site (Business A) for a long period of time and is no longer allocated work. But rather than submitting the application against their actual employer, the labour hire agency (Business B), they have lodged the application against Business A, which is incorrect.

3. The Applicant was not dismissed. The Applicant may have submitted an unfair dismissal claim on the basis that they were forced to resign or it was a constructive dismissal; the circumstances at the workplace gave them no other option but to resign from their employment. If the employer refutes this and the employer did not initiate termination, this is where you can jurisdictionally object to the application.

4. The dismissal was a case of genuine redundancy. Perhaps in this instance, the Applicant was made redundant, and the Applicant believes that the redundancy was unfair and not a genuine or true redundancy as there were suitable redeployment options in the business.

5. The Applicant's employment does not meet the minimum employment period. This objection refers to the qualifying period stipulated in the FWA, whereby the employee is only eligible to make an unfair dismissal claim if they have surpassed six months from the date of commencing employment.

6. The Applicant earned more than the high-income threshold. As the respondent, you need to provide details of the Applicant's earnings to make this jurisdictional objection.

7. The Employer is a small business employer and the employer complied with the Small Business Fair Dismissal Code.
8. Any other objection.

If you do submit a jurisdictional objection, you would need to explain this position in the form. In the event you do not jurisdictionally object as you did terminate Mr Mac's employment as he stated in the F3 form, you would simply not fill out the jurisdictional objection section and move onto the reasons for the dismissal, as well as a response to the Applicant's contentions.

What details you put in here is going to depend on whether the Applicant is represented by a paid agent, union representative or a lawyer, as you may opt that over-sharing or providing a detailed response is not the best way to approach this application. It may be decided that most of the responses will be provided verbally during the conciliation, as what is said during a conciliation cannot be used in a hearing.

Also, if the matter was to progress through to a hearing, you would then have the opportunity to supply detailed submissions for the Commission to consider prior to the hearing, or enough detail for the Commissioner to make a decision on the papers. Once the Form F3 is completed, signed by yourself or the person with the proper authority in the business you support, you can submit this to the FWC email address for your respective state along with any supporting annexures. This email must include the Applicant in the correspondence and the contact details of those attending/ running the conciliation.

As the HR representative, even if you are not leading the conciliation on behalf of your employer, it is recommended that you be in attendance.

185

With the Respondent's application successfully submitted, the FWC email address automatically provides a receipt that the email has reached their inbox. All you need to do now is continue to prepare leading up to the conciliation. Your degree of confidence and experience in leading these conciliations will dictate the level of preparation you make for this matter. If you're not comfortable and are nervous leading the discussion, I recommend preparing a script for yourself outlining the timeline of events, facts and the arguments you have as to why the dismissal was not harsh, unjust or unreasonable. You could make references to the relevant sections of the FWA and annexures included in the submissions.

Whatever process you choose to take, you need to be intimately familiar with the facts of Mr Mac's termination and be able to rebut any surprising arguments during the conciliation. Also remember that this is just the first step – it is a conciliation and not a hearing.

The conciliator is there as a third-party facilitator with the sole aim to try and resolve/close the matter before it needs to proceed to the Commission and use Commission resources.

The conciliator has targets and one of the targets is how many conciliations can be settled, before a matter progressed through to a hearing. Bear this in mind when approaching the conciliation.

General Protection claims follow the same process as unfair dismissal claims, in the sense that they are first listed for a conciliation process. With there being a reverse onus of proof, the Commission will assume that the business unlawfully terminated Mr Mac, based on a prohibited reason.

It is then up to the Respondent to prove otherwise, as it becomes a question of fact; why was the adverse action taken? If the adverse action was not taken, how do you go about arguing this and presenting this information to the Commission in a succinct way?

Relevant questions that the Commission will consider when digesting the facts is if a proscribed or protected reason was an operative factor in the adverse action. Using Mr Mac's case, was Mr. Mac terminated on the basis that he was ill and away from work for extended periods of time due to his illness (protected reason), or was it due to some other basis of the decision?

If there had been multiple reasons for adverse action, with one being a proscribed reason, then this would be a breach of the applicable GP provision in the *Fair Work Act 2009*. However, the breach must have been substantial and operative in the decision-making to terminate Mr Mac's employment.

The Commission also considers whether the adverse action was taken "knowingly and recklessly". What this means is that the Respondent was aware that terminating Mr Mac on grounds of his ongoing illness was taking adverse action, and the Respondent continued with terminating his employment regardless.

The Commission would try to understand what was the Respondent's intent; was it to terminate Mr Mac's employment for a protected reason or was it due to a combination of his dishonesty and his ongoing absenteeism? Therefore, it is important to rebut evidence provided by the Applicant, or the Commission will have no other choice but to presume that adverse action had indeed been taken. Now temporary illness is only one of the many protected reasons. The following are proscribed reasons protected by the FWA:

1. Protected workplace rights. If Mr Mac had exercised a workplace right such as refusing to perform unsafe work in the workplace, or if Mr Mac had made a bullying and

harassment complaint against a colleague, and as a result of this he was subsequently terminated, this would be in breach of this protected right. A workplace right also covers lawful industrial action and if Mr Mac had commenced court action or legal proceedings against the employer.

2. Protected freedom of association. If Mr Mac's employment was terminated based on his political inclinations and joining a political group, some other type of association than this would be considered adverse action. Mr Mac has the right to associate with any type of party or body he so chooses without being adversely impacted by this in the workplace.

3. Protection from workplace discrimination. If Mr Mac was terminated for any type of protected characteristic such as his sex, age, sexuality, carer's responsibilities, etc., then he would have been adversely impacted by the Respondent.

4. Adverse action can also include if Mr Mac was not given his legal entitlements during or after employment, changes were made to Mr Mac's employment without consultation and the changes disadvantaged him, Mr Mac was treated differently to others in the workplace, and Mr Mac was offered different and unfair terms to those of his colleagues. These would be considered adverse action and give license to Mr Mac raising a GP claim.

The above list of protected reasons would apply to Mr Mac as he was an employee of an employer. However, general protections do not strictly apply to only employees like unfair dismissal. Prospective employees, prospective contractors and contractors, or any member of an industrial association have the ability to lodge a general protection claim against an employer.

You need to understand this as a HR professional, particularly when engaging with prospective employees during a recruitment process. For example, if you were interviewing Mr Mac and decided to not give him his role as a florist due to his sexuality and this was made clear to Mr Mac, or he has the ability to demonstrate that this was the reason for him not being given the role, then he could make a GP claim. If Mr Mac was going for a volunteer position as a florist and wasn't successful, he wouldn't be eligible in this respect to lodge a GP claim on the basis that he was a prospective volunteer.

When an application is made by prospective employees, contractors or an association, the GP claim is non-dismissal based. In Mr Mac's current claim with being dismissed on the basis of his temporary illness from the workplace, this is referred to as a dismissal-based GP claim.

There are two different forms the Applicant can choose from in making a GP claim: a non-dismissal and a dismissal GP claim form. In Mr Mac's example, he would need to download the F8 form from the Fair Work Commission website. The form asks similar questions to the F2 form for an unfair dismissal matter. Mr Mac would need to provide his contact details, the date of the dismissal, the reasons for the dismissal, what the alleged contravention is and whether he is legally represented by a paid agent, association or lawyer. The form can be either lodged with supporting documentation via email or through the Fair Work Commission's online portal. Once this has been lodged, the respondent will need to fill out the appropriate form and submit with supporting evidence to the FWC.

With unfair dismissals and general protection applications now covered in detail, I'd like to take you through Stop Workplace Bullying applications, which can be made by current employees. Stop Workplace Bullying applications in my opinion are the least common applications made and are often unheard of by a lot of HR professionals. I believe this stems from employees not knowing that this is an option available to them and another jurisdiction that the FWC can become involved in to facilitate a resolution. The process followed by the FWC is identical to the management of unfair dismissal and general protection claims. Please note that the FWC will not investigate any allegations of bullying and harassment. The FWC performs the function of considering the evidence provided by both parties, and, in the event the dispute cannot be resolved, to then make an order.

In most circumstances, when the employer receives the Stop Workplace Bullying claim, this will prompt internal discussions and make the matter a priority for the business – if it hasn't already been to try and resolve any issues at a workplace level. Once the application has been received by the business, as the HR representative you may need to prepare a response. You can assert contentions on a number of different grounds:

- That the alleged behaviour by the Applicant has not occurred or has not occurred repeatedly. The respondent may indicate that an incident has occurred, but this was addressed and has not occurred repeatedly. This is where the respondent would refer to any type of counselling notes, investigation files or references to discussions that have taken place to address any type of bullying and harassment that the Applicant has made reference to in the application.
- The Applicant is not covered by national workplace bullying laws. To put forward this contention, you would need to check the national employment framework and

understand whether the employee is in fact eligible to make this application.

- The action taken by the respondent in relation to a matter or matters pertained in the Applicant's form was reasonable, and fitting for the circumstances in the workplace.
- The Application is false, vexatious and has no reasonable prospect of success. This contention indicates that the bullying and harassment claims either did not occur as they have been stated by the Applicant or have been fabricated to negatively impact the Respondent.

During the FWC's mediation and hearing proceedings, the FWC will consider whether the application fits the appropriate jurisdiction: if there is substantial evidence to reasonably believe that bullying did occur in the workplace and whether there is a risk for bullying to occur in the workplace of the Applicant.

If the matter has progressed through to a hearing, a determination will be made whereby the Commission can make an order for the bullying to cease and desist in the workplace, and the respondent to monitor behaviours or involved individuals and provide additional training and support to employees regarding bullying in the workplace.

The FWC cannot award any type of financial compensation to the Applicant for damages or psychological distress. The FWC can impose penalties to any party that fails to comply with a FWC order once it has been made. It is very important to understand what the FWC expects from the business you are supporting in these circumstances, as you will likely be the person responsible with implementing any necessary changes and monitoring employee behaviour going forward. If any workplace behaviour policies need to be reviewed and/or refreshed training needs to occur for the employee group, then you would also need to organise and implement this too.

So far in this section, only employee-based applications have been covered. Employers can also lodge FWC applications. Employers are able to lodge an application to interpret or enforce an agreement, when a dispute has arisen between an employee and the company and a resolution at the workplace level has not been reached.

An application can only be made by the employer once genuine attempts have been made by parties involved to try and reach a resolution; steps have been taken according to the governing modern award, employment agreement or any other industrial instrument; and still, despite these efforts, a resolution has not been reached.

The form, which can be submitted by either an employee or an employee, is an F10 form, which is downloadable directly from the FWC website. The form requests the FWC involvement in dealing with a dispute in accordance with a dispute settlement procedure.

Like other claims, which can be made by the commission, conciliation or mediation is the first step, and if the informal process fails the FWC may make an order that parties are obligated to follow.

Overall, there are a few different FWC claims you will need to gain experience in managing and advocating on behalf of your employer throughout your career. It is important to learn and observe how others construct arguments in their submissions and then deliver these arguments during conciliations, mediations and hearings. If you can observe how an internal legal resource or a senior HR Manager manage a claim, ask your manager to be involved or be a fly on the wall. The more exposure you have to these types of the matters, the more comfortable you will become in dealing with them, but also being able to put your stakeholders at ease when claims do come through to them via email.

Managers can be very nervous and uneasy when they see the FWC seal. This is driven by these claims being foreign to them and they can at times take the claim by the Applicant personally. Being equipped with the right level of information and knowledge to explain the process and that the FWC's goal is to try and resolve these matters as informally and efficiently as possible will help build your stakeholder management.

6

NEGOTIATING ENTERPRISE
AGREEMENTS

AN ENTERPRISE AGREEMENT (EA) is a document formed by way of collective bargaining where an employer engages in negotiations with their employees and nominated representatives. An EA is specific to a particular enterprise or employer and outlines the scope of employees the EA covers. It is important to note that an employer may have multiple EAs governing different types of employees' employment conditions.

Once an EA is formed, the document is rubber stamped by the Fair Work Commission and acts as an industrial instrument for how an employer will pay wages and minimum working conditions. Having a governing EA is not a requirement for all employers and is just one type of a number of other industrial instruments, which could influence a business' minimum employment conditions.

The terms and conditions of employment are regulated by the *Fair Work Act 2009* (FWA*)*. This is the overarching piece of legislation and has regulations that provide additional guidance for employers. The FWA is a critical legislation, which all HR professionals should read and familiarise themselves with as it forms the basis of a lot of advice provided in day-to-day responsibilities.

The FWA also includes the National Employment Standards (NES) – setting out the eleven minimum employment entitlements to be provided to all employees covered by the national workplace relations system. A modern award, EA or employment contract cannot override the NES and can only match or offer better conditions than the NES.

For an EA to be approved by the Fair Work Commission (FWC), the EA must meet certain requirements. One of which is that the EA must not exclude the NES or any provision of the NES.

The NES employment conditions will be subject to terms included in the modern award or enterprise agreement. An EA may include terms that are ancillary, incidental to or supplement NES entitlements. If an EA contains the same entitlements as the NES, then the terms of the enterprise agreement would operate in parallel to the employees covered by the EA NES entitlement. However, this does not give the employee the ability to double dip and have double the NES benefits. All these types of circumstances of an EA does not give rise to contravening the NES.

As a HR professional, it is crucial to understand the key differences between modern awards and enterprise agreements. Each modern award is vastly different to the next, and likewise with enterprise agreements as they are employer specific. (Please bear this in mind when comparisons are made in this book, as they are made generally speaking and focused only on the key points.)

Starting with modern awards…

Modern awards are created and published by the FWC. They were first introduced in January 2010 and were designed to cover all employers and their respective employees within a particular industry or type of occupation.

A modern award strictly applies to a covered employee when a governing EA does not exist, and must only include terms that are permitted or required by the Fair Work Act. As a HR professional, it is important to monitor the significant dates of when modern awards are subject to an annual wage review and any other changes determined by the Commission that impact the business you are supporting.

When an annual wage review does occur, it is recommended that HR review all employees' current payment arrangements and ensure that all employees are paid equal to or above the new modern award provisions. Any employee that falls below this minimum should receive an increase on the effective date of the wage review stipulated by the FWC.

Let's now move onto enterprise agreements and what separates them from modern awards. An EA is made between an employer and its employees or employee bargaining representatives by way of collective or in good faith bargaining.

Enterprise agreements have expiry dates and apply to all employees within scope of the agreement for as long as the EA is in operation. An EA will still be in operation and cover a group of employees even after the expiry date has passed, until either the EA is replaced by another EA or terminated through an application process with the FWC.

An EA is also a comprehensive document, which outlines the terms and conditions of employment made at the enterprise level between the employer and employees. EA's are drafted in a way to meet the requirements of the employer and can vary significantly between other businesses in terms of roles covered, duties and responsibilities, payment arrangements and conditions, which go above the NES requirements.

Bargaining Process

The bargaining process for an EA can take many twists and turns, and the success of the negotiations can at times be dependent upon how good the relationships are between the business and the members of the bargaining committee.

When an EA expires, the employer can agree to bargain and initiate the bargaining process, or the employees may request the employer to commence bargaining. The employer may then refuse to commence bargaining whereby a majority support determination will need to be held. If the majority of the employees are supportive of the negotiations commencing, then the employer must then issue all covered employees with the Notice of Employee Representational Rights (NERR).

Now, even before a NERR is released by an employer, there should be a lot of preparation done by the HR representatives involved in the negotiation as well as the business leaders. I recommend preparing for an EA negotiation at least three to six months in advance prior to the expiry date of the agreement, particularly for EAs that cover a large number of employees and have a significant impact on the business' overheads.

Preparation of an EA negotiation involves a number of different exercises to be completed. HR professionals should start with what is often the most important consideration for a business: the cost impact analysis of the current EA and what the EA could cost if increases are applied over the course of the new EA to wages, allowances and any other type of benefit.

The cost analysis can be put together by looking at the last 12 months of wage costs of all existing employees and use this to develop scenarios. For example, if the business is willing to give up to 2 per cent increase to all wages and allowances over the life of the new EA, which may be a three-year period, how much additional cost would this be?

You would then be able to work through two other examples of a 1.5 per cent or 2 per cent increase. You should also audit the current wage rates against the minimum rates stipulated in the governing modern award to ensure year on year over the course of a proposed agreement, the wages rates will not fall below the minimum wage rate required to be paid. To provide recommendations around what would be a suitable increase over the life of the new EA, you'd want to present the business with some industry-based research.

Industry-based research requires HR to look at what the business' competitors have offered in their existing EAs and what the industry standard looks like. I recommend writing a research paper that outlines what existing competitor EA's are offering in terms of wage and allowance increases; any additional benefits above the award and/or NES provisions; length of the EA such as whether it may be three or four years; involvement of the union/s in negotiating the agreement; and how the EA/s have been structured.

In setting a benchmark for the business you're supporting, you need to consider whether matching competitor offerings is beneficial or not from a commercial perspective. For example, a competitor may provide better employee benefits to their people but, overall, the business is losing money year on year as their strategy has been to outbid and out match their competitors leading to an inherent increase in labour costs.

Another factor to consider is perhaps that the competitors were not initially paying their employees as high as the business you're supporting, so a similar increase percentage to benefits is not required or recommended in the business you're supporting. This among future projections of revenue and contractual renewals with major contracts, account holders and forecasted volume is required to calculate what is the maximum offering the business is willing to agree to in negotiations.

An important factor in these calculations is also the consumer price index (CPI) over the past 12 months, current quarter and if there is any indication for future CPI figures. You can also drill down to what the CPI impacts on resources involved in the operational process are. For example, you may look at the CPI of fuel and oil if you're in a supply chain and logistics industry. If this is projected to radically increase in the next 12 months, the business can understand this and offset this against a lower percentage increase in employee benefits.

With all these intricacies to consider, I recommend having the final costing strategy approved by the relevant decision-makers in the business prior to releasing the NERR. Another important part of research is conducting both operational and payroll-based workshops. You need to understand how the EA currently works and applies to the business, and whether the EA is being interpreted correctly and translated into employee payments, as well as what aspects of the EA are not working for the business.

Prior to conducting these workshops, you can send out a questionnaire to the relevant peer group, which may include the following questions:

1. What would you like to change in the current EA?
2. Are the operational hours of the business still the same?
3. What would you like to be added to the EA?
4. What are the main questions you have received from employees about the EA?
5. Are there any parts of the EA that are no longer applicable to the business or are not actively applied to operational practice?

6. Do you foresee any immediate challenges if we were to start EA negotiations?
7. Do the union have a strong presence in your workforce?
8. What were the log of claims from the previous EA negotiation?
9. Does the union have a campaign or agenda for this EA negotiation?

Understanding the details to these questions is a critical exercise for your preparation as a HR professional, and also gives you an understanding of what terms the business is willing to agree to and not concede on.

There is a common misconception among HR professionals that when you're bargaining an enterprise agreement, agreement must be reached with all parties prior to going to a vote. This is not the case! I must admit that at one point in my career I too also had made this assumption.

When HR professionals are in doubt or unsure of technical points in any type of matter and not even just enterprise agreements, they should refer back to the governing legislation. In this case, what does the FWA state regarding good faith bargaining requirements? There is no ambiguity with the FWA in this respect. The good faith bargaining requirements stipulate the following:

- Bargaining meetings should be at reasonable times, where party members attend and participate in discussions.
- Party members share relevant information to support their log of claims, and that this should not include confidential or commercially sensitive information.
- Parties need to respond to proposals made by bargaining representatives in a timely manner.

- All parties should give genuine consideration to the proposals made by the bargaining representatives for the agreement, and provide reasons for the responses provided to these proposals to the bargaining representatives.
- Party members are to behave in a respectable manner and refrain from capricious or unfair conduct that undermines the collective bargaining process.
- Party members should negotiate with bargaining representatives for the agreement.

The above bullet points are a summary of the points captured in the Fair Work Act, and, as you can see, none of them prescribe that the employer needs to concede the bargaining representatives requests.

Mutual agreement does not need to be reached in order for the EA to go to vote. In saying this, an employer can finalise the negotiation stage of the EA and progress through to voting stage without reaching an agreement with the union and/all bargaining representatives.

If agreement is not reached, this could present difficulties for employers when the union have a strong presence or foothold with employees. This is why HR professionals also need to understand the risk profile of the organisation as a part of their preparation.

There are many types of workplace cultural models HR professionals can use to profile their business and understand the degree of influence the union may or do hold in EA negotiations. The purpose of this profiling is to generate awareness to senior management of what to expect during bargaining, and whether the business can reasonably expect a highly aggressive response from the union or a more docile response.

The reason I strongly recommend going through this exercise is that employees have the right to take industrial action when an EA is under negotiation. Industrial action is colloquially known as "going on strike" or the union "going out on the grass" and is when employees can stop work for a period of time.

Going on strike can be a co-ordinated effort led by the union or by employees alone to leverage their bargaining position. If the business were to lose productivity, on a large site this can have significant financial and customer implications, particularly if the strike is ongoing for a period of time. This is another component that should also be costed up and included within your preparation materials.

Once you have mapped your bargaining environment, have a costing model and you understand what the industry at large and your competitors are offering their employees, you can begin formulating a log of claims.

A log of claims is a register of all the clauses and sub-clauses of the existing EA and what changes you as the employer propose to make. When the negotiation has commenced, each party would present their log of claims to each other, discuss and bargain in good faith to finalise the proposed agreement document prior to going to a vote. You may be thinking, well what would this look like?

A log of claims can be developed in a number of ways. My preference is to copy and paste the existing EA into an Excel spreadsheet, with columns identifying the clause number, sub-clause number, name of the clause, the clause itself in full, if there is a proposed change (yes or no), type of change (semantic or technical) and the proposed change.

As you develop the spreadsheet and you progress through negotiations, you can insert comments from the bargaining committee or specific members against each item, so you have an accurate record of feedback. Please note that these comments would not replace the requirement for an accurate record of bargaining committee meeting minutes.

Although this Excel spreadsheet may seem like a very tedious exercise, this really does makes it a lot easier when you eventually need to track changes to the existing EA document to draft the proposed EA document. With enterprise agreements being lengthy and complex documents, you don't want to get lost in what changes have been agreed to or ones you have already made to the drafted document.

Another consideration is that enterprise negotiations can last for longer than six months. A six-month negotiation is considered very speedy in most industries. Over six months is a long period of time to remember all your ideas and suggested changes to each sentence in an enterprise agreement! This is why I highly recommend using the spreadsheet as a working document so that the final stages of the negotiation are easier for you and the business.

In your log of claims spreadsheet, you need to categorise the changes you are intending on making. I classify semantic changes as changing the wording of a clause or order of a clause to make the document read easier, for formatting purposes or a means of consolidating clauses that repeat itself.

A semantic change has no material impact on the way employees are paid and would not detract from the meaning for the existing clause. This is different to a technical change; a technical change is where a clause or a series of sub-clauses are being changed and would have a material impact on the way employees are paid. This may be the wages clause of the EA, which stipulates when any increases are applied to the rates as time passes.

Technical changes to the EA can be quite contentious and more attention is given to them by the bargaining committee parties. So now you might be asking yourself, how do you go about recommending changes?

If you haven't negotiated an EA before, this can seem like a very daunting task, not just from an administrative point of view, but also with the added stress of negotiating with unions and/or employees. This brings me to the next section, where I will take you through the general "clause headings" of enterprise agreements, and what you could be looking for to change, make consistent or remove from enterprise agreements. Please note that every EA is unique, and the next few paragraphs should not be followed exactly as they are general guidance. It is important to remember that enterprise agreements are underpinned by modern awards, which vary significantly!

Dissecting Enterprise Agreements

Let's start this section with a question. What should be put into an enterprise agreement?

I'm going to answer this question with another question, which is featured in this book on multiple occasions. What does the applicable legislation say?

Again, the FWA provides clarity to employers on what an EA should cover and what matters need to be stipulated in the agreement:

- Matters pertaining to the relationship between the employer and the employees covered or within scope of the enterprise agreement.
- Matters pertaining to the relationship between the employer and employee organisations (trade unions) covered.

- Deductions from wages authorised by an employee and what process should be followed by an employer.
- How the agreement will operate and for how long.

If you have never read an EA or are unfamiliar with enterprise agreements, I recommend downloading a few from the Fair Work Commission website from different companies to get a detailed understanding of what the FWA means by these bullet points. Pay particular attention to how these documents are structured and how the enterprise agreements have covered the above points. All enterprise agreements rubber stamped by the FWC have been deemed compliant and would be by default aligned to the above bullet points.

Moving onto the required clauses for an EA to be functional and meet compliance requirements of the FWA. These required clauses are not all stacked at the beginning of an EA but are ordered in a structured way so that the EA makes sense and terms are properly defined first before being referenced.

The first few pages of an approved EA are the FWC's rubber stamp and Commissioner sign-off of the EA. These pages outline whether the enterprise is a single agreement or not; that the Commission is satisfied that the requirements have been met under the FWA; the group of employees were fairly chosen; any bargaining organisation or representatives being covered by the EA; any undertakings that were made; and approval date of the EA and the nominal expiry date of the EA.

The approved EA has also been assigned a reference code, which is a combination of letters and numbers. This reference code needs to be used on the application forms to submit a proposed EA, which would eventually override this existing EA.

The top of each EA page should refer to the name of the enterprise agreement, which is often the name of the company, the state and type of work/employees covered and the year the negotiations commenced for the EA. An example may be Humesware Transport New South Wales Enterprise Agreement 2020, which provides a good indication of what the EA covers and the year the negotiation commenced. I'll be using this fictitious company name as a consistent example as this chapter progresses.

The first Clause is often called "Title", which states that the Agreement shall refer to the Humesware Transport New South Wales Enterprise Agreement 2020 (the "**Agreement**"). This first clause is numbered as 1, and the paragraph is referred to as a sub-clause, and labelled as 1.1. As the agreement moves from one clause to the next, the numbers change in order accordingly.

The heading for Clause 2 can be referred to as "Parties". Sub-clause 2.1 would state that the Agreement is made between the legal entity, which, for this example, is Humesware Pty Ltd, ("**Humesware**" or "**the Company**") and its employees eligible to be covered by this Agreement.

As you construct sub-clauses, it is important to use terms and language consistently. Every time you are to reference a term like "Agreement", a capital A should be used throughout the document consistently. This applies to all terms used such as "Full-time", "Part-time", "Employee", etc.

In this sub-clause, you would also refer to any bargaining representative who was involved in the negotiation and contributed towards the construction of the agreement. The sub-clause would also state the union's intention to be bound by the Agreement. If a union body was not involved in the negotiation, then this sub-clause would only refer to the employing entity and the covered employees. For an enterprise agreement to be approved, you do not need a union body to be involved in the negotiation as a requirement. If there was no involvement of any union, you should not reference a union body you may think is applicable. It is also important to reference the legal entity correctly, as this is important for the submission requirements of the proposed EA post the employee vote.

For Clause 3, I recommend having the "Definitions" of the key terms to be referenced throughout the document to be placed at the very beginning of the EA. Other EA's have opted for the definitions to be included in the EA as Schedule or Appendix at the back of the document, with the Schedule clearly labelled and referred to throughout the document.

Both methods work and are compliant. It is up to each individual business' preference. It is my personal preference to have the definitions section at the front of the Agreement. In saying this, each sub-clause would be a definition of a term, for example 3.1. **"Act'** means the *Fair Work Act 2009 (Cth)."* Attention to detail with sub-clauses is also important. If you have a full-stop at the end of sub-clause 3.1., then also have a full-stop at the end of 3.2. and so on. This may be me being a little picky, but attention to detail is a must when drafting these documents. Other terms you would need to include in this clause are the modern award that the EA is underpinned by, and the abbreviated term that references the modern award, and any other key terms used frequently such as **"FWC"** for Fair Work Commission.

The EA should now talk about what type of employees and locations the enterprise agreement covers. This section of the EA is titled "Scope". The sub-clauses would need to stipulate that the Agreement applies to Humesware Transport employees engaged by the Company at the listed sites and whose employment has been covered in the Classifications in Clause 21. We will cover in detail what the purpose of the Classifications Clause is and how it can be written.

As a HR professional, it is reasonably expected that this Scope clause is written clearly and there is no ambiguity as to which employees are not covered. This is very important, as you don't want employees in the future to make claims that they are or are not covered by the EA once it has come into effect. This could add additional cost to the business if the Company needs to recognise more employees and that would thereby give them greater entitlements to their existing arrangement. This also leads me to another important point that when you are drafting an EA, it is very helpful to have multiple people check and read through the proposed document prior to going to vote. Once an agreement is drafted and goes to vote, it cannot be changed.

If changes are required to the document, the business would need to make those changes and then conduct another vote, which is a frustrating process. To avoid this, have colleagues and your manager read the document to ensure this clause and all other clauses are not ambiguous and they have the same interpretation as you do in writing the document.

So, when does the Agreement come into effect and when does the Agreement expire? These are very important pieces of information and are part of the required information stipulated in the FWA. This is why it is common practice to have a whole clause dedicated to this information, often titled "Term of Agreement".

The Agreement can only come into effect or in operation seven days after it have been approved by the FWC. EA's would have a sub-clause indicating this and the nominal expiry date such as "30 January 2022". This clause may also cover how the agreement may be varied or terminated prior to the nominal expiry date provided that parties agree and the process is followed in accordance with the FWA requirements. The variation and termination of enterprise agreements process will be covered later in this chapter. For now, it is important to understand that both of these are options to an employer, and, if it is to be referenced in an Agreement, the "Term of Agreement" clause is a sensible section to add this.

As I have briefly mentioned previously, the Fair Work Commission assigns every EA a unique reference code. The purpose of this code is so that each proposed EA document includes what EA document it is planning on superseding. It is for this reason that EAs have clauses titled like "Previous Agreements Rescinded and/or Varied".

Using my fictious example, the 6.1. sub-clause could read "This Agreement shall replace and rescind the Humesware Transport New South Wales Enterprise Agreement 2017 (HUM1234/2017)".

I'd like to also bring your attention to the use of the language in constructing these sub-clauses. There is a significant difference between "may" and "shall". When a sub-clause uses "shall", the EA benefit or term is binding, whereas "may" is not binding. Referring to the previous paragraph, employers may vary or terminate an agreement prior to the nominal expiry date; the use of "may" demonstrates that none of the Parties are obligated to carry this out as a term of the agreement. Keep this in mind when you are drafting sub-clauses and if the union or bargaining representatives propose changes to the wording of sub-clauses. A slight change in wording can make a huge difference, particularly when it comes to working through a dispute on the interpretation of an applicable EA.

We are now at our proposed Clause 7 in our fictional EA, and we need to consider what other pieces of information is critical to cover in the beginning of the document. One critical piece is how the EA relates to the modern award/s and how the modern award and EA will relate to one another.

At the beginning of this chapter, I explained how the EA conditions cannot be worse off than the governing modern award, and the modern conditions are commonly mirrored to an extensive degree in a respective EA. This relationship will be captured in our EA, with Clause 7 "Relationship to the Award".

For the purpose of our example, Humesware Transports New South Wales Enterprise Agreement 2020 will call up terms of the Road Transport and Distribution Award 2020 ("**RTD**"). Our clause would need to stipulate that the provisions of the EA were made to the extent allowable under the modern award at the time the Agreement is in operation. This is a fancy way of saying that the conditions of the EA reflect the statement of the RTD at the time the Agreement was drafted, and any changes made to the RTD after the Agreement came into effect are excluded unless otherwise agreed by the Parties. This is to not say that modern award increases applied as time passes does not impact the EA, because it most certainly does.

All employees covered by an EA in operation must be made equal to or above the modern award minimum rates throughout the life of an Agreement. This Clause would also need to include a sub-clause outlining that in the event inconsistencies arise between the Agreement and the provisions of the modern award, in this case the RTD, then the provisions of the EA shall prevail. However, in the event the Agreement is silent on a matter, such as a benefit or how an allowance is applied to a particular statutory entitlement, then the governing award conditions shall prevail. Please take note of the use of "shall" as it is purposely written into these sub-clauses so that this is binding and all Parties understand this.

It is also important to include in this clause that the Agreement is to be read in conjunction with the NES and that nothing in the EA will provide an entitlement less than what is stipulated in the NES. Although this is a given in writing EA documents, it is important to state this in the EA for employees to read and understand, as they generally are not as informed as HR professionals in how the NES, modern awards and EA's interrelate with one another.

Another requirement for a compliant EA is a "Consultation" clause. A lot of companies choose to insert the model term clause from the FWA, word for word into this clause so that all the requirements are legally met, and it covers the key ingredients of genuine consultation with employees. I think this is an effective method, rather than draft your own sub-clauses, particularly if you are writing your first EA.

Some businesses also elect to use the Consultation term of the governing modern award, which is also an acceptable method. If you are looking to draft or make changes to the model term in the FWA or a modern award, you need to ensure that the sub-clauses you draft cover "major change", and specifically if a "major change is likely to have a significant impact on employees".

So, let's start with what is "consultation"?

Every modern award created by the FWC includes a consultation term, which describes the process by which an employer is required to consult or engage in genuine discussions with their employees and representatives (a union body if covered by the EA) when the employer intends on implementing significant changes to the workplace.

The employer is obligated to conduct consultation when the employer has decided to make major changes to production, program, organisation, structure, change to an employee's roster or ordinary hours of work. So, these examples are when an employer needs to consult.

Let's now get into how an employer should go about genuinely consulting with employees. Genuine consultation would require the support of HR professionals to draft and distribute a notice of significant change to the employees and their respective representatives. If a union body is covered by the enterprise agreement, to maintain positive working relationships with the union, I recommend giving the union advanced warning of the upcoming consultation: a day or two at most. It is important to give them a bit more background on the reasons why the business is considering the change, so they are equipped to try and answer their members' questions as best as they can and are not be put on the spot.

Alleviating this pressure on the union is a good measure to try and win the union's buy-in to the change and show as an employer you are trying to genuinely involve them in the consultation process. By having this conversation before the employees are notified, it may raise questions that the business and HR haven't considered prior to deciding on the changes. It may also help the company to anticipate some of the questions managers will face when delivering the notification and having those direct conversations with impacted employees.

If the change involves bulk redundancies, it may be appropriate to present the state of the business and where the redundancies will be coming from to the union. In this presentation, you shouldn't include commercially sensitive information, but why the redundancies are necessary to preserve the business. Perhaps the redundancies are in response to a loss of a major contract or an industry down-turn in volume that needs to result in a reduction in associated labour costs. Whatever the major change may be, I have always found it helpful to have these preliminary discussions with the union whether they are aggressive or a more passive union.

I've gone off track a little… Getting back to the wording of the Clause as a whole, you want to state that the business is not required to disclose confidential or commercially sensitive information to relevant employees impacted by the change or changes. Although employees may find this aspect frustrating, particularly if they are potentially going to be made redundant, the FWC understand that the business' vitality is dependent on keeping this type of information private.

The Clause should also address how the employer does not need to consult with all of its employees on the change, and only the relevant employees being impacted by the change. Your role as a HR professional is to support the change beginning to end and understand that employee agreement is not required for the business to delay or not go ahead with the major changes. However, the consultation process is not a tick and flick exercise and must be followed as per how the EA stipulates. Employees have the full right to dispute the changes as per the "Dispute Resolution Procedure" clause.

The *Fair Work Regulations 2009*, Schedule 6.1 provides a model term on how an employer can deal with disputes under an enterprise agreement. Again, it is up to the preference of the employer and how their existing EAs have been written as to whether they use the model terms available or have a differently worded clause. If you're working on a greenfield agreement (the first EA for an employer to cover a group of employees who have not been hired yet), then you may wish to use the model term to meet compliance requirements and save yourself some time!

The model term starts out by describing that employees raising a dispute should first try and resolve the issue, with their chosen representatives at a workplace level, with relevant management. As a HR representative, you should be involved in working through this dispute and trying to see if a workable solution is available.

If the dispute cannot be resolved at a workplace level after a reasonable attempt has been made by both parties, the dispute may be referred to the Fair Work Commission. Once the dispute has landed with the FWC, the FWC may try to resolve the dispute by way of a conciliation, mediation or making a recommendation. If the dispute is not solved using these more informal methods, then the FWC may formally arbitrate the matter in a hearing and/or decide which is legally bindings to both parties. Your clause needs to cover these degrees of escalation. It is always the preference to try and resolve these matters at a workplace level before they escalate.

Our fictitious EA is now on its tenth page and for learning purposes, let's say that the Humesware Transport New South Wales Enterprise Agreement 2020 was put together with the involvement of a union body, HWA (fictitious union).

Our EA should have a clause outlining when an employee may choose to have representation and the limit to this representation during discussions with the employer. You may choose to have the title of Clause 9 as "Employee Representation". Sub-clause 9.1. could state that "Nothing in this Clause shall imply that an Employee must be represented by a Representative, a Representative of the union or an elected Union delegate".

As a HR representative, you need to also be able to hold discussions with employees without the need for a representative to be present, such as performance appraisals. The employer would also want to limit the number of representatives allowed in these types of discussions, as well as the number of nominated HWA union delegates allowed at any given time on a site. This is a reasonable sub-clause to include, and I recommend having a limit so that discussions with Employees are not overwhelmed with representations.

This is going to be a very long chapter if I try to describe every type of clause in an enterprise agreement. So, going forward I just want to focus on the last type of required clauses, and the clauses I recommend you having in your EA. That way we can return to how to go about starting your negotiation with employees. The last three required clauses of a compliant EA are an individual flexibility arrangement clause, shift worker leave definition and base rates of pay equal to or higher than the modern awards.

As a HR professional, you need to keep abreast of the information released from the Fair Work Commission around compliance requirements for approving EAs, as changes can occur mid-way through your negotiations or even after this book has been published. Always check what the Fair Work Commission published information has to offer, the relevant legislation stipulates and if you're still unsure, seek legal guidance. This book is not written by a qualified lawyer or solicitor and offers only general guidance. So, these three additional clauses may change or remain the same when it comes to writing your own EA.

An individual flexibility arrangement is by way of mutual agreement when an employee and an employer agree to changes in their working arrangement. This may be a change to the employee's respective working hours, days of work, over-time rates, penalty rates, allowances and leave loading. These can only be regarding permitted matters underneath section 172 of the *Fair Work Act 2009* and cannot include any unlawful terms. The arrangement must result in the employee being better off overall if there was no arrangement in place.

The FWA also outlines how an employer should treat and respond to an application made by an employee for flexible working arrangements. The terms of this cannot be less than what is stipulated in the FWA, and the sub-clauses can either refer to the process stipulated in the FWA or outline the terms in sub-clauses. Some EA's have the "Individual Flexibility Arrangement" clause as a schedule at the back of the EA or as a clause towards the end of the EA. Again, whatever is the format or structure that the business would like to take.

Another compliance requirement of enterprise agreements are to stipulate the definition of a shift worker for the purposes of paying annual leave. In recent times, there have been disputes and cases regarding the annual leave accrual and loading applied to shift workers. This is why the Fair Work Commission has made it a requirement to define this is all EA's in order to be rubber stamped.

For your understanding, a shift worker is defined as an employee who is employed on a site in which shifts are continuously rostered 24 hours a day for 7 days a week and the employee are regularly rostered to work those shifts on Sundays and public holidays. An employee often likes to make claims to be a shift worker when they are not, as shift workers are entitled to five weeks of annual leave a year instead of four weeks. As a HR professional, it is important to be able to distinguish between employees who are shift workers or not shift workers. Differentiating between shift worker employees

217

needs to occur for payroll purposes so that they can accrue annual leave correctly and be paid accordingly.

The last requirements, which we have already covered is that employees covered by an EA cannot be paid below the minimum base rate of pay of the governing modern award. The purpose of creating an enterprise agreement or negotiating an existing EA is to create a document that provides more benefits than the modern award.

If you weren't going to pay employees higher than the modern award under an EA, then you would just construct employment contracts, which have the provisions of the modern awards. To ensure your EA is compliant, it is important that the HR professionals conduct a review of the existing employment conditions and construct a log of claims with proposed base rates of pay, which would be above the minimum awards rates across the length of the proposed agreement. If you're unsure how to conduct this review, seek legal advice.

Recommended Clauses

I've covered the required clauses in order for an EA to be rubber stamped by the FWC. More clauses should be added to an EA to outline how employees will be paid; what they will be paid according to what role; what types of employees are covered in the EA; what allowances are applicable and when; how will employees accrue their statutory entitlements; and will the employer offer any additional benefits such as the cashing out of leave? Ordinary hours of work and associated penalty rates shift work, breaks, crib breaks, superannuation, notice to terminate employment, redundancy provisions and employee obligations.

That is a lot of clauses and details to work through, and some of these recommended clauses may not be applicable to your business. As a HR professional, you will also need to work out which order to put these clauses in so that the document flows cohesively and references to clause numbers in a sub-clause are effective. This can take years of experience and to give yourself a head start, you can use this book as a guide for the required clauses and research EAs in your current industry to see how other businesses have constructed their respective EAs.

Better Off Overall Test (BOOT)

Before the FWC approves an enterprise agreement, it must be satisfied that the EA has passed the BOOT. This test demonstrates that all employees covered by the EA are not worse off than if they were only covered by the employment terms of the governing modern award.

An EA would not pass the BOOT if not all the employees covered by the EA are better off, even if the majority of employees are better off. Performing a BOOT requires HR to go through the proposed clauses and understand how they are more beneficial or equal to the terms of the governing modern award, and which ones may be flagged as worse off than the current modern award. Remember that BOOT is not a line-by-line test, but an overall assessment as to whether all employees covered by the EA would be better off overall than if they were merely covered by the conditions of the modern award or modern awards.

There are circumstances where enterprise agreements are covered by more than one award, so as a HR practitioner you would need to ensure that the BOOT accounts for this.

Special attention will be given by the FWC to the monetary components of the proposed EA. Therefore, I recommend creating a table of the key monetary clauses and making a direct comparison to the modern award, like the following:

- Rates of Pay.
- Applicable allowances and loading.
- Full-time, part-time and casual definitions.
- Shift workers definition and associated loadings.
- Leave entitlements.
- Redundancy and notice provisions. Are they strictly NES or above NES provisions?
- Gazetted public holidays and how these are paid.
- Additional benefits such as Picnic Days, additional payments such as a mobile phone allowance, Rostered Days Off (RDOs), etc.

For non-monetary benefits, the FWC would not be able to make a mathematical assessment to an equal better off overall scenario, as circumstances would differ between each employee and their relevant classification under the EA.

Notice of Employee Representational Rights (NERR)

As the title of this chapter is "Negotiating Enterprise Agreements", I should really return to how to go about negotiating an EA now that I have dissected what is included in an EA, and how to start building a log of claims and conduct a BOOT.

With all the research you have conducted, you're now in a good place commercially and administratively to release the NERR to all of your covered employees. A NERR is a document, which needs to be correctly completed in accordance with section 173 of the *Fair Work Act 2009* in order to notify employees of the employer's intention to start bargaining.

The form is updated regularly and should always be downloaded straight from the Fair Work Commission website. Some enterprise agreements, which have been submitted to the FWC for approval, have been rejected due to the wrong NERR being released to employees, an administrative error on the form itself, or not all employees had received the NERR. Getting this first step right is pivotal in starting a negotiation, as well as ensuring no roadblocks occur when you go to have the EA approved by the FWC.

Once you have downloaded the form as a word document, there are some highlighted fields that must be completed. You must correctly enter the name of the employer.

In our case this would be Humesware Pty Ltd as this is consistently referenced in the EA as the employer entity. You will also need to enter the name of the proposed agreement exactly as it is, with no abbreviations.

In our case this is Humesware Transport New South Wales Enterprise Agreement 2020. The last field asks you to provide a description of employees covered by the enterprise agreement. The wording should mirror what you have in your "Scope" clause, so for our example it would say "Transport employees performing work in New South Wales".

Before releasing the NERR, have your manager or your legal counsel if you have one internally in your business to review the document. As once the NERR has been released to all employees, if you need to make changes you will need to re-release the NERR again.

With your NERR document ready, you need to confirm which employees are going to be covered by the EA and how will you go about distributing the EA to them all at the same time. When you go to submit the application forms for the proposed EA to the FWC, the FWC asks you to provide proof and records of you achieving this.

I recommend firstly performing an employee verification exercise, confirming your current employees are using a payroll report. You should send the list of employees to their respective managers and see if anyone has been left off the list in case, they are incorrectly categorised in the payroll system, or if employees have departed the business. You don't want to miss any employee and you also don't want to send the NERR to any employees who have departed your business.

If the payroll report doesn't include an accurate record of their home address and email address, you can ask the managers to confirm these details also with their direct reports. Once you have a final list of employees and their correct contact details, you need to determine whether you will be sending out the NERR via email, or via registered post of a combination of both methods.

In the past, I have used both methods to ensure I have covered everyone as best as I could. Also, if your employees do not regularly use their email address, registered post may be a better option. You will need to conduct this assessment for your business.

Now, you also don't just want to release the NERR to employees without some type of communication plan. If the EA will involve the negotiation involvement of a union body, you can give them advanced warning of your intention to start bargaining. This could be over the phone or via email, and you could also send them a copy of the NERR prior to releasing it to your employees.

On the day you do decide to release the NERR to employees, I recommend organising a briefing session with the respective managers so that they understand the process of bargaining, and how the NERR is the first step in the process. You can ask them to arrange toolbox talks on the release date so that employees are verbally informed of the employer's intention to negotiate and to expect the NERR in their emails and/or mail.

When the NERR is sent to employees in hard copy or electronic form, it cannot be attached or accompanied by another document. So, if you're sending the NERR via express registered post, the NERR cannot be stapled to any other document. In an email, the NERR needs to be sent as the only attachment. This is an administrative requirement of the FWC. Also, if you're emailing the NERR in bulk, you can bcc all the email recipients so that employee's personal email address is not shared among the other employees. When you send the email, you can also request a read receipt as proof of distributing the email. The tracking numbers of the registered or the email receipts need to be stored in a safe place for record-keeping, for the FWC application process.

When you have released the NERR or at the same time of releasing the NERR, you could have also informed your employees that they can nominate employee representatives to be a part of the bargaining committee. This can be done by way of a vote/nomination process.

(Please note that there is no limit to the amount of employee representatives that can be nominated, and employees can self-nominate themselves onto the bargaining committee.)

In more circumstances, you will have one or two employee representatives. In some industries, almost all of the employees self-nominate themselves and the bargaining committee becomes huge. This is unavoidable and is a part of bargaining in good faith.

Bargaining Committee

Once the NERR has been successfully released and you have your nominated employee representatives, as the supporting HR business partner you need to form the bargaining committee. As the HR representative supporting or leading the negotiations, you most certainly need to be a member of the committee, along with a senior manager/s involved in leading the operations covered by the proposed EA. Ideally, you would have had management buy-in for their participation when conducting the operational and payroll workshops three to six months in advance of the NERR being released. If the union is covered by the existing EA, you need to have a union organiser or secretary assigned as a bargaining member. This is often the union organiser you have a standing relationship with and would have provided an advanced notice of the business' intention to negotiate.

With your bargaining committee now formed, you need to arrange the first meeting with all members at a mutually agreeable time and place. The agenda for this discussion is really to establish ways of working or a "team Charter"; how you intend on bargaining; each committee member's role; how often you will organise a bargaining committee meeting; how you intend to present the log of claims and at which meeting; and the business can also present an overview of business performance and plans going forward, which may have a bearing on the proposals made at a later stage.

As my mission is that you can read this book and have a solid idea on how the process would run in a real-life scenario, I'll now take you through in detail how your first meeting could run. How smoothly this will run is dependent upon your preparation, the cultural model and influence of the union on the business, and the state of the relationships between the members of the bargaining committee.

An email has been sent by you with the following subject line: "Humesware Transport New South Wales Enterprise Agreement 2020 – Bargaining Meeting #1". The email has the time and date, location or meetings virtual link included in the email along with the attached agenda.

Leading up to the meeting, I recommend having a catchup with your management members (excluding any employee representatives) and briefing them on their roles and what is agreed to say and not to say. You are to brief them that the first bargaining meeting is an introduction and no offers or proposals are to be made. You should also educate them on the approval process required to be followed prior to making any offers in later stages. A chairperson is to be appointed, usually the operational leader and a record-keeper; the record-keeper needs to keep an accurate record of meeting minutes. These meeting minutes need to be distributed at the end of every meeting and agreed that these are indeed an accurate record by all members of the bargaining committees. You can send the email with the attached meeting minutes at the end of the meeting, and request all members to reply "yes" or "this is an accurate record". You should collect all these and save them where they can easily be found, at a later date. Try and have all these confirmations prior to your next bargaining meeting.

Now that your debriefing is done, and your agenda has been distributed, you attend your first meeting. Introductions are in order – what each member's position is and their assigned roles (if applicable).

You would ideally hand over to the chairperson to provide a business update on how the business is performing overall, and any influencing factors in the industry at large. This may be a recent loss or win of a contract and change to a piece of legislation. The business may be recovering from an industry down-turn or from the global pandemic of COVID-19.

Whatever business overview is provided, the information should not be confidential or commercially sensitive. Just the right amount of information for all members to understand the current state of play – this provides a nice segue into the team charter.

As the HR member of the committee, you are well placed to lead this agenda item, as the "team charter" in a lot of respects mirrors a code of conduct. You would want to position the team charter as a means for all members to bargain in good faith and discuss matters in a respectful manner. When I have presented a team charter, it is a list of statements, which I ask every bargaining member to acknowledge and agree to abide by. These may include the following:

- All members will be punctual to each meeting, and in the event a member cannot attend the meeting they are to provide notice of non-attendance.
- All parties will treat each other with mutual respect. All members will have the opportunity to speak and have the right to speak without being interrupted.
- During the meeting, we ask each member to have their phone on silent so that the discussions are not interrupted.
- All members will understand that an agenda has been set for each bargaining meeting and all members should abide by this agenda. Additional agenda items may be delayed and/ or discussed at the next meeting if the appropriate response is not available or the business needs to confirm details.
- All members will actively participate in good faith bargaining.

Once you have all the members agreement to abide by these statements, you may move onto the next agenda item. This may be discussing how frequently the committee should meet and when, and to agree that at the next meeting the first version of a log of claims can be presented. Depending on the business' relationships with the bargaining committee, you may want to discuss the first version of these log of claims and have a general discussion about them.

All these discussions points need to be accurately recorded in meeting minutes. All parties should provide copies of the log of claims or updated points of discussions prior to the next bargaining meeting. At the conclusion of the meeting, any action items should be summarised and also added to the meeting minutes.

With your first meeting finished, you would distribute the meeting minutes and ask each member to confirm that this is an accurate record of discussions. It is important to get these confirmations prior to the next agreement. Meeting minutes can be relied upon if the union or bargaining representatives make an application to the Fair Work Commission that the employer is not bargaining in good faith. This argument may be based on the fact that there is a current disagreement on a log of claims, or the representatives feel as though their positions are not being genuinely considered. An employer's argument against this is to provide the FWC a copy of all correspondence – how the log of claims has progressed during bargaining as well as the detailed records and recognition of bargaining members that the meeting minutes are a true and accurate record of discussions.

If an employer is found to have breached good faith bargaining provisions of the FWA, then the FWC may deem that a serious breach and this may progress through to an arbitrated determination. This is just one avenue whereby the bargaining can go off track and involve the Fair Work Commission.

The bargaining representatives and/or union may make an application that the scope of the enterprise agreement is incorrect and does not effectively cover all the necessary employees. These scope applications to the FWC can be used as a tactic to win employees more benefits, if being covered under the EA is more beneficial than the current employment conditions they are under. The FWC would see the employer's and the Applicant's perspective and determine if a Scope order is required.

Another application that can be made by either party in the event that negotiations are stalled is for the FWC to assist with the negotiations. Another point of escalation may be an application by the employer to suspend or terminate the EA if the negotiations or vote is not going as planned. An application to terminate an EA is considered a last resort measure to get an EA voted up. However, this may be the business' upfront industrial relations strategy if the business needs to radically remove additional costs from the business. If any of these types of applications are made and you are the supporting HR representative, you would be instrumental in putting together the required information, formulating responses, and ensuring that the employer's needs are met.

Explanatory Documents

Once a business has reached the final stages of bargaining, it is up to HR to lead the drafting of the proposed agreement. My recommendation is to use the log of claims spreadsheet you have been building to make the appropriate changes and tick that this has been done by you. You should have two documents: one being the tracked changes in a word document so that any reader can see what has been changed, removed or added to the proposed EA, and the second document being the "clean" version.

The clean version is essentially the final proposed EA document you would want the bargaining representatives and the union (if applicable) to agree on prior to releasing to your employees to consider and voting on. You would need to email the clean and tracked changed documents through to the bargaining committee members to review and gain their confirmation of support in writing prior to releasing communication to employees.

Throughout the bargaining process, it is important to keep your covered employees informed and updated as to where the negotiations are up to. This is so when you're at the stage when you are ready to release information on the proposed agreement and explanatory document/s, it is not a complete shock to employees, and they understand the reason for the communications.

Having an explanatory document along with printed copies of the proposed agreement and governing modern award/s issued to all covered employees prior to the vote is a requirement to have the EA successfully approved by the FWC. The business will need to provide supporting documentation that this occurred and that the explanatory document was sufficient to explain the major changes to the document. Using our example, the documents you could release to your employees prior to instigating a vote may be the following:

• Hard copy printout for each employee of the Road and Transport Award 2020.
• Hard copy printout of the proposed EA, Humesware Transport New South Wales Enterprise Agreement 2020.

- Explanatory document.
- Communication script (for managers only).
- Frequently Asked Questions (FAQ) fact sheet (for managers only).

The communication script and the FAQ fact sheet content would be driven by what is included in the explanatory document. The explanatory document's purpose is to provide information about the fundamental changes to the terms and effects of the Humesware Transport New South Wales Enterprise Agreement 2020.

The document is a summarised version only and is read in conjunction with the proposed Agreement. It is also important to notify employees that the Explanatory document does not form a part of the Agreement, and that the terms and conditions included in the Explanatory document will be further explained to employees. If you have made major changes to the formatting of the existing Agreement, such as changing the order of major clauses, or removed Schedules from the back of the document and created clauses into the bulk of the Agreement than those details should also be included in this document.

The Explanatory document can include a table with the clause number and title, and what has been changed in the Agreement. I recommend including as much detail as possible on the changes that matter the most to your employees – what changes have occurred to the rates or pay, any applicable allowances and benefits. They need to clearly understand any increase if it is being applied over the course of the Agreement. What is the per cent increase and the new proposed rates?

If there have been a lot of semantic changes, such as wording, these don't necessarily have to be included in this document but referenced that this has occurred. The main purpose of this document is to provide a detailed overview of the technical changes that have occurred in the proposed Agreement, which have a material impact on how employees will be paid in the future.

When employees are issued these documents, I recommend having a sign-off sheet for receipting these documents and noting employees' attendance at the organised information sessions.

At these information sessions with employees, it is important to have HR and management present and prepared to answer as many questions as possible about the proposed EA. As preparation for these sessions, HR should hold a briefing session with managers, so that they are familiarised with the changes and can ask any questions they have upfront prior to facing their employee cohort.

The FAQ fact sheet may be a list of questions originally posed by management and suggested questions who managers believe employees would ask. Having this fact sheet along with a drafted script will make the delivery of these information sessions more consistent and help guide the discussions. If questions are asked during the session that management or HR do not have an immediate answer to, these should be noted and addressed prior to the access period commencing and going to a vote.

A few of these information sessions should be held to ensure every covered employee can attend one. The details of when these information sessions will be held can be distributed to the relevant managers via email, and put on employee noticeboards so that they can also see when they are occurring.

Access Period and Voting

The Access period is defined as a clear seven days where you provide access to the proposed EA and other supporting documents prior to the vote period commencing. Once you have held the preliminary information sessions and addressed employee questions or any type of resistance to the agreement, the business may make the decision that they have reached the stage where a vote is the correct course of action.

To open up the access period, I recommend having a letter signed-off by a senior leader of the business, a CEO or a general manager involved in the negotiations outlining the next steps. This notification letter would note the name of the proposed agreement and the business' intention to go to a vote. The letter will outline when the access period commences.

For our example, the access period for Humesware Transport New South Wales Enterprise Agreement 2020 will commence on Monday 7 December 2020 and conclude on Wednesday 16 December 2020. This provides more than seven clear days for employees to have access to the Explanatory document, the Proposed EA, and a copy of the governing modern award/s. The letter would also indicate the dates and times in which the vote opens, the method of the vote and when the voting period closes. During the Access period, it is important that one or two more information sessions are held during the Access period for employees to consider the issued documents and ask any last-minute questions regarding the proposed Agreement prior to going to a vote.

The notification letter to employees needs to include the method of voting. There are several types of ways a vote can occur, which include a secret ballot, a digital vote (via text message confirmations), postal and online voting, and telephone voting. With the use of technology becoming increasingly more important in everyday life, digital voting methods are becoming more popular as it is almost a guarantee that all covered employees have a mobile phone and are able to receive and reply to a text message.

Whatever method your business decides to use or as a HR representative you choose to recommend, the business needs to satisfy requirements under the FWA. These requirements are to take all reasonable steps to notify the relevant employees of the following by the start of the access period for the agreement: the time and place at which the vote will occur, and the voting method that will be used.

There is a high threshold test, which must be satisfied during the access period in order to demonstrate that the business has taken all reasonable steps to ensure that the terms of the proposed agreement, and the effects of those terms have been properly explained to the covered employees. The FWA indicates that the explanation provided must be in an appropriate manner, taking into account the particular circumstances and needs of the relevant employees. This is why the drafting of the Explanatory document is so crucial.

The Explanatory document and the information session must cater to employees with culturally and linguistically diverse backgrounds, young employees who may not properly understand what is captured in the documents, and employees who do not have a bargaining representative for the agreement. As the HR representative, you need to ensure that you satisfy this test, and this can be supported with evidence in your future application to the FWC to have the EA rubber stamped.

Let's assume that all covered employees under Humesware Transport New South Wales Enterprise Agreement 2020 have received the notification letter, the access period has finished, and the vote has commenced. What does voting look like?

With there being a list of various voting methods, I'll only go into detail on one of them, being the digital voting method.

As the votes need to be counted fairly and with no opportunity for the bargaining representatives and/or union to claim that the votes were not accurately counted, I recommend using an external company specialising in business EA voting to conduct the vote. This can be done by providing the external company a list of all covered employees, and their mobile numbers. The Company will need to also understand the details of the vote included in the notification letter and the name of the proposed enterprise agreement. When the voting period commences, they will send out a text message to all covered employees, asking them to confirm their vote as a "yes" or a "no". This would require the employee to text back their vote. Any employee who does not respond to the text message is considered to have not placed a vote. Once the voting period has closed, the external company would then count the votes and release the results along with the report to the employer. This result would then be released to the organisation at large, the covered employees and the bargaining committee members.

For a vote to be successful, it cannot be conducted less than 21 days after employees were issued the NERR. The majority of employees who cast a valid vote must support the enterprise agreement. If 100 per cent of all covered employees casted a valid vote, the business must receive 51 per cent of employees having voted yes to the proposed agreement. If only six out of the total 10 employees covered by the agreement voted, and five of those employees voted yes then the agreement has been made. However, if five out of the 10 employees vote yes, then the agreement has not been made. So, this is how an enterprise agreement would be voted up if no industrial action was taken. If the union or bargaining representatives would like to take industrial action in response to the enterprise agreement, a protected action ballot must first be conducted before lawful industrial action can be taken.

Protected Industrial Ballots are normally conducted by the Australian Electoral Commission (AEC). When a bargaining order makes a claim for industrial action, the FWC can make a protected action ballot order. Once the order has been made, all covered employees are requested to vote as to whether industrial action is to occur. Industrial action only becomes authorised once if at least 50 per cent of those on the voting poll voted, and more than 50 per cent of the votes that were cast were in favour of taking industrial action. Both parties can elect to have a scrutineer present during the voting process at the AEC office to watch the votes be counted. The FWC are then required to publish the results of the ballot as soon as reasonably practical.

Lodgement of Agreement to FWC

Humesware Transport New South Wales Enterprise Agreement 2020 has been voted up by the covered employees by a landslide... Excellent! Next comes the rush for HR professionals to finalise the paperwork for the FWC within 14 days of the vote being finalised.

The two forms, which need to be completed by the employer, are the F16 and F17 forms; they are downloaded directly from the FWC website. These forms need to be signed and completed by the representatives of the employer who have the authority to sign the completed EA and the forms.

A copy of the signed EA with employer representatives and employee representatives and union (if applicable) also needs to be submitted with the forms. The EA needs to have at least one employee signature. The bargaining representatives should be copied into the email when the forms are lodged to the Fair Work Commission. When this is lodged, you will also need to provide any other supporting documentation. Supporting documentation would include the copy of the notification letter, NERR distributed, the explanatory document, as well as any relevant bargaining correspondence.

Before an EA is approved by the FWC, the FWC would conduct their own BOOT to ensure that the agreement is more beneficial overall than the underpinning modern award. This BOOT can result in lengthy delays in the FWC approving enterprise agreements.

If the EA requires an undertaking to be completed, this would further delay the approval process. An undertaking is when the FWC has identified a minor error or issue with the enterprise agreement. If this occurs, the FWC would request the employer to make an undertaking to clarify the issue in the enterprise agreement. Once the FWC is satisfied that the undertaking has satisfactorily addressed the error, contains the necessary clauses in the FWA and passes the BOOT, the FWC will approve the enterprise agreement. Once approved, the Fair Work Commission will send correspondence to the employer designated contacts with the approved version of the enterprise agreement. This is now the final version of the EA cannot be changed in any way. This is the copy, which needs to now be issued to all covered employees and must be made accessible to all employees.

7

ORGANISATIONAL DEVELOPMENT

IN MY EXPERIENCE, A lot of entry level HR professionals or those with only a few years of experience will not gain exposure to organisational development (OD) programs and how they are designed and rolled out until later in their career. Without this exposure, you would not know what OD is and how it is a specialist area within the HR realm.

OD specialists often start out in either a HR generalist role or a learning co-ordinator position, whereby they start to focus on how a business can maximise employee productivity and efficiency. This is what OD is all about – how a business can support an employee's personal development, through training initiatives and leadership programs, and by doing so having a two-fold effect of increasing employee engagement and uplifting productivity. OD functions with specialist resources can be found in large organisations, but when these functions are not yet formed in a business these duties and skills fall into the HR remit.

Learning and Development

The most common component of OD in a business is learning and development. All businesses regardless of size need to have learning and development (L&D) to teach new and existing staff members across various roles and levels. This can be as simple as a site safety induction, an on-boarding learning module for new employees to understand the business' history or more complex training such as Anti-Bribery and Corruption Policy.

Types of learning and development programs can be administrated in a range of different ways and formats, whether this is face-to-face training, online delivery, or a combination of both. When a business does not have the allocated resources or expertise to deliver a particular training program or specialist course, they can engage an external provider.

If you are seeking out a quality external course provider on behalf of a business, you can start by looking for registered training organisations (RTO). For an organisation to gain this degree of certification, they would have needed to satisfy a large array of compliance criteria and would have been required to deliver detailed and structured programs designed by qualified trainers. Despite this, as a HR professional it is an expectation and component of your role to be able to develop training programs (sometimes from scratch) and in some cases deliver the training yourself.

Training programs, which a HR practitioner may be asked to design and roll-out, can vary from stereotypical HR-related topics such as the Code of Conduct training and can be a specific program developed to address a gap in the business. An example of this would be the requirement to develop a two-full day training program to upskill frontline team leaders.

The need for the training is that the team leaders are promoted to this position for their technical aptitude, and not necessarily their capability in managing a team. With this gap in knowledge and skills, team leaders are struggling to appropriately manage their team members when issues arise pertaining to performance, absenteeism, misconduct or bullying and harassment. They are solely reliant on escalating these difficult conversations to their manager one-up and this is overwhelming middle management. It is also the expectation that the team leaders are able to address these problems and challenges when they arise, but if they have been appointed to these roles without training, then the business has not positioned them for success.

Now what exactly would a two-day training program look like, when it is to specifically address this frontline management and give them enough knowledge to start addressing these types of issues in their teams?

If you were to start designing the program, the first stage would be thinking about what learning outcomes you're trying to achieve and list them. You then need to break them into categories such as understanding expectations, communicating effectively, performance management, understanding company policies and procedures, and developing a personal action plan.

Looking at these categories a title of the program could be "Basic People Leader Skills". Under each key learning outcome, you would then start listing the relevant topics and content to educate the target audience, which examples and learning exercises are going to be included and if there will be any supporting material to be distributed during the workshop.

Starting with the first topic "Expectations of People Leaders", relevant points may be the following: what makes a good leader, leading our (company) values, leading your team and leading with integrity.

For the second topic "Effective communication", you may deem it important that team leaders understand what active listening is; how to give feedback whether it is positive or constructive; and how to deliver this ensure the right message has gotten through to the employee.

Understanding what content is relevant and will have the greatest impact on the target audience is a critical part of designing a program that effectively delivers its intended learning outcomes.

As you start to integrate more material and content into the training, you must consider how you are going to keep your target audience engaged. You can achieve this by providing training exercises, which are relevant to them in the business, industry and profession they are performing.

An exercise may provide a detailed scenario they can relate to and challenge them to think about the correct way to manage the situation. Let us say for instance that the team leaders are responsible for overseeing the correct use of forklifts in the warehouse and they notice that one employee has failed to complete the pre-start checklist on multiple occasions. How should a team leader address this non-compliance with the employee? As not completing a pre-start checklist is a safety breach and if the forklift was in fact faulty, not completing the checklist would jeopardise the team member's own safety in the workplace.

A group discussion or dividing the work group into smaller discussion groups to brainstorm this example is one way this could be workshopped. Another method could be to have a mock meeting, whereby a volunteer from the group is asked to re-enact how they would have conducted the discussion or disciplinary meeting with the employee not completing the checklists.

During the mock-situation, the remaining work group would be able to critique the feedback provided and the trainer facilitate the discussion. You may decide that these types of exercises are the most practical and incorporate one in each topic covered over the course of the two full days. Whatever you choose, the exercises need to be engaging, relevant to the team leaders and allow them to understand what the expectations of the business are moving forward using these types of scenarios.

To keep your audience focused and engaged during the face-to-face workshop, a PowerPoint presentation may be the most appropriate. The PowerPoint presentation would keep the facilitator on track with the time schedule, and break up the day with snacks, breaks and lunch time. The PowerPoint presentation should not be overwhelmed with sentences but must capture the key points and learnings under each topic as the workshop progresses.

One slide for the "Effective communication topic" could list the key learnings to deliver constructive feedback fairly and effectively. These can be bullet points such as the below:

- Don't withhold constructive criticism.
- Notify the employee about the underperformance concerns (if applicable).
- Provide constructive feedback in a timely manner to the event/ incident of concern.
- Pay attention to the language you use to deliver the constructive feedback.
- Be factual and limit your comments to performance rather than the personality of the individual.

- Get to the main point of concern, and do not delay the important parts of the conversation.
- Describe the consequences of the matter of concern and if it is to continue occurring.
- Encourage the employee to provide their version of events and explain the reasons for their actions or under-performance.
- Decide what specific actions must be taken.
- Summarise the discussion that has occurred at the end of the conversation.

If the above points are all captured on one slide in the presentation, the level of detail is not overwhelming, and the facilitator can talk to every point. If HR is going to develop a program about effective communication, then the training needs to be effectively communicated.

Towards the pointy end of the program, you may decide that it would be beneficial for each team leader to have homework after the workshop in the form of a personal action plan. The personal action plan would be a distributed template given to each participant to complete about what they personally need to improve according to the courses' topics.

Two weeks from the date of the course, they would need to sit down one-one-one with their manager and go through the action plan about how they are going to cement their learning outcomes in the business. The personal action template would also encourage them to think about other areas of personal development they may have in their current roles.

Using this feedback along with a course survey, HR and the business would be able to improve upon the course delivered and understand whether participants found the content useful and applicable in the business. Fine-tuning learning and development modules and programs are all a part of ensuring they are providing the required value they were intended to for the participants.

If the team leaders provided overall positive feedback about the course, you may determine that a larger audience would also benefit from the learning outcomes. With employees geographically dispersed throughout Australia in the business, delivering the training face-to-face would not be economical or achievable on a large-scale. This is when HR should consider whether the training program could be converted into an online training module, delivered through a Learning Management System (LMS). A LMS software (portal) integrated into a company's intranet page or in its standalone form whereby employees are assigned learning profiles, provided log in details linked to their company email address and are required to login and complete all assigned training modules.

The easiest method to convert the existing face-to-face training team leader course would be to use the existing PowerPoint presentation and voice over a script. The script would include the explanation the facilitator would have provided in person. As the examples cannot be workshopped online with multiple participants, the exercises would need to be adapted for the online delivery. An added benefit of using LMS modules is that at the end of the course participants can be requested to complete a quiz to demonstrate that they have actively listened to the module and understood the content. A set pass mark can be made, and the quiz could be true or false questions, multiple choice or a combination of these types of questions. As many or as little questions can be asked and once, they have passed the quiz, their completion would be recorded against their learner profile.

If all enrolled participants need to complete the course by a particular date, HR can run a report to see the completion rates of the course and who they need to follow-up. If the business would also like to recognise participants for finishing the course, the business can integrate an electronic certificate, which can be downloaded by the user and kept for their records. There is a lot of functionality an LMS has to offer a business!

A well-integrated LMS program offers a lot of benefits to the HR function and the overall business to meet its strategic objectives and compliance requirements. If a business is listed on the Australian Stock Exchange and has a board of directors, there will be corporate governance obligations that can only be satisfied through a stream-lined training platform. A part of this requirement is the delivery of modules like Anti-Bribery and Corruption (ABC), Code of Conduct and Ethics Policy, Gift Policy, and a Whistle Blower Policy, to ensure employees are aware of the expectations and how they can escalate concerns in the business through the appropriate channels.

The LMS portal makes the delivery of the training and reporting on the completed training extremely easy and accessible to HR. LMS portals have dashboards, which can be extracted and used as a scorecard you can present to the board of directors.

The Board is accountable for ensuring they are meeting their obligations under the *Corporations Act 2001*, so having this information on hand is useful so they can monitor progress and make decisions if the legislation changes or new compliance requirements are imposed. Employees would also have the ability to update their learner profiles to include their own experiences, other certifications and qualifications they have that are not associated with the business, tag their skills and list their career aspirations and goals. If a business is looking internally for a particular skill set, such as speaking and writing fluently in Mandarin, the business can locate this and request for that specific individual to become involved in translating a confidential document from English to Mandarin. By having this performed internally, the business saves money and safeguards against the risk of the document being leaked outside of the organisation. Having employees update their learner profiles is also useful when a business is looking to implement succession mapping and Hi-Po Programs.

Succession mapping is a part of ensuring that a pipeline of talent and potential leaders is ready to be promoted when a vacancy becomes available or an opportunity is created in the business. HR need to map out who are the identified high potentials (Hi-Po), what are their gaps in knowledge, skills and experience hindering their succession and if they are a flight-risk for the business. The individuals marked as Hi-Po may not be notified or know that they have been marked as such until the succession mapping has been finalised, and a personal development program has been developed to support their career.

When I have been required to create a succession-mapping program, my preference is to keep the program simple, easy to understand by managers and shows the levels of a business, who the Hi-Po is and what is required for them to be promoted with the right capabilities for the next level up.

An excel spreadsheet with inserted organisational chart style can be used to map out each team, who is in the team, what are their skills, and if they are identified as the next potential leader in that area.

Once HR have made the initial draft, the organisational chart details need to be confirmed by collaborating with the current leader of that area. If a Hi-Po individual has been identified as a flight-risk, which is someone looking to leave the business as they are not satisfied with their current role or don't have an opportunity for promotion internally, the business needs to create an action plan to address this. If a Hi-Po leaves the business, this creates a gap in the succession chain and would take a long period of time to replace that degree of talent than if they had been given an opportunity or invested in by the business.

To prevent a Hi-Po from leaving, HR may suggest investing time in mentoring the individual, enrolling them in a course of their choosing or a course such as a master's in business administration (MBA) – a course preference that supports individual's progression into a senior management position. If someone is a flight-risk, it may flag to the business that more action is required to keep top talent engaged and could provide the necessary justification for HR to develop and roll-out a leadership development program.

As a HR professional, the number of projects and opportunities to develop programs in the OD space is phenomenal. If you're entrusted with designing a leadership development program from the very beginning to the implementation phase, this is a difficult feat if you're not an OD specialist. Unless you have experience in this area, you may want to consider outsourcing this program to expert facilitators and be the internal resource to endorse and co-ordinate participation in the program instead.

The first step before a leadership program is kicked-off is to identify who will be the participants and how they should be selected. Will a group of senior managers discuss the succession map and choose the most highly rated Hi-Pos, while also considering those that are a flight-risk? Or will employees be able to make program applications and explain why they would like to be considered in the future for management positions, and thereby be invested in by the business through this program?

Understanding what the most appropriate method is will help understand how many participants the program will have and what the key deliverables of the program need to be. There are many ways to design leadership program and I am far from being an expert on the subject. In acknowledging that, all I can really do is provide you an overview as to what programs I have been involved in.

A comprehensive leadership program would have regular meetings whereby participants are assigned work groups, and in these groups, they must collaborate equally to complete a major project that benefits the business. The aim of this is to demonstrate the importance of working together, gathering stakeholder buy-in and the necessary funds from the business to implement the changes, and demonstrate the impact of the project on the business' performance.

How they deliver this project must be according to the teaching of the program. These teachings may be in relation to an assigned text or book, which is mandatory for the participants to read and reflect on at each meeting. Other meetings may be brainstorming sessions on how to solve an industry or business specific problem, and proposing reasonable solutions to these. The main focus of the exercises in the program must be on developing their leadership capabilities, and not necessarily their technical skills to deliver solutions. Therefore, leadership programs may involve the assignment of mentors in the business.

Coaching and mentoring is an effective method for developing a person's leaderships skills, through the transfer of critical thinking abilities and imparting years of knowledge from the mentor to the mentee. If a leadership program is to include a mentoring aspect, then the business would require willing and committed mentors from the business to be assigned with one or two of the participants in the program. The benefit of this pairing is that the participant will be able to learn directly and have this personal contact when they need advice or would like some guidance on the program material or any other matter in the business. Having a mentor inside the business means that the advice would be incredibly relevant and practical to the participant and would not be out of touch with the specific circumstances of the business.

There are also benefits for the mentor. The mentor who has volunteered or been requested by the business to participate in the leadership program has been recognised as someone with a lot of knowledge, and as a good leader to then have people shadowing them. It is complimentary recognition and can also provide a degree of intrinsic value to the mentor as they are giving back to the business and helping another develop their career with the business. The mentor would also act as a sounding board to review assessments and presentations before they are submitted or made in front of the working group.

A leadership development program would require participants to complete assessments and make presentations to the workgroup throughout the duration of the program. Considering most programs last for a twelve-month period, there is ample opportunity for each participant to practise these presentation skills and ensure they are meeting the criteria on their assessments.

An example of a presentation would be explaining to the workgroup on how they have applied their learnings from the program to making an impact to the business, their own department or team members. The presentation may specifically address a group project, which has been finalised or share an update on the progress.

The challenges faced by resistance from team members or any revisions that needed making to the project scope, design and delivery. The participants may also have to demonstrate how they have personally become a more effective leader through their own accountability, style of communication, ability to deliver change management, influence and negotiate with decision-makers in the business, and also be able to coach and mentor others. This is not an exhaustive list of what may be covered and are just examples of what may be included in a leadership program.

Workplace Culture

Organisational development embodies how HR can improve the vitality of the business through various initiatives. One way of achieving this is by first understanding the current workplace culture, where the business' culture should be in terms of values and employee satisfaction, and understanding what actions need to be taken to transform the workplace culture.

Large organisations would have an established company vision and mission statement, and the governing ethos or value set that all employees are expected to abide by and demonstrate prior to joining the business.

This company ethos would be the foundation of what the business' workplace culture is aiming to become. Using this as a starting point, HR can then take action to understand what the gap is (if any) between what the business ultimately desires in terms of workplace culture and what the state of the workplace culture currently is. One effective tool used by HR professionals is an engagement survey.

An engagement survey is a tool used by HR to quantify how valued employees feel in a business. The measure used to determine this is the employee's engagement levels on different measures included in the survey. The survey can vary in length and how it is delivered to a business. How long and comprehensive the survey will be is dependent upon what outcomes a business is looking to achieve from the survey, and use the information gathered to create meaningful actions in the business.

Depending on the workforce, the survey may need to be distributed online via a link and/or available in hard copy form for employees who do not have access to a computer. If the business is aiming to get the highest response rate possible, the access needs to be fairly accessed and distributed to all employees within the business.

Another means to increase participation rates is for the responses to remain anonymous; the business would not be able to identify each participant and trace back any comments of feedback made by individuals. This is a good way to negate any hesitations employees may have about providing honest and perhaps negative feedback about the business. The business would also need to set a deadline as to when participants need to complete the voluntary survey and provide regular reminders leading up to the date. With the distribution sorted, let us get into the questions asked of the employees.

An employee engagement survey should not just include any type of question HR deem to be relevant or a "feel good" question. Every question must be trying to elicit specific feedback from the employee, which can be quantified ultimately into an overall engagement score. The questions should align to a category of engagement. For example, an employee's views on how the business approaches safety or whether they feel fairly remunerated for their position. For the answers to be quantifiable, each response provided must produce a score.

At the start of the survey, you want to gather some demographical information about the participants. This is not with the purpose to identify them, but so you're able to understand trends and patterns in the business when it is time to analyse the results. When it comes to determining categories, you could start with the list below.

- Leadership: Is there adequate transparency of the strategic objectives of the business and do you understand the "bigger picture"? Are you getting the required direction from your direct manager and is your direct manager supporting you to succeed?
- Job Satisfaction: Do you have a clear understanding of your role, responsibilities, and your accountability? Do you understand how your role fits into the "bigger picture"? Do you enjoy your role and the type of work you perform? Do you feel empowered to make decisions in your role?
- Communication: Is there transparency from the top down on business performance and strategy? Is important information regularly disseminated from your direct manager? Do you feel you have enough information to perform your role effectively? Does information flow quickly throughout the business, or can the communication become lost?
- Career development: Is adequate training provided for you to perform your role effectively? Do you feel you will have the opportunity to continue your career with the business in the long-term? Have you had the opportunity to participate

in training programs to develop your won skills, knowledge and capabilities?

- Recognition and Reward: Do you feel fairly compensated for the work you perform? Are wins regularly celebrated in the business? Do you regularly receive recognition for the work you contribute from your direct manager?
- Work-life Balance: Do you feel you have flexibility in your role and how it is performed? Do you have flexibility in your working hours and place of work? Do you feel the business is supportive of alternative working arrangements in general? Are you able to maintain a healthy work-life balance?

The above are suggested starting points. When constructing a survey, my preference has always been to use the five-point Likert scale, where a question or statement is posed and the respondents need to answer with "Strongly Disagree" to "Strongly Agree".

For these questions or statements to be effective, they need to be simple; don't have a long sentence. If the question is quite complex, break the question into multiple sections or separate questions so you can get the proper feedback you are after.

What you are aiming for is to be able to provide a statistical analysis on the number of respondents, the type of respondents who participated (age, sex, department, if they are management) and the overall engagement score in each category and across all categories. You would also want to provide employees the opportunity to provide open-ended feedback and commentary for each category and/or at the end of the survey.

In my experience, the comments provided can be quite revealing and may even lead to a formal investigation as it allows employees to raise a confidential complaint without having to approach HR directly. From the statistical analysis, HR would need to produce recommendations that would address the lowest score areas and present this to the business. One such recommendation may be the introduction of a wellness program; a wellness program falls into the OD remit and is conducive to a healthy workplace culture.

When a business is considering introducing a wellness program HR will be tempted to introduce all the exciting bells and whistles like social and networking events, along with getting involved in community support initiatives. These are all a part of supporting employee wellness, but to give the program direction the strategic objectives need to be set first like any other program before launching into the implementation phase.

The core objectives of a wellness program can be to achieve higher productivity and loyalty from employees, decreasing absenteeism, reducing injuries and workers compensation, supporting workplace diversity and a work-life balance.

As a HR professional, you will need to interpret the needs of the business and add or amend these objectives as you see fit. As you can see from these objectives, a wellness program has quite a broad scope and a lot of opportunities for HR to implement change in the business. Workplace diversity, which feeds into the business' recruitment campaign and employee value proposition, is a good starting point for any HR practitioner.

When promoting workplace diversity in a wellness program, there are some commitments the business needs to make upfront first. These include ensuring that recruitment and selection continues to be based on the merit of each applicant, sustaining awareness of the importance of diversity in gender and the demographics of the types of people employed and who continue to work for the business. Commitment to workplace diversity can manifest in several ways. These include the following:

- Demonstrate workplace diversity in leadership: This involves having a diverse management group, varied in gender, ethnicity, age, and any other type of characteristic. It would reflect poorly on the business to say that they are committed to workplace diversity and leaders in the business are not representative of this.
- Support flexible working arrangements: Allowing employees to work flexibly whether it is at home on some days of the week, alternatives hours or days of the week provides employees a work-life balance. It also supports employees with outside work commitments such as children or caring responsibilities to be able to manage their obligations with work, which may have not been possible without the flexibility provided.
- Workplace diversity and culture: For workplace culture to be inclusive and tolerant, management need to uphold these values in how they lead their teams. They need to be self-aware and recognise cultural clashes or tensions when they arise in their teams. They also need to be able to address communication breakdowns and behaviours, which are not engendering of tolerance and acceptance. Management needs to embody treating everyone with respect and dignity, and set the zero tolerance for any type of bullying, harassment and discrimination in the business. Company policies and procedures need to provide management guidance on how to handle these matters if they arise in the workplace, and what the expectations are for all employees to support workplace diversity.

With workplace diversity now addressed as a means of safe-guarding employee wellness and inclusion, the program also needs to consider how to improve the quality of connections in the business. This is all about fostering an internal community where people come together for a common cause, activity or networking event. This is where I find a lot of HR professionals have a little bit of fun, as they can essentially gain control of a business' social event calendar.

HR also can engage with surrounding communities by building partnerships with other businesses, non-for profits and supporting specific causes. One way to bring employees together is to get them involved and rally towards a common cause, which is endorsed by the business. This may be a non-for-profit (NFP) organisation that has existing ties with the business, or the work performed by the NFP is aligned to the business.

By building a partnership with a NFP, employees would be encouraged to support their campaigns and initiatives in the community. The business would thereby internally promote these events and campaigns in the business and support employees taking time out during working hours to attend events, join in any activities and support the initiatives in their own way, such as separate fund-raising campaigns.

By having a common cause to rally behind, employees that may not have ordinarily met or socialised are brought together and networking opportunities are born. These types of events and community engagements nurture employee engagement and allow employees to give back to their community, especially when they may have not found the time to do so out of working times. This provides intrinsic joy to employees and supports their overall wellbeing.

Another wellbeing initiative could be internally organised without the involvement of an external organisation or partner.

Every month or cyclical period, HR may organise a company-wide wellness initiative distributed on a "social calendar". One example may be that in the month of March, there is "walk to win" campaign, where employees can sign-up and record their number of steps per day. The team with the highest number of steps at the finish line earn recognition and may even be awarded a nominal prize, like the business will pay for them to all treat themselves to a nice dinner or a team-building exercise. These fun challenges and social events inspire teamwork and can create banter and a healthy level of competition between teams and departments.

The activity encourages employees to maintain a level of exercise and to introduce activity into their day to maximise their number of steps. Fit-bits may also be supplied by the business so that each team has a fair and consistent means of measuring their output. Wellness champions may also be elected across the business to tally each team's results and announce the winners. There are so many ways to make this fun for a lot of employees. If the business wants to go one step further to taking employee wellness seriously, they can create sponsorship relationships, which benefit employees.

A business may decide to become a sponsor and establish an agreement with gym providers, nutritionists or other businesses that promote employee wellness. By having these established relationships, employees would be eligible for staff discounts or preferential treatment with these service providers. Another agreement can be with an Employee Assistance program (EAP), which is a service provider that provides confidential counselling and coaching services.

The EAP provider would allow any employee and their immediate family members to access the counselling services for free and the records of discussions would not be accessible by the organisation. EAP service providers may also offer financial assistance and guidance, and have the ability to make referrals to other medical practitioners.

Having an established agreement with an EAP provider can be very helpful, as you can direct employees to this when they are experiencing difficulties in their working life and/or personal life.

EAP providers may also be requested to attend locations when major changes such as bulk redundancies are being rolled out and employees need that extra level of support. EAP providers may also attend site when the business has experienced an unfortunate death and employees need someone to speak to. EAP services are great for organisations to offer and again speaks to how the business cares for their employees' overall wellness.

In this chapter, I have covered how there are a multitude of ways HR professionals and a business can develop and implement OD programs. There is such a broad scope of initiatives that HR can consider, and it may be daunting for HR to be able to prioritise which program provides the greatest impact. You will need to be able to make this assessment based on the compliance requirements and strategi objectives of the business. If the business has started focusing on building its Employee Value Proposition by way of streamlining recruitment and talent acquisition, then perhaps a focus on workplace diversity and inclusion is the first on the list. If a business instead is investing in developing the exiting culture and making employees more collaborative, then a partnership with a NFP may be the way to go to encourage those social interactions. Whatever the company's agenda may be, as a HR professional you are now able to see what your options are and how you can start thinking about supporting your own and your client group's wellness.

8

REWARD AND RECOGNITION

THIS CHAPTER WILL TAKE a deep dive into how HR professionals develop frameworks and implement programs to generate a consistent approach towards reward and recognition in a business.

Reward focuses on how employees are compensated for their contribution and efforts towards the business such as payment of wages, salary, additional bonuses, allowances and perks. Recognition refers to various types of opportunities to identify high levels of performance or a specific achievement in the business, which could be finishing a difficult project, exceeding safety results, or contributing an innovative idea.

To attract talent into the business and the ensure fairness for existing employees, HR need to lead the development of a compensation framework. The compensation framework needs to take into account what the market offering is for particular roles; what current employees are currently paid and at what range (the top, middle or low end of the compensation spectrum); and what the business needs to achieve through the employment of new or replacement positions. These types of considerations are also imperative when conducting merit reviews and pay parity exercises for existing employees. Without a uniform approach to employees' reward and recognition, employees can become disengaged, feel underappreciated or unfairly treated if employees performing identical roles have vast differences in pay or may even threaten to leave the business to gain more compensation. Therefore, having a framework in place is critical in large organisations and HR play a significant role in establishing what this looks like.

In the Recruitment chapter, an explanation was provided on how a job description should be graded according to the role's skills, responsibilities, level of experience and the overall seniority of the role within the context of the business. The grading number or category can have an assigned compensation range, with a recommended offer composition, and any associated bonuses (short-term or long-term) or benefits that a new or existing employee would be eligible for in this role. These types of recommendations need to be put forward by HR.

Assuming you are new to HR, you are probably thinking well how do you come up with these recommendations? HR need to be well versed in what the current market is offering and how offerings differ between each state in Australia, as well as rural areas for white- and blue-collar roles. So that HR are not having to become well versed for every type of role, there are industry-based guides and guidebooks released by large recruitment agencies, which are available at a cost to businesses. HR need to keep in mind that these are guidelines only, and wide variances can exist depending upon the type of role and the candidate the business is looking to attract.

For learning purposes, let us say that Humesware Pty Ltd are looking for first year Automotive Apprentice to work on the fleet vehicles, provide vehicle services and overall maintenance functions. HR could rely on an industry guide or a combination of this and understanding what a reasonable offer would be.

The first step would be looking at the applicable Modern Award, which is the *Vehicle Repair, Services and Retail Award 2020*. In this Award it provides what the minimum rates of pay and applicable allowances are for a junior employee (if they have finished year ten or year 12 education) and an adult employee over the age of 21 years. These rates of pay are the absolute minimum the business may want to pay employees and may set the benchmark in the compensation framework. However, if the business was looking to offer above the modern award provisions, a base salary offering range would need cementing. This may be a range of $38,000 to $42,000 base salary. When an employee is placed in the range, it may be based on their level of experience and whether they have completed their year 12 high school certificate. Having this range is also important for existing employees in the event a merit review or pay parity exercise is undertaken.

Continuing with this example, Humesware Pty Ltd has 50 apprentices with a mix of junior and adult apprentices in their first year and all the way up to their fourth year of the apprenticeship. They have been issued base salaries based on what the hiring manager felt was right at the time, as there was no consistent salary framework in place. As a HR representative, you have generated a report to see how they are all paid, what arrangements they are on and which type of employee they are: junior with year ten or year 12 certifications and if they are an adult apprentice. You then insert the correct salary range for each job level in the apprenticeship and calculate each individual's compensation ratio. What is the percentage of their base in comparison to the maximum bandwidth?

If an apprentice is on $35,000 base salary as a first-year apprentice and the maximum salary on offer is up to $40,000 base salary, the compensation ratio is 0.875. Employees on a compensation ratio of one or higher should not be eligible for a merit review or a pay parity increase as they have already met or exceeded the maximum remuneration offering for the position. The framework may also include bandwidths on any type of commission or bonus scheme, as well as applicable allowances to be offered per annum. When employees are compared against each other and the bandwidths, HR can also identify those employees who are paid a lot lower or higher than their peers. Those on a lower salary could be subject to a pay parity increase to bring them into alignment with the rest of the working group. Organisations perform these exercises on a large scale when various scenarios occur.

An orchestrated pay parity exercise would be important to conduct when the business has a group of employees who have been loyal and with the business for some time. As market conditions change over time, new candidates brought into a business may be offered more than what the existing employees are currently on due to CPI and other influences. This can create a scenario whereby long-term employees (who are performing satisfactorily) may be paid a lot less than new starters, creating a gap in remuneration. To ensure fairness and equity in pay, a pay parity exercise may help address these gaps and ensure that long-term employees are paid according to the job they perform.

Employees sometimes also disclose their pay arrangements to one another in organisations where the classification and pay-scale is not transparent. When colleagues come to realise they are paid significantly less than someone else performing the same role as them, it can have negative impacts on their attitudes and performance. A business does not want employees who are disengaged, particularly when these issues can be addressed!

So now that you understand how much the variance is, how do you go about determining how much to increase each employee eligible for an uplift? As increasing each employee to the maximum bandwidth is not ideal due to the increase in overhead costs and leaves little room for an increase in the future if they remain in that role.

Using the compensation ratio, HR may decide that those who are between 0.2 to 0.6 rating are eligible for an uplift. The uplift may aim to get them to the median remuneration across the entire group or may even aim to get them all at a satisfactory level of 0.7 ratio. Whatever the benchmark, it is not recommended to increase all employees to the maximum benchmark. By having an established framework across all areas of the business and an ideal compensation ratio, this removes the uphill battle for human resources in rectifying the remuneration inconsistencies, as a business is a lot more receptive when you are not drastically increasing overhead costs. Once all the necessary approvals have been received from the business, HR need to then support processing these increases and communication of the end results to the employees.

With all the increase amounts applied to the existing remuneration arrangement, HR can calculate what the new offerings and how much the increase is in total using a consistent effective date of the increase. The effective date of the increase can be either a date in the past so that a back-pay is processed, or a day in the future. HR create a letter template on a business' letterhead addressing the employee, subject of the letter being "Pay review – Salary Increase" with an outline of the increase applied and the applicable effective date. The letter should include that all other employment conditions contained in their employment contract remain the same. The letter should also be signed by the direct manager or a senior manager in the business, and also requests the employee to sign and date the letter acknowledging the change. The letter templates can also be linked as a mail merge template, particularly if there many letters to complete. When the letters are distributed by the managers, they should let the employee know they will have one copy for their records, and copies of signed letters should be returned through to HR so that this spreadsheet and letters may be forwarded through to payroll for processing.

Direct managers can assist by collecting the signed letters in their respective teams. The HR representatives co-ordinating these efforts should as a courtesy give payroll a heads up of the increases coming their way. This is also useful to HR as they will be able to provide an indication of when all the changes would be processed by and when employees could reasonably expect to see the changes come through on their payslips.

An annual merit review process is similarly executed to the pay parity exercise prescribed above. HR need to use the bandwidth's established for each role and the assigned budgets to determine whether employees are or are not eligible for an increase.

When I refer to a merit review, this is an annual process conducted by large organisations to ensure offerings remain at market and industry rates and increase in line with the Consumer Product index (CPI) each year. The average merit review increases applied to ranges between 1-3% on base salaries.

To be eligible for a merit review, HR have guidelines to ensure employees underperforming, have been issued disciplinary action in the last 12 months or are too highly remunerated are not included in the process. Another consideration is when the employee commenced with the company, as new starters joining a company beyond a certain date should be excluded from the merit review process.

Some managers use the merit review process in order conduct a regular pay parity exercise and align team member's pay if they are performing satisfactorily. This isn't the primary purpose of the merit review, but managers are often given control over their team's budget and can assign this evenly in terms of percentages or allocate a higher percentage of increase to individuals needing more of a bump in their salary. Apart from the merit review and pay parity exercises, a business can reward employees for their performance with short-term and long-term incentive schemes.

Bonuses and Share Plans

A short-term incentive (STI) or long-term incentive (LTI) scheme is generically referred to as performance bonuses issued to specific employee groups when they have, and the business has performed well over a 12-month period. These types of bonuses are often reserved for middle to senior management in large organisations to ensure they have accountability for their team's results and are rewarded accordingly.

The scheme used to calculate organisation-wide bonuses are governed by the human resources function and may rest specifically with a remuneration and benefits specialist. In collaboration with senior management, HR need to draft a document that outlines what the business' performance expectations are, what threshold needs to be met for the bonus to be payable, and how high the performance needs to be for the bonus to be paid 100 per cent in full.

Common performance indicates is the amount of revenue, cash-flow and other financial targets are made or maintained, safety performance for lead and lag indicators, number of safety incidents, lost-time injury (LTIs), medical treatment injury (MTIs) and serious injuries. Another category may be a people measure, such as turnover or retention rate and the overall performance of the team on delivery project initiatives by designated timelines.

The Key performance indicators set are dependent upon the organisation, as well as how the bonus will be paid when thresholds are met or not met. There may even be a sliding scale available, whereby exceeding target performance by a certain percentage may make employees eligible for 110 % of the allocated bonus and above. Thereby exceptional performance is not just rewarded with 100 % of the bonus. HR also need to consider whether employees become ineligible for a bonus if they resign within the financial year and the bonus has not yet been processed, or as long as they have completed a certain portion of the year, they are eligible for a pro-rated amount. These finer details are important to remove ambiguity and so it is clear when employees can resign without their bonuses being impacted.

The STI and LTI document should also outline how employees must prevent inappropriate eligibility of benefits. This may refer to forfeiture or clawback provisions in the event employees engage in misconduct or fraudulent activities such as adjusting performance reports and measures to benefit their bonus payment amount or treating other employees in an unfair manner in order to meet performance thresholds. Another section or clause of the document needs to outline how bonuses are not considered guaranteed earnings. Thereby, the business has sole discretion as to whether they will be paid and can significantly vary.

Businesses may decide not to process any bonus or only a small portion of a bonus if the business is not performing financially well or does not have adequate cash flow to justify the pay-out. If HR is met with scenario, there needs to be adequate communication provided to employees well in advance of payment date as to the reason for the decision, and what this means for their bonuses. Team or one-on-one discussions may be appropriate for this communication also, particularly if employees were expecting to be paid their bonus in full that year.

If a business is listed on the Australian Stock Exchange, senior leaders and HR executives may decide to invite a selective group of employees to own restricted shares of the company or allow every employee the opportunity to own shares when they join the business.

When share plans are implemented that are to be administered by the board members, and they are charged with ensuring that the business meets their obligations underneath the *Corporations Act 2001*. Alike the bonus incentive schemes, the share plan needs to incorporate what steps will be taken when an employee with shares leaves the business – whether they can retain their full portion for a period of time, only retain a certain portion of shares, or if all shares may be relinquished at the cessation of their employment. Whether employees retain their ownership may also hinge on the reason for the employee's departure; if they were dismissed for misconduct or any other reason, this may immediately forfeit ownership of their shares.

In the event an employee tries to sell their shares at any time, there would be restrictions in place in how these shares are sold. Regardless of the specifics of a share plan and how much an individual may own, this has no bearing on the nature of the employment relationship and cannot be used to increase compensation or damages brought against the company for loss of employment.

Most entry level or junior HR professionals would not have exposure to the intricacies of STI, LTI and share plans until much later in their career. The reason for this is that these types of programs and documents are managed by senior HR professionals in a business, and they are not distributed widely even among fellow HR team members. These documents are considered private and confidential, and may in some instances be tailored to certain individuals in a business. Please keep this in mind if you're starting out in your HR career and you're curious around your current business' bonus scheme and share plan structures. Despite this, junior HR professionals will generally have exposure to most frameworks, policies and procedures in large organisation. One such remuneration and benefit document is a company's parental leave policy.

Parental Leave

Chapter 4: Employee Entitlements covers in detail the 11 National Employment Standards (NES), which includes parental leave, which is available when employees have worked for their employer for over a 12 month period are then eligible for 12 months of unpaid parental leave.

Section 70 of the *Fair Work Act 2009* outlines this provision for unpaid parental leave, the criteria and when the leave must be taken in relation to the expected date of birth. When most people think of parental leave, their mind goes to the mother taking the time off with her newborn baby. However, parental leave can apply to both the primary and secondary carers regardless of whether they are the mother, father or partner in the relationship.

Before I delve into how a business may decide to pay above and beyond the mandatory NES requirements, it is necessary to understand how parental leave applies in a business to its employees. Couples can take leave as per Section 72 of the *Fair Work Act 2009*, as long as the leave is taken consecutively and so their leave occurs at the same time. For instance, if the first employee is the female who is pregnant and takes leave first as the primary carer, and then the partner would like to take leave; the leave taken must be taken before the first employee's leave period has ended. The partner would then be able to take a period of leave (concurrent) no longer than eight weeks, which can be taken in two separate periods with the agreement of the employer with each portion of leave not being shorter than two weeks.

There is also a provision in the *Fair Work Act 2009* for unpaid special maternity leave; this is provided to a mother when she is unfit to continue working due to illness in relation to her pregnancy, if there are workplace risks if she continues working while pregnant or in the unfortunate event the mother has a stillborn baby. In these scenarios, the mother can choose to take unpaid special maternity leave or use any accrued personal leave. The option of special maternity leave is only available within 28 weeks of the expected date of birth of the unborn child.

If a mother is experiencing an unsafe work environment, the employer is obligated to transfer the employee into a safe job prior to commencing parental leave. The criteria for the safe job alternative are that it would provide the same number of ordinary hours the employee would normally work so that the employee is not financially disadvantaged, or the safe job may provide a different number of ordinary hours (more or less) with the employee's agreement to this change in working hours.

For the employer obligated to provide a safe job alternative, the pregnant employee would need to provide a medical certificate or documentation, which indicates that working in the current capacity would give rise to hazards or that the employee is too ill to perform that job up until parental leave commences. If this medical certificate and information is provided by the employee and a safe job is available in the business, the employer is obligated to offer the transfer without any changes to existing employment conditions and terms occurring. The employee must not be financially disadvantaged by the transfer in position.

Once an employee has commenced their parental leave, whether it is paid or unpaid they are guaranteed their position when they return to the workplace. This guarantee is irrespective as to whether the employee decides to take the full 12 months of leave, arranges to only take a portion of the leave or decides to return back to work earlier than expected by the employer.

When the employee returns to work after parental leave, they must assume the same position and conditions prior to their parental leave period commencing. So that the transition back to work is easier for employees, during their parental leave period they can request the employer to provide "keep in touch" days.

A "Keep in touch" day is when the employee performs work for a day or part of a day during the parental leave period, and is paid as per the employment contract conditions. If there is an agreement between the employee and the employer, the employee may work up to ten days of "keep in touch" days during the parental leave period. These can be done all in one go, the employee working part days, full days or a few days at a time. An overview of how parental leave can be taken and enjoyed for up a 12-month period has now been explained.

As a HR professional, it is a requirement for you to provide guidance to employees and managers on how they may be paid during parental leave as per the NES and/or as per a specific company policy. If a business like Humesware Pty Ltd had not developed and implemented a company specific parental leave policy and purely relied on the legislative requirements, eligible employees would only be entitled to the 12 months of unpaid parental leave.

Unpaid parental leave in this sense refers to the employer who will not be paying the employee during this period of leave. However, employees eligible for parental leave can be paid a nominal daily rate via Centrelink (Human Services) for up to a period of 18 weeks during their leave period. Employees are eligible for government payments if they are the primary carer of a newborn or newly adopted child, individually have earned less than $150,000 in the last financial year, will not be working during the parental leave period and the child's birth has been registered in the territory birth register.

There may be some other requirements, and so as a HR representative you should recommend that employees directly liaise with Human Services rather than the business to co-ordinate these payments. The employer becomes involved as Human Services will pass on the government payments to the employer to process the payment. This is to ensure that the employee is not working while double-dipping the government entitlement. Another advantage of this arrangement is so that if the business has a paid parental leave scheme, the total payments made to the employee is visible and can be organised accordingly.

It is entirely at a business' discretion to make payments to employees during parental leave, as it is not a mandatory legislative requirement. HR would be actively involved in determining the type of payments available and which employees are in scope for the company paid parental leave policy. An example of paid parental leave policy is a "top-up" scheme, whereby the business will make up the different between the government payments over the 18 weeks of parental leave and the ordinary earnings the employee would have received had they worked. This top-up scheme may be at 100 per cent for the entire duration of the 18 weeks, or may be on a sliding scale, being at 100 per cent for the first four weeks, 75 per cent for the next four weeks and so on. Another option may for the employee to instead receive half pay spread over a six-month period instead of the top-up tiered arrangement. Employees may also elect to use some of their accrued annual leave and long service leave (if applicable) entitlements to cover periods of unpaid leave throughout the 12-month period. This leave taken needs to be agreed by the employer and may also be another option available in isolation or as a part of a scheme in the company policy.

There are some large organisations that have elected to pay 100 % of an employee's pre-parental leave conditions throughout the duration of parental leave. These organisations may have made this decision to support employees during parental leave to retain top talent, and to encourage women to remain working in their business. This parental leave policy is an attractive benefit for women considering working for a business offering this to their employees and is a competitive advantage if a business is looking to promote and increase workplace diversity.

Openly advertising or making this information available to prospective and existing employees is a draw card and something a woman about to or considering having children in the future would seriously consider. This is such a great opportunity for HR professionals to become involved and see how a change or review to the existing parental leave policy (if available) can contribute to a business' workplace diversity campaign or strategy. This may also be a means to solve the lack of females in particular positions, as some women are unable to continue working for the business if they lose income while on parental leave.

Another option is to provide employees the ability to apply for an additional twelve-months of paid or unpaid parental leave; this is not an obligation to provide an additional 12 unpaid months and again is discretionary as to whether it's granted and/or paid by the employer. Whatever the business' circumstances may be, I encourage you to understand how the business could potentially position itself to go above and beyond the NES provisions for parental leave. If a parental policy does not exist in the company, there is a golden opportunity for you to make a difference for the employees and the business at large. How exciting!

Awards and Gifts

It is incredibly important for a business to keep their employees engaged. There are many benefits gained by this as employee engagement has an inherently positive impact on productivity, the workplace culture and how successful the operation is overall.

One method of keeping employees happy and engaged in the workplace is by having a structured recognition program, whereby employees are publicly awarded or even when it is appropriate giving gifts to acknowledge their efforts, unique contribution to the business or to celebrate an important milestone.

In large organisations, these types of recognition are often expected by employees and when they do not occur it can become a strong point of resentment and can lead to employees becoming dissatisfied with the company's treatment towards them.

In my experience, businesses need to understand how recognition of performance and loyalty is key in keeping employees engaged. When a business gets this wrong, HR will definitely hear about it! Employees reach out to HR when they are not satisfied with the degree of recognition they are receiving in a business.

The most common complaint is when years of service are not recognised and celebrated by the business, particularly for milestones such as five years' service, ten years' service and beyond. To ensure there is a fair and equitable recognition for all employees, HR should iron out the details of a recognition of service program. This would instruct managers on what is required to ensure the employee receives consistent recognition. This type of program must as a minimum state whether each year of service is recognised with an award or a gift, or if only specific years of service are acknowledged as they are considered milestones; an award may be given for each milestone, but the value of the gift provided may increase over time. Deciding on what is appropriate as a gift (if any) needs to be approved and costed by the business, as this may be adding significant additional costs particularly if the business has thousands of employees. The award provided can also be signed by a senior management in the business, personalised to the employee, printed and framed by an external company so that this is professionally executed. Having awards printed on standard A4 paper is a little tacky and won't be as valued by the employees receiving them. Another component of the document should provide guidelines to managers on how the employee should be given the recognition.

The award and/or gifts provided to employees to celebrate milestones is just one component of providing recognition. Managers need to execute this recognition properly and this shouldn't just be given to the employee out of the blue. Their achievement should be celebrated among their team members and peers. For a business to properly celebrate and recognise achievements, an event could be held formally or informally, depending upon the achievement and how many people are being recognised. An example of this, is that there may be upwards of 20 employees in a building or area celebrating a service milestone within a month or the last six months. Therefore, an organised event whereby all employees can be publicly recognised at the same time would be appropriate. This event may involve sending out invites to all employees in that location, and catering a lunch or a morning tea with some treas. The managers or a nominated senior manager may say an opening business update and introduce the purpose of the event, and then proceed to formally recognise the milestone with each employee's name being read out one by one. The setting would be similar to a student accepting their graduation certificate at an assembly; they come up, shake the manager's hand, accept their award and gift among an audience of their peers. There could also be a PowerPoint presentation with all the recognised employees and their years of service listed for all to see. There are many different ways to do this.

Making these types of events special makes a difference to the company culture. The choice of the gift provided (if any) is subject to the business' discretion. The gift provided may be related to the business' own products and services provided, or related to an ongoing partnership. The gift could also be completely unrelated to the business and be gift vouchers for various retail stores. A business may opt for gift hampers or an experience voucher, to go hot air ballooning, sky diving or whatever the employee elects to use the voucher for. Another recognition approach I have seen over my career is that the important milestone is recognised by the business organising a team dinner or lunch, in the employee's honour to celebrate. That way, the entire team acknowledges the milestone and all team members benefit from the achievement fostering stronger working relationships. When this approach is adopted, the business may also combine recognition for achievements other than service milestones into one event.

Another aspect of an effective recognition program is to recognise outstanding performance, demonstration of company values and a unique contribution to improved operational excellence or innovativeness. Depending upon the company's ethos, this may manifest into an employee of the month award, or a specific company value self or peer nomination process. Recognising employees in the business does not solely need to rest on the shoulders of managers, as self-nomination or per-nomination processes are a fantastic initiative. An example of this would be when an employee observes their peer going above and beyond to solve a problem, or demonstrates a company value, they would be able to nominate their peer for a monthly award or category for this contribution in the workplace.

When a nomination is submitted, there would need to be an assigned committee that assesses each application and determines whether this satisfies the criteria for an award. An individual employee would be able to receive multiple nominations with the open period for applications, and would be required to provide examples of why the nominated employee is worthy of recognition. Employees may also have the ability to nominate a peer based on them providing a unique idea contributing towards continuous improvement. The business may also decide to have different category awards such as a safety award (which department or individual had contributed the most towards safety in a period of time), or which employee has uniquely contributed towards continuous improvement leading to operational excellence. There are just so many opportunities and ways of recognising employees in a business, that there really isn't a reason why this shouldn't be occurring in a business where there is a dedicated HR function.

As a HR professional, you can take the lead in implementing a recognition framework or improving an existing program in place. Gain employees' feedback as to whether the program is working and if the program is being well-received. Ultimately, if the program is not having a positive impression and lasting impact on employees then the program is a detractor from employee engagement.

9

REPORTING AND SYSTEMS

THIS CHAPTER IS ALL about how a business can measure HR effectiveness and quantify the impact of HR business partnering to the bottom line. A lot of HR practitioners do not focus on quantifying and measuring their efforts, and the impact of initiatives implemented in the business. Without this focus, a business can build a perspective that HR representatives are very "fluffy" and aligns to the stereotype that HR like to talk to employees about their feelings, and only hire and fire employees. This is inaccurate! This fallacy still exists today and is exacerbated by HR traditional methods of not reporting on value adding activities and speaking a similar language to the rest of the business.

Organisations crave regular reporting analytics on cash flow, profit and loss, which is all about numbers, and these are the reports that appeal to senior business leaders. When HR start to speak in numbers, they begin to understand the value HR can bring to a business despite being a non-revenue generating function and the potential cost savings that can be introduced by supporting HR initiatives. Having a HR strategy complemented by periodic reports helps evolve the

HR function from one that purely serves administrative tasks, to a group of professionals who partner with the business to enact real change.

There are four main categories I recommend that HR functions should as a minimum report on. These are measurements on HR effectiveness and how HR projects have produced a Return on Investment (ROI), performance management of individuals and work groups, workplace diversity and inclusion, and workforce analytics. Starting with the first category, implementing processes and reports on HR effectiveness supports the HR function to position and build business cases to generate endorsement for new projects and initiatives. Having the capability, systems and processes to be able to quantify how HR's efforts have made a difference to a business encourages senior management to buy-in into new projects and ideas so that a reasonable budget is assigned to these pursuits.

Human Resources Information Systems

How does HR report on their efforts? The foundation of a report is the collection and analysis of accurate data. When you are working in a large organisation, it is common practice for systems to be integrated in the business to collect employee information. This may be solely through a payroll system and/ or a Human Resources Information System (HRIS).

HRIS is a type of software used to manage human capital information, can track recruitment activities, employee departure from the business, compensation information and generate organisational charts. When a HRIS is used properly and to its full functionality, accurate reports can be generated and communicate directly with the payroll system or module.

Having a downstream feedback mechanism allows information plugged into HRIS to filter through to payroll for processing. This would thereby give payroll the opportunity to become the source of truth, for all employee data, which is incredibly important for compliance requirements.

An example of how HRIS is used is when a vacancy has become available the job requisition number is generated by the HRIS and used to recruit for this role. Once a new role or replacement role has been filled, the new employee details are assigned to the requisition number and the business is able to track which new starter has filled the vacancy.

The employee details includes all necessary information that payroll would require to process their first payment. Other aspects of functionality include having a document archive, where HR representatives and managers can upload documents assigned to employee profiles with varying degrees of accessibility. With this basic level of information, HR would be able to extract how many open roles the business has, how many have been filled and what is the average time taken to fill these positions, what percentage of open roles are new versus replacement roles, and what are the details of these new starters. All this information from one piece of HRIS functionality!

Continuing with this example, the business would use the recruitment reports generated from the HRIS to measure the effectiveness of a workplace diversity and inclusion project. Assuming the entire recruitment module is activated in a HRIS, a business would be able to track how many applications were received for each role; their demographic characteristics; if they are female or male or unidentified gender; if they are Aboriginal and Torres Strait Islander; and the characteristics of the successful applicants.

If the business had a quota for a percentage of women interviewed and placed in specific positions, this report would be very helpful for HR to understand how successful the business is tracking. Using this report, the business would also be able to understand how much overhead and campaign costs have been dedicated to these efforts and what the ROI is. If more female applicants applied and were placed in the business after a recruitment drive for "Women in the Workplace" was held at various conferences, then this would be tracked.

Based on the costs associated with this recruitment drive, HR would be able to calculate the material impact this has had on recruitment deliverables. Going one step further, from these female appointments what added benefit have they contributed to the business could be measured in comparison to hiring their male counterparts? This is how HRIS reports can be used to measure ROI.

If HR professionals are required to monitor recruitment or any other type of performance indicator weekly, monthly or quarterly, HRIS software allows automatic reports to be generated and emailed directly to a list of assigned contacts. HRIS software also can send relevant managers and HR alerts when a job requisition has been raised or a new employee needs to be on-boarded so that the appropriate approvals are requested and made.

By having an approval chain built into HRIS processes, a business can achieve governance over recruitment activities, a level of consistency on compensation offered to new and existing employees, transfer of employees between departments and locations, and termination payments processed and sent through to payroll. From a compliance perspective, there are a lot of benefits to having a HRIS in place. Assigning various levels of access to different types of users of a HRIS means that a business can track who has changed what information, and gives HR a higher level of access to make compensation changes and co-ordinate redundancy payments.

If a manager was to accidentally add an extra zero to the end of a base salary, that can make a world of difference to the end result processed through by payroll!

For a business to set-up the approval chains and levels of access appropriately in a business, I recommend that HR develops and implements a governance council. The governance council oversees the data integrity and use of information captured in the HRIS, and is also accountable for the correct transmission of information from the HRIS to the payroll. The council also needs to ensure only relevant information is sent through to payroll and that the information is sent in a timely manner to safeguard against the payroll cycle being delayed.

HRIS software has the capability to integrate performance management tools for bi-annual performance appraisals and any associated merit review processes. Organisations with systematic methods of conducting performance appraisals with employees, whether it is via 360 degrees feedback, one-on-one conversations with the direct line manager, and an initial self-assessment, a business can capture these records in a performance management module of HRIS software. This would involve HR working with the software designers to implement a customised form and progression chain for the business, allowing goals to be entered with KPIS, comments to be made against each goal by the employee, manager or any other relevant party and for final sign-offs to occur.

By having these all captured in one place, HR can follow-up with managers and individuals to complete these discussions and forms by a designated time. HR would also be able to understand what stage the form is up to and conduct quality audits to ensure the performance appraisal comments are not "copy and paste" and are specific to each person's role.

When a performance management scheme has been integrated with a merit review process, the overall performance rating of an employee would impact whether they are eligible for an increase in compensation, and what percentage of increase may be awarded. When a percentage increase has been allocated by a manager and approved in the HRIS, this would feed through to payroll for processing. The business would also be able to analyse the number of increases allocated against the budget and understand how much monies have exceeded budget restrictions and accrue this in the month the compensation increases are effective. By HR using the full functionality of HRIS software for performance appraisals and compensation reviews, HR will be able to demonstrate the software's ROI and also draw meaningful actions from the extracted reports.

If a merit review report demonstrates significance variances in compensation for roles of the same or similar grading, HR should be reviewing the reasons for those variances and developing an action plan to address any significant gaps. A merit review report may also reveal that males and females performing the same graded role are paid differently across a range of departments, and a program of work may be required to address these variances.

By HR having access to this data and reports, HR professionals can be empowered to develop business cases to address issues in the business. HR representatives may have already known these issues existed, but without the necessary data the business may not have been convinced of their existence or the extent of the problems. The reports would also reflect the importance of a manager's role in managing their team fairly and equitably with feedback provided during performance appraisals and awarded compensation.

With HR having full visibility to these discussions HR can conduct calibration sessions to ensure merit reviews and overall gradings are consistently allocated and aligned to what is the expected trend for a cohort or group of employees. Without a HRIS software to draw upon this information, these calibration sessions would have been conducted manually using spreadsheets. This would cause significant additional hours of work and complicates a process, which most managers do not openly embrace in organisations. However, there are some processes and reports senior management look forward to from HR as it has a direct impact on their budget and bottom line, which speaks to one of their key priorities.

Workforce Analytics

In my personal experience, line managers and senior managers look forward to workforce analytics and reports generated by HR. They genuinely get excited and like to understand how they are performing in comparison to other work groups, the state they are based and nationally. Line managers may even have set people targets and accessibility to workforce analytics can influence their decision-making to try and reach these. When I refer to workforce analytics, I am speaking broadly on the human capital of the business, an important pillar above cash flow and asset management. Workforce analytics provides meaningful insights into the composition of the workforce, changes and trends occurring and empowers HR and managers to make decisions to influence these trends and achieve strategic objectives.

One of the fundamental workforce reports management would expect from HR and rightfully so is an accurate head count report. This report would need to break down the head count by each role and type of role – full-time, part-time, casual or contractor – with the ability to drill down into the details of each headcount which each worker's full name, as well as a rolling average month on month.

HR can also provide graphs for peaks and troughs whereby head count is fluctuating in a full financial or fiscal year. HR may also make a comparison between the recruitment activities to hire replacement positions and any deficiencies in relation to the turnover rate. This would explain any trends in a slow decline in overall headcount, or if recruitment activities are over-achieving then this may explain a steady incline in overall headcount. Other explanations for a stable head count or increasing headcount would be a healthy or downwards trend in turnover rate; the turnover rate is the total number of separations divided by the average total headcount.

On face value, a turnover rate of 20 % may seem quite high, but in comparison to an industry average of 35 % this may be exceptional. Providing commentary to results and explaining trends is a useful exercise for HR to undertake so that the results are not misinterpreted and subject to harmful assumptions. Other useful detail for a headcount report would be the workforce composition.

A workforce composition report and supporting graphs would be a deep dive into the current worker pool. This would look at the type of workers currently engaged in terms of gender, grade and role, average compensation, comparison of compensation to the industry comparator, the average age of tenure per age group, average age across work groups, and the number of departures per month by manager.

Having these characteristics available to line and senior management allows them to scrutinise the type of retained employees and the type of employees being newly recruited. From this, the business could discern that certain roles attract more females and other roles are more male-dominated. The business may be also see a particular trend where one manager in the business has a significantly higher turnover in their team in comparison to other managers or a national average, which would be a red flag!

Identifying these trends and highlighting these in reports and scorecards provided prompts meaningful discussions and can lead to meaningful changes. With reference to a scenario where one manager has a high turnover rate, this trend may lead to further investigation by the manager in conjunction with HR to understand why employees are leaving and if there is anything untoward occurring, or a direct result of the nature of positions and pressures in that team. Understanding why and how employees depart the business is another core piece of workforce analytics.

When an employee decides to leave the business by their own volition, it is best HR practice to have a feedback mechanism where their feedback can be captured. HR need to be interested in the key contributing factors as to why an employee decides to leave the business, particularly in their first 12 months of employment. The most common method is to distribute an exit survey to employees who resign.

The exit survey should be quantifiable as that is what this chapter is all about, and this can be done by categorising each question and using numbers to rate each response. These categories may be safety, your role, management, benefits, overall satisfaction.

Having these categories will help HR discern how they personally viewed safety and how they observed the business to prioritise safety, how satisfied they were in their own role, what their experience was with their direct manager and management holistically, and other factors that may have influenced their decision such as pay and work-life balance (or lack thereof).

By quantifying this feedback, HR would be able to make recommendations and provide commentary around the main reasons for employees resigning, and which areas a business needs to focus on improving. If for example a common trend was that there was a lack of personal development and career development, it would be in management's best interest to invest necessary resources to ensure their team members feel invested in. Management would have an opportunity to develop their team and hopefully see a two-fold effect: a reduced turnover rate and a higher productivity rate. This is a value-adding action taken from HR reporting.

HR reporting should similarly provide an analysis and updates on non-voluntary departures from a business; these are terminations and redundancies. A business needs to be aware of the main categories for these departures, and HR are in the prime position to provide commentary on these matters.

The type of categories a business could use for terminations are drug and alcohol breaches, misconduct, under-performance, workers compensation, bullying and harassment, and redundancies. This is not an exhaustive list but would be a good starting point if you're looking to build your own HR report. One way of measuring this would be to compare the total number of non-voluntary departures versus voluntary departures on each month, the rolling average non-voluntary and voluntary departures, the total number of departures for each category listed above, and what the total departures was in the last financial year. Managers respond well to visual graphs and images to illustrate this information and any trends.

From this report, HR and managers may identify some concerns or common challenges across different areas of the business. Again, having the information available and then discussing what the reports demonstrate leads to meaningful discussion and real change.

If HR was to merely distribute the reports and this is where the process ended, then there would be limited value in generating the reports in the first instance. HR need to constantly challenge themselves around why they complete certain tasks and how they can successfully partner with the business so that strategy objectives are obtained.

One strategic objective of a business may be to reduce the overall annual leave liability of employees. Employees with an excessive annual leave balance should be encouraged by HR and senior management to take their annual leave to promote wellness, work-life balance and also reduce the liability carried by the business.

Unused annual leave is paid out to employees when they depart a business and these accruals also have the potential to increase in a value overtime. If an employee has an annual leave accrual of 52 hours and carries over these accruals untouched into the new year, and as of 1 January the employee receives an increase to base salary all the accruals have been raised in value commensurate to the increase applied to the salary. Therefore, a business and HR should have an ongoing initiative to regularly monitor annual leave accruals and encourage employees to take annual leave regularly throughout the year.

A HR report to address this initiative can calculate the overall dollar figure of the current annual leave liability per department, per employee and overall. The annual leave liability can also be averaged per employee and an average balance of annual leave days provided to managers.

A similar report can be generated for personal leave accruals, but with negative or zero balances being the focus. Unlike with annual leave, HR and businesses would not encourage their staff to take personal leave unless they require the type of as they are ill or need to care for a family member. Identifying which employees have low or negative personal leave accruals would highlight those individuals who may be excessively absent or using their personal leave on a Friday or Monday on a regular basis, to pro-long their weekend. Any negative personal balance is essentially a credit given by the company to an employee, which impacts the business financially. If an employee with a negative balance was to leave the business and they do not have enough earnings and other accruals to reconcile the credit, then the business is essentially forfeiting money to the employee. Adjusting the HRIS so that employees cannot go into negative leave balance and excessive personal leave automatically defaults to leave without pay is one solution a business may employ to prevent this from occurring. By providing this report and discussing the data, this solution may be implemented if it was not already and thereby preventing cash leakage.

As effective middle management and frontline leadership is a strong indicator of business success, HR should devote focus and resources to understand how employees are internally promoted and what are the characteristics of the business' leaders.

HR can start by delving into the average age of each management level throughout the organisation, and understanding which individuals are outliers to the average. In addition to their age, what are their qualifications, years of relevant management experience and average tenure in the business. What proportion of each management group were internally promoted versus recruitment externally?

If there is a low percentage of internal promotion at each management level, then this would indicate to HR that there may not be enough focus on personal development and succession mapping. If succession mapping is not a priority in the business, then "hi-potential" individuals may become disengaged, their productivity decreases, and they may eventually decide to leave the company. Having a succession pipeline, identifying Hi-Pos and reporting on these are essential to achieve stability in these key roles. It is also critical to ensure current managers remain engaged and not have a toxic impact on their teams and colleagues. Having HR reports that identify individual employees, whether they are a flight risk and whether they are in line for a promotion is essential for senior management and C-suite executives to understand the state of the business. HR can use the reporting results to posit the need and importance of leadership development programs and the overall investment into the training and development of middle management.

From looking at various factors and trends on HR reports, HR may also identify areas of improvement. On face value, if a site or location in a business has a higher turnover rate and decreased average length of tenure in comparison to the set benchmark, this would be a concerning finding. HR should then pose questions as to whether there may be an unhealthy workplace culture on site? What has the management stability been like recently? Is there any major significant change/s that have occurred on sites? Is the site profitable? Is the site facing any challenging market or industry implications?

Considering these questions and trying to find the answers will ensure that HR professionals are not making negative insinuations and are getting to the root cause of these results.

A methodology HR practitioners use to understand these types of anomalies or the state of a workplace culture across the broad is to implement an engagement survey. An engagement survey uses quantifiable categories to understand the workplace culture and which factors are impacting employees the most to create a positive or negative working environment.

For an engagement survey results to provide meaningful findings and for HR to make pragmatic recommendations, the survey needs to execute correctly. The survey needs to be taken by a variety of different types of employees in the organisation and have a reasonable level of participation from employees.

The most common form of delivery is for an email to be distributed to emails. However, some employee types may not have access to emails and HR need to develop an alternative means of collecting this feedback, which may be a collection of hardcopy feedback forms through management.

When these surveys are designed, you need to firstly decide what is the core purpose of these surveys? What outcomes is the business looking to achieve from the results and how will the results be used to achieve these outcomes? Addressing these agenda items will support HR to develop the appropriate questions and associated categories.

Once a survey has been rolled out with a deadline for employees to complete the survey, HR should be periodically encouraging employees to participate. HR can position that the survey will be confidential and will not identify the participant, and it is an excellent avenue to provide commentary on the workplace culture. Once the findings have been collated and analysed, a summary of the findings should be distributed to all employees so they understand the state of the business and how the business will be responding to this feedback.

Before this happens, HR need to present the findings to various levels of management. Providing real feedback that they may or may not be receptive to is pivotal in creating real changes to the business. HR can produce a report with supporting graphs to demonstrate the overall score for each engagement category per state and location, and how these locations scored in comparison to the average and benchmark. If the business has reservations around how the results of a survey are analysed and the quality of the information produced, then HR can co-ordinate the implementation and analysis of the survey via an external party. This delivers a level of independence and leaves little room for managers to question the integrity of the information gathered. Having transparent and meaningful conversations is required for these reports to be useful to a business and to empower HR professionals as change agents.

A fundamental component of a HR professional's role is to lead and assist in the management of employee relations matters. In large organisations, there may be a high volume of ER matters per month, which can be reported on using similar categories to the non-voluntary departures.

By reporting on the workload and amount of ER matters HR are involved in, it demonstrates the function's contribution and type of matters being addressed to uplift the workplace culture. ER matters can range in complexity and degree of financial risk to the business. These details can accompany the average length taken to close out each type of category. The business may also be interested in seeing which HR representative is managing cases most effectively in terms of outcome delivered and the time taken to close the matter.

If the business has a whistle-blower policy or hotline, the matters coming through this channel can also be analysed using the same metrics. In my experience, I have found that board members are incredibly interested in these types of reports and like reassurance that serious matters are being addressed in a timely manner. Although HR may have a detailed report with every ER matter, the employee names involved, etc., HR need to develop a suitable HR scorecard to summarise key pieces of information for targeted audiences such as a board of directors, or the direct reports of the Chief Executive Officer.

Building a HR scorecard is a necessity for large corporate organisations and businesses that need an update on all the moving pieces involved in the people agenda. A HR scorecard can be designed in a variety of different formats, with a variety of graphs and visual aids – with red colour to signal negative results and green to signal positive results. Arrows may be used to indicate downward and upward trends in data. In essence, the HR scorecard summarises all the types of detailed report examples provided above and enables the business to set new strategic objectives and understand how existing objectives are tracking. Ensuring that the HR scorecard remains relevant and allows important decisions to be made helps secure HR's role as a true business partner. Merely providing reports to the business is not an effective means for HR to break the mould of being an administrative function. As a HR professional, you need to have the mindset of how you can partner with managers to influence and make decisions, which will benefit the business.

10

BUSINESS POLITICS

So, I HAVE LEFT the best chapter until last. This chapter is all about learning how to navigate the wonders of corporate politics… and I say "the wonders" sarcastically. It is an unfortunate fact of life that in HR or any profession in a corporate environment, you are going to face the unpleasantness of corporate politics. I personally loathe getting involved in corporate politics.

In the first few years of my career, I was naïve and had no inclination on how to deal with corporate politics, or even the basics for that matter. I was even unsure on how to approach a situation with my direct manager when I disagreed with their point of view. Any feedback I was given I took to heart, and I was easily influenced by older and more mature players in the corporate game. I felt lost and not in control of my own career path. I actively rejected getting involved or taking sides in any political drama and tried to stay as neutral as possible.

By reflecting on my own experiences, I made a lot of mistakes. It was only from observing the behaviours of others that I built my own political savviness. It is my ambition that by you reading this chapter, you can avoid having to make as many mistakes as I did and learn from my blunders.

The way I view corporate politics, and as it was explained to me by a seasoned professional, it is like an ancient Roman court. Imagine a bunch of people dressed up in white togas, discussing their opinions and stating arguments that suit their agendas. Alliances are formed and people make plans to take down their enemies, whether it is in a subtle way or more explicitly like what happened to Julius Caesar. Before you know it, people around you have changed sides and are the ones digging the figurative knives into your back. It is a colourful analogy, isn't it?

Well, this is what it can be like working in a corporate environment. As you rise the corporate ranks, the stakes become higher, and, without your own initiation of these behaviours, you will find yourself stuck in the middle of the political drama. As your career progresses to a senior management level, you will be forced to deal with more seasoned politicians with established alliances and relationships in the business. The purpose of this analogy is not to frighten you, but to make you aware of how barbaric some people can act when trying to gain a career promotion or safeguard their future in the business. Not everyone who is involved in the political game is vicious and will switch alliances to suit their agendas. Some players are loyal while ambitious and will make more behind the scene moves. This is the unfortunate reality of working life. Some organisations have healthy cultures and supportive colleagues, and other businesses foster competitiveness and a culture where you do anything you can to benefit yourself and only yourself. So, what can you do to survive the political nightmare? The first lesson I had to master was the art of managing upwards.

Managing Upwards

There is nothing worse than working for a manager who is not as technically competent or has limited people management capability, and working for them is overall an unpleasant experience. Knowing that they may not be as good as you are and are paid more than you can really be demotivating. Your manager may also be a master delegator and thereby have less tasks and projects to complete. When the projects and tasks have been completed by you, they would then sign off on the work, provide feedback and may even claim credit for the work as their own.

Research supports that these experiences make many hard-working and deserving people frustrated and disengaged from the work that they love. If you are not in this situation, you are incredibly fortunate, as the main contributing factor towards leaving a company is having a bad boss. So how do you go about managing upwards or doing the best you can in an unfortunate circumstance?

When you are in a workplace and you are experiencing a negative dynamic between you and your manager, it can be difficult to not be emotionally impacted by it. Most of our waking adult life is spent working and can form a large portion of our identity and sense of self. When you are at the point when you are dragging your feet to get to work because of your manager's behaviour towards you, and the effect this has on your job satisfaction, you have only two options. The first option is to leave the business by finding another job and resigning. The second option, which does not necessarily have to just be in response to a bad boss, is to manage upwards.

Managing upwards is all about managing your relationships, the expectations of your direct manager and, at times, your manager's own direct manager. If you're in a situation where you have a bad boss, you need to firstly understand the parameters of your working situation.

If you feel you are more experienced or more technically competent than your boss, how did you reach this conclusion? How have you concluded that the knowledge and skills gap between you and your direct manager is not that large? Is your manager younger than you? Were you passed up for the opportunity to take your manager's position? Understanding why you have negative feelings towards your direct manager will help you overcome them and effectively manage the relationship going forward. Your resentment may be the cause for you having negative interactions with your manager, or it could mainly be due to the way your manager treats you and others in the business.

Once you understand what is going on with yourself emotionally and you're able to rationalise this, you can move forward. Having the ability to effectively manage upwards is an important skill to have to safeguard your vitality in the business and manage the expectations of senior management. It is also a means to minimise the negative impacts a direct manager may have on you by controlling your own emotional state.

With your own self-assessment and analysis of your working circumstances, you will come to realise that going head-to-head with your direct manager is not an effective strategy. I've had my own personal learnings in this respect when I was in my early twenties. Despite feeling passionately about a subject and the way something should be handled in the business, blatantly disagreeing with your manager and not picking which battles to fight does not bode well.

The reality of corporate politics is that your direct manager does hold a great deal of influence over how you succeed and progress in the business. Going head-to-head with them when there is a disagreement and when you cannot understand their perspective on a decision made only makes an enemy out of your manager. You must have the wisdom to know when to let matters go and when to pick your battles. I'm not suggesting that you should be a pushover and agree to everything your manager says, and to not raise opposing viewpoints on a subject. It is just to be measured in your approach when you do this. If your manager feels very strongly on a course of action and you disagree with this, don't push too hard. Ultimately, the decision will be made by your manager, and it is their job to make difficult decisions. Your direct manager may have insight and information you do not have access to and has considered this in making the decision. Whatever it may be, you should always aim to maintain a positive working relationship with your direct manager, and fighting with them or writing sharp, blunt emails is never a good idea. Again, I am not suggesting you suck up to your boss, but merely hold your ground when you can, and on matters where you will have little influence over your manager's decision, it may be better to let it go.

If you are looking for more advanced strategies because your manager may be toxic and is overwhelming you and others in the workplace, I have constructed a list of suggestions and factors for you to consider.

Once you have considered these points, I will provide examples of what managing upwards effectively looks like. Here is the list to get your thinking cap on and warmed up:

- If you focus on developing a positive workplace environment with your direct manager and your team members, it will make working together a lot more manageable. This is particularly effective if the relationship is already strained.

By you initiating the first efforts, it demonstrates to others that you are willing to move past any issues or challenges that have transpired. Making positive relationships with people you interact with at work should be your normal ethos in the workplace. However, when it comes to your relationship with your direct manager, despite the challenges that may exist, you should devote more effort to this area.

- When you disagree with the decisions your manager is making, try your best to understand their rationale for the decision. Is there something you may be missing or pieces of information you're not necessarily privy to that cannot be widely shared? Is the decision being made differently as your manager has more expertise or knowledge in this area? Does anyone else agree with your manager's decisions at a higher level, or is there a general feel of disagreement across the board? Try your best to understand your manager's perspective, even when you disagree with their points of view.

- Do you understand the bigger strategic picture of the business or are you limited by the information your manager chooses to share with you? Do you have a clear appreciation for the contribution your individual role makes within the team and the broader business? Is your opinion of your contribution in alignment with how the business views it, or is there incongruity here in this assessment? Are you invested and involved in the establishment of the short-term and long-term goals of the business? Answering these questions will help you in managing your own efforts in your role. It will also help you to appreciate the necessity of your manager's position and may refresh your perspective on your manager's contributions towards the business.

- Is your manager giving you difficult tasks and challenging you on the quality of your work to provide you with constructive criticism? Is there a chance that your manager is trying to develop you further and may be treating you differently as their own way of mentoring you? Is their management style synonymous with "tough love" and is there a possibility that your manager is an advocate of your abilities and potential? Some managers have an unconventional means of coaching their team members and this may not be obvious to those on the receiving end.

The above bullet points are all in the pursuit of building a positive relationship with your manager to benefit your dynamic and your overall satisfaction in the job. This is the foundation of being able to manage upwards effectively. Managing upwards is not just solely about having a good relationship with your manager and the other managers up the chain of command. It is all about using this positive working relationship to benefit you in the workplace.

Everything about this chapter is what you can do to further yourself in the workplace. It is not about what you can do for others or what the manager's or your team member's experience may be. Although that may be relevant in the context of these teachings, this chapter is central to your experience and what changes you can make to excel and become a political player.

Based on the assumption you have a positive working relationship with your direct manager, you will be able to lay the groundwork for managing upwards. A mistake many professionals make is limiting advocacy of work only to your direct manager. You cannot put all your effort in managing just your relationship with your manager. You need to diversify and ensure the management level above and to a senior level are aware of your contributions and quality of work. If you instead divest all your energy into your manager, if they leave the business or move into a different position you essentially have to start building your reputation all over again from scratch.

Having a strong personal brand in a business is part of managing upwards and is a net that needs to be widely cast. Making efforts to ensure people know that you were involved in, led a major project or were behind a successful endeavour is just one step in managing upwards.

Having the ability to influence your manager and other people in the business is a part of managing upwards. To be able to have this type of pull, you will need to devote time and energy into building alliances. Going back to the analogy of the Roman court, in a workplace it is important that you have a range of different players on your team who will advocate for you. The stronger your circle of influence, you will find the more say and influence you will have in the business and the safer your position will be from threats or being challenged in the business.

Creating this circle of influence comes from networking, developing relationships over similar interests, and more specifically similar ideals on the way things should be done in the business. People tend to bond over similar annoyances or when they have a "common enemy". When you are voicing your views and if they may be in contradiction to your manager's, you need to be wise and careful around who you speak with.

If you're not familiar with the political landscape, who already has alliances and long-standing relationships, you may actually be telling your manager's friend that you disagree with your boss. That would be very awkward for you, and you may not find out about this pre-existing relationship until much later.

To familiarise yourself with the political landscape, you should study the existing organisational structure. Look at the direct reports to the Chief Executive Officer and from senior management downwards. This will only get you so far, as the organisational structures will not identify the alliances, and those who have more influence than others. The degree of influence may also be incongruent to the position they hold, as someone who has been in a business for a long period of time and not necessarily ascended the ranks may be very well-respected and hold a great deal of influence. These gems of information will help you avoid awkward interactions as navigating corporate politics is like navigating land mines. One wrong step and it can really backfire on you and your reputation in the business.

With the political landscape essentially mapped out and your network in the business proverbially budding anew, you need to concentrate on how you will play the political game. Will you be an active participant in the game with an aggressive approach, someone who remains neutral and only gets involved when there is really no choice in the matter, or someone that influences behind the scenes?

This may seem very weird to read in a HR related book, but this is honestly what corporate politics is like in a workplace. Some people get a thrill from it, using people or turning people against others to suit their agenda and playing the blame game. Other people like myself really do not genuinely enjoy observing or having to participate in these types of escapades. Unfortunately, as a HR professional you will often become dragged into these types of matters when issues become personal and there is conflict in the business. When this happens, although in your role you are charged with being neutral and resolving issues objectively, you need to manage how parties perceive you. In the way you handle these matters, you need to avoid being perceived as taking sides in the political nonsense yourself. Being aware of this and how by doing your job you may be adversely impacted, you may need to consider what a win-win solution is. A win-win solution will benefit both parties and leave your reputation out of their crosshairs.

Keeping your manager informed regarding any project updates or challenges in the business is a normal part of the team member to manager relationship. This dynamic can become strained if you're not managing up correctly and not keeping your manager informed of any political movements or issues that will come their way. Managers and people in general do not like to be blindsided, whether it is receiving an angry customer's phone call or a manager is expected to provide updates on a project and they have not been provided the necessary information to do this.

Ensuring your direct manager remains informed and is well equipped to also "look good" when they are under pressure or managing a problem will benefit the both of you. Exercise your discretion when informing your manager of certain matters, as you need to also value their time, and they may not want to know the details in depth pertaining to every matter you are managing.

You may also gain information informally about movements in the business in your own circle of influence and network. You will have to make the decision whether you reveal your sources and these insights with your manager or keep this information close to your chest. Sharing information with your manager this way may also gain you some favour, or it may make your manager feel inferior as their own network have not provided these insights. Manage these types of conversations delicately. If you're unsure, you can play it safe and keep your cards close to your chest.

Playing the Game

Playing the game of corporate politics day in and day out can be quite taxing, unless you enjoy these types of behaviours. To manage these interactions with minimal emotional impact to you, it really does require having resilience and grit to wear the tough times. Corporate politics can spike during periods of unrest, transformation in the business and where there is a lack of job security.

If the workplace culture is toxic, then the workplace may have a constant flow of rife politics. Having a grasp of the political landscape will help you understand how to play the game and what the unspoken rules are. If you're new to the business, I recommend not becoming an active player until you have full visibility of the players and their bench strength. Network ferociously and build up your alliances. Before you start playing you will also need to make the decision as to whether you are willing to do anything necessary to protect and benefit yourself, or you will abide by your own moral code. There are good people who choose either path to achieve their goals; it is more so a question as to whether you're willing to sacrifice your ethics during these interactions or take a hard stand even though it could politically go against you. Once you have made up your mind which path you will take, you need to now learn how to play.

There are a lot of learned behaviours and strategies people use to promote themselves and diminish other people's reputation. Gaslighting is a term used to describe when people act maliciously against selected individuals, by manipulating them, driving down their confidence and reputation. A gas lighter will make active attempts to isolate an individual and make them perceive that their team members or the business at large is turning against them, which may not be the case at all. Gas lighters on one hand are very rude and manipulative to selected individuals, and then to senior managers and colleagues they deem to be useful, they will turn on the charm. The problem with being gaslighted is that because your experience is unique to you or a specific individual, when you raise your concerns with others, they will not share your experience. People may also not believe you about your experience with the gas lighter and defend that person, further exacerbating your sense of isolation.

Gas lighters are also clever in how they manipulate their targets. They will almost always ensure that the interaction is one on one, so that what is said or what is done can be easily denied. They will use examples such as this: "The team think you're not pulling your weight and are too slow to close off the purchase orders. The team don't understand your workload... Don't worry, you're doing a good job".

This is an example of manipulation and will leave the listener feeling awful despite the reassurance provided by the gas lighter. The gas lighter may also have other conversations with the team members, indicating that the targeted individual believes that they are not pulling their weight in return; this would encourage all the other team members to form a mutual dislike for this poor victim. You do not want to be the person getting gaslighted and you need to recognise these types of individuals. They are often quick to provide criticism themselves but cannot deal with criticism given to them. Gas lighters are notorious for being "control freaks" and want to exert control over everybody in their reach. Recognise these tell-tale signs and if you find yourself in the position being gas-lighted, just remember that they are doing this to try and manipulate you. Confront them on their untruths and rely on the alliances you have formed. If you have a strong network, they will believe you when you describe what is occurring and act as your advocate in case things at work become even messier.

Gas lighters and other types of workplace politicians can be a master in misdirection. Just like the Kansas City Shuffle anecdote, whereby you are so focused on the left-hand waving that you forget to even look at what is going on with the right hand. Misdirecting attention from problem areas and core areas of concern is what seasoned politicians do to take themselves out of the spotlight when things are not going their way. Misdirecting the attention on someone else so they personally avoid criticism and that person is apportioned blame is their ultimate goal. These behaviours can be demonstrated in both simple and serious matters.

Another example of misdirection is when someone pretends to be very engaged and interested at work, and all the while they are planning their escape. By pretending to be engaged in the workplace, no one would suspect that if you called in sick, or were late to work a few times in a month, that you were in fact attending job interviews. However, if you were vocal about how much you disliked the place and you took this time off, people would more readily assume you're in the job market. Misdirection is all about managing perceptions of you to benefit yourself and to make people believe something that may not necessarily be the truth.

Another strategy workplace politicians use is called white-anting. White-anting is an Australian specific term used to describe when a person leaks private or sensitive information about a group, team members or an individual to cause disruption. Leaking this information can have the sole purpose to diminish someone's reputation, sabotage relationships or a project's progress. The sole purpose of this approach is to cause chaos to benefit the workplace politician.

Let's say for instance a guy called Bob has just been reprimanded for lack of budget control, but Bob also knows about the customer service team run by Maria. Maria has also blown out her budget, along with making purchases that have not been approved by the appropriate management level. To take the pressure off Bob and turn the spotlight of scrutiny from him to Maria, he leaks the information about Maria to a colleague of his, Melissa. Melissa is a confidante of Bob's, but she is also connected well with Maria's direct manager. Bob knows of the relationship between Maria's manager and Melissa, and purposely highlights the budget issues in customer service to Melissa. Using Melissa to relay the message to Maria's manager, this makes Bob seem as though he is not being malicious, and so the message lands better as it is coming from a well-known source.

The integrity of the information is not questioned when delivered by Melissa, and it is also not tainted by Bob's own personal gains. Using these back channels is how workplace politicians can effectively white-ant. As a result of Melissa's conversation with Bob, and then Maria's manager, Maria was also schooled on her budget, and this made Bob's position not look as tumultuous. Melissa could have also been unaware of Bob's agenda and was just a pawn in Bob's game to make himself look better.

To keep ahead of these political manoeuvres, at times you have to keep your enemies close so you can observe their movements. If you keep your enemies at a distance, you will not have the necessary insights to understand their motivations, their ambitions, how they like to play the game, who is in their inner circle and whether they may be planning to sabotage your reputation or someone else's in your inner circle. These insights will help you anticipate their movements, and, if they are planning to bulldoze someone's reputation, you can steer clear of their path. Unfortunately, some enemies can be wolves in sheep's clothing appearing to be an ally or friendly so that they can gain information and your confidence, using this to their advantage. If they are good at this game play, it can be hard to differentiate the rabbits and snakes in the grass.

As you develop your political savviness, it will become easier to differentiate between the genuine and kind people minding their own business, and those that are willing to do whatever it takes to better themselves. When you are new to a business, you will be trying your best to build your network and understand who is who in the zoo. Applying this same adage, it is in your best interests to quickly ascertain who you can trust and who you can't, which are the snakes in the grass.

Business people and myself alike find it very helpful to discuss and explain corporate politics using a range of sayings and analogies. This is common in business and is a "shared language". A popular saying used in a business to explain an approach is "if you give someone enough rope, they will hang themselves". The saying is a little morbid... I know, but it is a simple way of explaining a paradigm. If you have a workplace politician too big for their boots, or is acting in a certain way that is viewed as harmful, or there seems to be an obvious gloomy end, this saying is applicable.

Your intervention or participation in their detrimental behaviours may not be required, and it may serve your interests to let that person suffer the consequences of their actions. This could be the case if this person is a rival of yours, someone you deem as an enemy or bully in the business. Using this approach is classified as the long game and can try your patience. If you're more of an active player in corporate politics or do not have the patience to simply observe, then you may be tempted to add fuel to the slow-burning fire. However, getting involved may compromise your position. Exercise your discretion and make a decision around what course of action you will take.

If you're inexperienced in these types of scenarios, my advice is to observe before taking action. Although the long game may be painful and exhausting, it is always more rewarding in the end to see someone "fall on their own sword".

Here is another saying at the risk of sounding cheesy: "knowledge is power". The more you know about your political landscape and the players, the stronger your position will be in achieving your own goals. Having a network work for you to gather information is very useful in establishing your influence in a business. Seasoned workplace politicians understand this and seek to either get information from you or others. If you have a public social media account or do not exercise discretion in who you share information with about you and other business movements, you are making it too easy for others to use this against you.

I personally have a strict social media code I abide by; anyone I am currently working with will not be added to my personal social media accounts, and I will not share with them what side projects and hustles I have in the works.

If I am informed of information that is not widely known and I choose to share this with someone in the workplace, I will not reveal my source. If you happen to be sharing this information with your direct manager, you need to be prepared to share who was the source if they ask. These are some measures you can take to prevent information leakage on yourself, so that it is not misconstrued into rumours. It is also effective in preserving your information channels and alliances you have built. Although it may be cheesy, having knowledge really does elevate your power in corporate politics.

As a HR professional, you will have the luxury of increased visibility to various political landscapes. When leading transformation projects or managing ER matters, you will be informed by your direct manager, employees and other parties of the political happenings so that you're better equipped to manage people's expectations and outcomes.

If corporate politics is the catalyst for a toxic workplace culture, HR professionals would become involved to understand the contributing factors, who are the main players and what can be done about it.

If an employee has lodged a formal complaint regarding a person or manager that is gaslighting them, again, this will fall into HR's remit.

To be an effective HR business partner and leader, you will need to become a proficient player in the political arena. This means not only understanding each player, their individual goals, and who is on which proverbial team, but also how all of this will impact how you manage various circumstances.

If you're not politically savvy enough for a situation, this can be perceived as you not having enough experience or "stakeholder buy-in" to deliver. Remain wary of this and how, by just being in your HR role, you can get placed in the firing line. Use the lessons explained in this chapter to suit your individual circumstances, as you may need to use different approaches across your career, as no one approach is better than another.

GLOSSARY OF TERMS

"**Australian Taxation Office**" is an Australian statutory agency and the principal revenue collection body for the Australian Government. This body is charged with ensuring employers and individuals meet taxation, administrative and superannuation requirements.

"**A support person**" is someone nominated by an employee to join them in a formal meeting with management. Nominated support persons may be a colleague, friend or family member that is not directly involved in the matter being discussed so that there is no conflict of interest. During the formal meeting, the support person cannot advocate on behalf of the employee, and may only act as an observer. During the meeting, the support person may take their own notes. Once the formal meeting has been officially closed, the support person then may ask questions.

"**Balance of Probabilities**" is the standard of proof used by HR when conducting workplace investigations and trying to establish whether allegations have substantiated or unsubstantiated.

"**Business Acumen**" is the ability to comprehend how a business operates to generate revenue, cashflow and profit. Business acumen is not limited to a particular profession, and is synonymous with having commercial savviness.

"**Collective bargaining**" describes the process of negotiation between an employer and their employees to reach an agreement on matters, which may pertain to entitlements, working conditions, payment of wages and worker rights.

"*Corporations Act 2001*" sets out how companies and business entities must conduct themselves and the legal requirements pertaining to specific roles, such as an Officer and PCBU.

"**Enterprise Agreement**" is an industrial instrument that is established between an employing entity and their employees.

"*Fair Work Act 2009*" is federal legislation that outlines and protects workplace rights, industrial activities, and entitlements.

"**Fair Work Commission (FWC)**" is Australia's national industrial relations tribunal charged with hearing matters and claims made by workers and employers.

"**Fair Work Ombudsman**" is a statutory government body that provides free advice and guidance on employment matters. The body may also become involved in informally resolving disputes and concerns between employees and employers.

"*Fair Work Regulations 2009*" is a key piece of Commonwealth legislation regulating employment and workplace relations.

"**Gaslighting**" is a form of psychological manipulation in which an individual or group of people covertly target a person, and deceptively make them question their own abilities, perception and attitudes. Gaslighting can have serious negative effects on an individual's mental health when they are the victim of this behaviour.

"**General Protections Claim**" is made by an employee against an employer for taking adverse action against them.

"**Genuine Redundancy**" is when the employer no longer requires the person's job to be performed by anyone because of changes in the operational requirements of the employer's enterprise, and the employer has complied with any obligation imposed by an applicable modern award or enterprise agreement to consult about the redundancy.

"**HR function**" is an interchangeable term for HR department or the HR team in a business.

"**Industrial action**" can be taken by union bodies and/ or employees to temporarily demonstrate their dissatisfaction with a dispute or an enterprise agreement negotiation.

"**Keep in touch days**" allows an employee who is still on unpaid parental leave to go back to work (paid) to keep up to date of what is happening in the business.

"**Loss Time Injury (LTI)**" is something that results in time lost from work, a permanent disability, or a fatality.

"**Medical Treatment Injury (MTI)**" is an injury or disease that has resulted in a certain level of treatment given by a physician and more care was required than just first aid.

"**Minimum Employment Period**" is commercially referred to as the probationary period, which is the first six months from commencement of employment.

"**Modern Award**" is an industrial instrument created by the Fair Work Commission and sets out the minimum employment conditions above the NES.

"**National Employment Standards (NES)**" set out eleven minimum employment entitlements that must be provided to all employees.

"**Notice of Employee Representational Rights (NERR)**" gives formal notice to employees that an employer is intending on negotiating an enterprise agreement by which they are covered by.

"**PCBU**" refers to a Person Conducting Business Undertakings and is a role defined under the *Corporations Act 2001*.

"**Performance Improvement Plan (PIP)**" is a formal document used by employers to performance manage their employees. The PIP document builds an action list.

"**Return to Work Plan**" is a developed program to assist an injured worker returning to work and pre-injury duties.

"**Rubber stamped**" is the colloquial term used when the Fair Work Commission approves an enterprise agreement and the document is sealed with the official stamp.

"**Single Touch Payroll (STP)**" is an Australian government initiative to reduce each employer's reporting requirements. Each time employees are paid, the payment information is directly sent through to the ATO.

"**Unfair Dismissal Claim**" is an application made by a former employee when they are seeking an unfair dismissal remedy.

"**Vexatious Complaint**" is a false complaint made with the intention to cause harm, distress and impact the reputation of the individual or group the complaint was made against.

"***Workers Health and Safety Act 2011***" is a significant piece of legislation governing an employer's and employee's obligations in a workplace to maintain and protect worker health, safety and wellness.

ABOUT THE AUTHOR

Melissa Hume is a Sydney-based HR professional with over ten years of human resources experience. She has always felt passionate about helping the community and coaching upcoming generations of HR practitioners. Her first book *Career Guidance for Now and for the Future* focused on how to secure employment through CV writing and interview techniques. In August 2020, Melissa was inspired and founded *Career Guidance Now* to support those who had lost their jobs due to the global pandemic.

Your HR Ally is Melissa's second book. She noticed an inherent lack of Australian resources for those studying HR or seeking to pursue a HR career. Taking matters into her own hands, *Your HR Ally* was written to kickstart a HR career. In 2021 Melissa became an Excellence Awardee for 'Australian HR Manager of the Year'. She has a Graduate Certificate in Business Administration, a Bachelor's Degree majoring in Psychology, as well as certifications in safety and payroll.